Simulation Teaching
of Library Administration

· · · · · · · · · · · · · · · · · ·

Bowker Series in
PROBLEM-CENTERED APPROACHES TO LIBRARIANSHIP
Thomas J. Galvin, Series Editor

SIMULATION TEACHING OF LIBRARY ADMINISTRATION

· ·

by Martha Jane K. Zachert

R. R. Bowker Company
A Xerox Education Company
New York & London, 1975

Published by R. R. Bowker Co. (A Xerox Education Company)
1180 Avenue of the Americas, New York, N.Y. 10036

Printed and bound in the United States of America.

Library of Congress Cataloging in Publication Data

Zachert, Martha Jane K   1920-
    Simulation teaching of library administration.

    (Problem-centered approaches to librarianship)
    Bibliography: p.
    Includes index.
    1. Library administration—Study and teaching—
Simulation methods.   I.   Title.
Z678.Z33   658'.91'021007   74-32041
ISBN 0-8352-0612-2

TO:

>Connie Bergquist
>Sidney Cone
>Liz Cropper
>Dorothea Johnson
>Veronica Pantelidis
>Sally Robertson

Former students who, through graduate assistantships, directed independent studies, and continuing interest, have contributed substantially to the development of simulation teaching methods and materials.

CONTENTS

• • • • • • • • • • • • • •

B. Governmental Library Simulation: Federal Library Model

LIST OF FIGURES

LIST OF EXHIBITS

FOREWORD

. . . .

Martha Jane K. Zachert's *Simulation Teaching of Library Administration*, the ninth title to be published in the Problem Centered Approaches to Librarianship series, is truly a landmark volume. It represents the first book-length treatment in the literature of librarianship of an exciting new departure in the pre-service and in-service preparation of library managers—simulation learning. Included here are a detailed presentation of the rationale and objectives of this most recently developed of the experiential teaching approaches to library administration, explicit guidance for teachers and training leaders in application of the method to learning situations ranging from the informal one-day workshop to the semester-length course, and, most valuable of all in my view, extended samples of simulation models and problem materials directly adaptable to a wide variety of instructional settings. The result is a handbook, sourcebook, and *vade mecum* suited to the needs of both the experienced teacher of library administration and the volunteer organizer or leader of an in-service management training program for library personnel.

This book is the outcome of more than ten years of careful research combined with creative, innovative, developmental work by a dedicated and gifted teacher. It is the impressive record of a conscientious, determined search for a *better way* to prepare librarians for supervisory responsibility, and to assist both students and practitioners to appraise more effectively their own potential for the managerial role. *Simulation Teaching of Library Administration* offers both the instructional materials needed by those wanting to experiment with a further alternative to traditional methods, and the basic information, in the form of shared experience, requisite to the creation of a larger body of new teaching resources by others in the field.

The limitations of conventional textbook-lecture-group discussion approaches in management training have long been apparent, and have been enumerated in sufficient detail elsewhere so as not to bear repetition here. Similarly, it is generally understood and accepted by both library educators and library administrators that the managerial and supervisory aspects of librarianship are, in many significant respects, similar to the counterpart activities in other fields. Thus, it becomes entirely appropriate, as Dr. Zachert has done here, to adapt the methods and objectives of simulation teaching, already well established in other disciplines, to the field of library administration. Like the case method of instruction, which has been presented extensively in earlier volumes in this series, simulation teaching provides a participative learning experience in which the application of theories and principles, through the exercise of professional judgment, is emphasized. By "presentation of the 'real' in a representational mode," the simulation affords an invaluable opportunity to acquire and develop managerial skills in an environment that is without risk either to the learner or to the organization. Above all, in its diachronic aspect, the simulation technique offers a realistic and memorable demonstration of the sequential character of managerial decision-making, along with a chance to experience that most painful occupational hazard of the administrative trade—having to live with the consequences of one's mistakes.

The Bowker Problem-Centered Approaches to Librarianship series is designed to make a wide variety of problem-oriented learning materials available for both formal and informal instruction in the several subfields of librarianship, as well as to demonstrate the value of the case study and related techniques in the presentation and analysis of contemporary problems of professional practice. Dr. Zachert's *Simulation Teaching of Library Administration* is a major contribution to this literature and a distinguished addition to this series.

Thomas J. Galvin
Series Editor

PREFACE

· · · · · · · · · · · ·

The now-classic model for teaching library administration calls for the input of theory by lectures and reading, and the classroom activity as teacher-centered discussion, with perhaps a soupçon of practicality through field trips. For small classes, especially with learner–practitioners of some degree of experience, traditional seminar study can be a meaningful methodology. In recent years case study has been introduced to library science teaching, and it has found wide acceptance as the preparation of appropriate cases has become a well-defined art. And yet, for many learners—and many teachers—some elements of meaningful instruction are missing. Lecture/discussion, seminar, and case study are all contemplative modes, and the reality of administration is anything but contemplative. Some would claim well-directed contemplation an advantageous mode for serious study, stimulating by virtue of its degree of difference from reality and its potential for the development of perspective on that reality. For others, it is simply not enough. Contemplation is too far from reality; transference does not happen across the gap. The would-be learner is left faltering, confused, and often resentful.

Simulation is offered as an alternative. Not a panacea, not a total replacement, simply an alternative that meets some of the criticism. Through it, learners are confronted with realistic problem stimuli. Their reactions, both cognitive and affective, constitute learning. The advantages claimed for simulation instruction include realism, individualization, immediate feedback, challenge, and power to sustain learner interest.

The underlying concepts of simulation and experiential teaching methods presented in this book have been borrowed from other fields—business, governmental and education administration primarily. The values for library educators are not hypothetical, however, for the methodology has been successfully used over a period of time by a number of teachers, and in a variety of educational settings related to career training for librarians. Neither is the approach overpersonalized. Much of the telling is in personal terms, in order to limit generalization, to induce acceptance of responsibility and to provide concrete examples in terms of teaching *library* administration. The assumption is that it will be easier for library educators to react creatively to methodological discourse couched in library science terms than if the same methodology were described in terms of high finance, international politics, militarism, or secondary school planning.

As the learning materials and activities are different in simulation teaching, so is the teacher's role. He is in many ways more detached from the learning group than in traditional instructional modes. He holds himself in readiness as a resource person and demands of himself the ability to lead the group in relating theoretical abstractions to the practical side of administrative reality. He maintains a position of centrality to the group through his creative and resourceful management of learning rather than through his delivery of lecture-packaged "truth."

The pitch for simulation as a preferred teaching/learning mode for library administration is not a claim that it guarantees more or better learning for all. In fact, comparison studies of teaching methodologies in general show that no one method can be decisively labeled "best," and there is no reason not to believe that the conclusion applies to teaching library administration. Still, enhanced learner interest, motivation, and personal responsibility for learning can be demonstrated in simulation instruction, as can student affective response to this experiential mode. Many teachers will readily settle for these advantages.

This book is offered as a practical manual to teachers of library science administration in master's programs and advanced classrooms and in a variety of continuing education formats collectively referred to herein as "workshops." It explains, it gives examples, it advocates personal trial of simulation teaching. It is not a review of practical experience with simulation in other fields, nor of general or specific research about simulation. It does not consider the almost certainly valuable application of simulation methodology to other areas of the library science curriculum; nor does it consider the enormous potential of simulation for research in relation to administration and other aspects of librarianship. Neither is this book a flight of fancy; every bit of it has survived repeated library science classroom trial. I owe a debt of gratitude, which I am delighted to acknowledge but can never repay, to those who have tried my material and relayed criticism along with, in some instances, samples of their own creative efforts: James Matarazzo, Simmons College; John Miniter, Texas Women's University; Denis St. Laurent, University of Toronto; Miriam Tees, Royal Bank of Canada, teaching at McGill University; Sara Thomas, Environmental Protection Agency, teaching at The Catholic University of America; and Wiley Williams, Peabody College for Teachers.

During my years of learning how to adapt simulation techniques to the teaching of library administration, encouragement and support has come from four deans, past and present: Louis Shores and Harold Goldstein, School of Library Science, Florida State University; and Father James J. Kortendick and Elizabeth W. Stone, Department of Library Science, The Catholic University of America. Paul Howard and Vivian Templin of the Catholic University Project Staff were indispensable. In various ways members of the Florida State University Computer-Assisted Instruction Center and the Division of Instructional Research and Services have helped. The former students to whom the book is dedicated have gone beyond the requirements of the student/teacher relationship. Nothing, however, has meant more to me than the sincere enthusiasm and criticism that has come from my advisees in FSU's Program in Special Librarianship and students in LS548, "Special Library Service."

The conversion of classroom techniques into a monograph for other teachers and group leaders was instigated by Dr. Thomas J. Galvin, Associate Director of the School of Library Science, Simmons College, and editor of the series Problem-Centered Approaches to Librarianship. His confidence and enthusiasm for my work, in addition to his ever-willing ear to the phone, have provided the stimulus and much assistance in the writing. The problems of publication have been borne by Madeline Miele, and Julia Raymunt of Bowker. These words are written to express minimally what is a great debt to all of these people and to absolve them of any responsibility for the ways in which I have failed to take full advantage from their proffered help.

Grateful acknowledgment is hereby made to: *Educational Technology*, John D. Krumboltz and Beverly Potter for permission to reprint Table 1, page 50, from an article originally published in 1973; Elizabeth Stone for permission to quote, on page 60, from *Human Resources in the Library System, Leader's Handbook* by Stone and Goodman; ERIC Clearinghouse on Educational Media and Technology of Stanford University; and Addison-Wesley Publishing Company, Reading, Massachusetts. Special thanks are due the U.S. Department of Health, Education and Welfare for permission to reprint with slight changes *The Governmental Library Simulation, Part I, Federal Library Model* and to adapt and excerpt from Parts II and III, *Participant's Resource-Log* and *Director's Guide*. "The project presented or reported herein was performed pursuant to a grant from the U.S. Office of Education, Department of Health, Education and Welfare. However, the opinions expressed herein do not necessarily reflect the position or policy of the U.S. Office of Education and no official endorsement by the U.S. Office of Education should be inferred." In the case of this material copyright is not claimed either for the original or for the modifications included in Part VI, B of the present work.

Finally, to Edward G. Zachert, my husband—whose role as idea-scout, sounding-board, and critic in my research and teaching extends far beyond that customarily and perfunctorily mentioned in prefaces, far beyond that of marital support and accord, and far beyond the dreams of women's lib—acknowledgment, thanks, and love.

MARTHA JANE K. ZACHERT

Columbia, S.C.
November 1974

PART I.
Introduction to Simulation Teaching

1.
What Is It?
· · · · · · · · · · · ·

Moon shots have shown us what simulation is, for television has pictured the astronauts in mock-ups, or models, of their spaceships and ground transportation vehicles. As they went about practicing in simulated environments the skills needed for space exploration, the astronauts learned without risk to themselves or to expensive equipment. "Representation of the real" is the definition of "simulation," i.e., reality that is too large, too far distant, too complex, perhaps too secret or too risky to be experienced directly.

Simulations of moon shots are variations of methods often used in other kinds of teaching. In classroom simulations the student participates in the operation of the model, just as the astronauts do, learning by his personal experience. Simulations have been designed to facilitate learning at every formal stage from the elementary grades through graduate school, as well as in such informal situations as in-service workshops and institutes. Simulation teaching is adaptable to a wide variety of subjects including science, medicine and allied medical sciences, business administration, public administration, social welfare, and educational administration and supervision.[1]

Basically, simulation teaching makes it possible for learners to experience the "feel" of reality in a controlled situation, without risk. The representation of reality is supplied by a model, and the learners interact either with each other in terms of the model, or with the model itself. Since the simulation is a representation of reality and not reality itself, the learner is protected against hurting himself or inflicting harm on the reality. Astronauts, in their simulated environments, experience many of the aspects of real space exploration. They make the decisions required in flight and receive feedback on the results of their decisions. They experience the physical sensation of a moon shot, and perfect the timing of routines they may be called on to use at split-second notice. Similarly, in a course in librarianship taught by simulation methodology the learner is in an environment controlled by a model. He makes decisions, receives feedback, experiences physical sensations, and demonstrates behaviors without risk to himself or to a real library.

Thus far, very little simulation teaching has been tried in library science. Nor has any specific research been carried out to determine whether or not simulation is an appropriate technique to use in teaching the particular subject matter called "library science." Arguing by analogy with other disciplines in which it has proved valuable, there is no reason why it should not be appropriate, especially in those areas that constitute applications of theory.

Although the materials used as examples in this book were originally prepared for teaching courses in the administration of special libraries, teachers of administration in other kinds of libraries and of general administration will find that the methodology is not limited in its appropriateness to the education of special librarians. Nor is it limited to the formal classroom; its usefulness in informal situations has already been demonstrated. In fact, it appears from pilot efforts that simulation methodologies are not limited to the teaching of administration. Any of the techniques described herein may be applied to teaching other areas of library science. Only the background research to provide valid models and problems and the teachers' willingness to experiment are needed to bring the considerable potential of simulation teaching to fulfillment in library science classrooms.

ADVANTAGES OF SIMULATION TEACHING

Many educational researchers have concluded on the basis of their experiments that simulation offers a great advantage over other teaching techniques because of its demonstrated capability to produce a high level of learner interest and involvement.[2] It appears to be nearly impossible for a student to remain passive when engaged in simulation learning activities. Participation enhances perception, reinforces theory, heightens motivation and exercises skills; it accomplishes these results with less physical and psychological risk to the learner than accrue from the same lessons in "real life." From the standpoint of learning the skills of administrative decision-making, simulation also accomplishes its results with less risk to the organization than if the lessons were learned in operating libraries.

There are other advantages of simulation teaching. Students find it enjoyable, thus enabling the teacher to capitalize on the demonstrated fact that the enjoyable situation is conducive to learning. Each student acts independently but in interaction with others much of the time, learning strategies of teamwork. Simulation emphasizes communication by offering opportunity for the development of this important skill. Immediate feedback and evaluation reinforce successful strategies and discourage those less successful.[3, 4] The use of a model based on salient *selected* characteristics is also an advantage, for omission of some of the detail of real situations serves to reduce complexity to manageable dimensions for the novice.

The learning effectiveness of simulation teaching comes, at least partially, from the *accuracy* of the representations contained in the model and in the problem-solving situations in which the learner is placed. Another important part of the effectiveness, however, comes from the *unreality* of the simulation. For, although the model moves in time, it does so unrealistically. Real time is sometimes speeded up (to omit real incidents and periods of time unrelated to the specific problem under study), and sometimes slowed down (to allow for more intensive study than would be possible in real time). The simulation may be interrupted, for explanations or speculations on alternative strategies, or it may be repeated under varying conditions or with different participants, neither of which is possible with real time.

In the opinion of many educational psychologists and teachers the development of new experiential teaching/learning methods does not portend the cessation of traditional methods. Rather, it suggests that we may, through research, learn more precisely which teaching methods are most likely to result in successful learning in given situations and for given learning objectives. Traditional teaching methods have been used as if they were multipurpose and all equally effective. Research now tends to indicate that most are potent for fewer, more specific purposes. The lecture, for example, can be very economical of time for the student when it summarizes widely scattered factual information. Well-related reminiscences can assist the neophyte in his modelling process. Case studies can give valuable experience to the student in diagnosing problems and formulating solutions. Incident method can give practice in asking pertinent questions about problem situations and in selecting data pertinent to viable solutions. Group projects rate high as spurs to individual effort and in giving team experience. Individual projects test the personal resourcefulness of the student. To these traditional values, we can now add the affective and cognitive values of the experiential methods. Simulations and games can be especially useful for practice in decision-making and for feeling the responsibility and trauma of decision-making and the importance of sequence in decision-making. Roleplay, in-baskets and games can contribute significantly to the development of communication skills so vital to the administrator. The specific methods chosen for given situations should depend on the learning preferences of the students and on the objectives of the specific learning experience.[5]

THE SIMULATION LEARNING SYSTEM

In general terms, the objective of simulation teaching of library administration is to provide opportunities for the student to experience the kinds of decision-making characteristic of the responsibilities of a manager. For practical reasons this objective must be accomplished without risk to any existing library—or to the student. In planning a simulation of administration to be used in the initial instruction of library school students, it must be assumed that the students need experience in all administrative functions. The same assumption does not apply, however, in using simulation in continuing education. Rather, for in-service training, needed experience can be identified and appropriate segments of a comprehensive simulation learning system can be selected, or simulations with limited objectives can be designed.

There should be, in addition to the general objective of gaining experience, specific objectives in relation to each administrative function: planning, organizing, directing, staffing, coordinating, reporting, and budgeting (to use the terminology of one well-known expression of administrative theory). The specific objectives are to be met through a series of problems in which learners perform administrative tasks in the given environment without risk—that is, by simulation. It should be pointed out that the specific objectives of the given problems appropriate for continuing education differ from those used in a master's level course. Examples of both kinds of problems appear later in this book.

Analysis of the use of classroom simulations in other disciplines shows that there is a recurring sequence of steps in the procedure, and that this sequence is relatively fixed and predictable. In fact, a well-defined learning system has emerged. This system, as shown in Figure 1, may be implemented in a single class session, may constitute an entire course, or may be applied in a variety of time schedules. The experiences from which illustrations for this book have been drawn are "sustained simulations," i.e., simulations used as the basis for an entire course in library administration. The techniques described, however, can be used in simulations for any desired curricular segment: a unit, a course, a workshop, an institute, or any other.

It is assumed for purposes of this learning system model that the learners have had no prior experience in simulation and must, therefore, be introduced to simulation techniques in the course at hand (Module 3). This is probably a wise assumption in relation to current library science students and practitioners. Simulations are being widely used in the lower grades, however, and it is entirely possible that learners who are experienced in the techniques will soon appear regularly in library science classrooms and eventually in continuing education sessions. In that case (and the teacher can determine this only by asking each new group of students), Module 3, "Explanation of Simulation Techniques," may be omitted or may be used only as a brief review.

Of greater importance in the teacher's planning is the question of whether or not the learners have had prior instruction in administrative theory. It is assumed in Figure 1 that they have, and no module for theoretical instruction is included. If, in fact, the learners have not had such instruction, obviously it must be provided before they can be expected to practice its application.

If a major objective of the instruction is to include the theory of administration, at least two modifications of the basic learning model appear feasible. There is, at the present time in library science education, no basis in research for choosing between them. Figure 2 shows these alternatives: (a) presentation of the total amount of theory to be considered in the given course, followed by all of the the problems in application; (b) presentation of the theory in smaller segments, following each presentation with a problem relating to

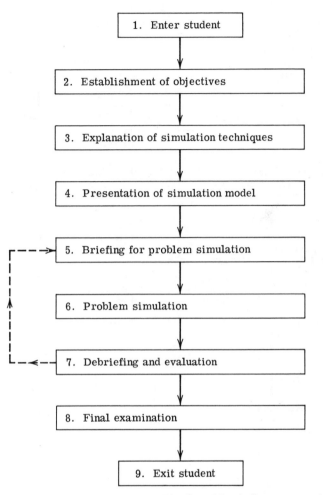

Figure 1. The simulation learning system. The dotted line indicates a repetition loop during which the learners advance from problem to problem. This loop (which includes as many problems as the teacher wishes) constitutes the main body of the course timewise.

the application of that bit of theory. For some kinds of instruction—for example, those in which the theory of administration is to be reviewed rather than presented initially—a third alternative appears feasible: (c) principles emerge from problem-solving.

EXPERIENTIAL CLASSROOM TECHNIQUES

Classroom techniques used in simulation teaching are characterized as "experiential" methods, meaning that the student learns through personal involvement and experience. For example, in teaching library administration,

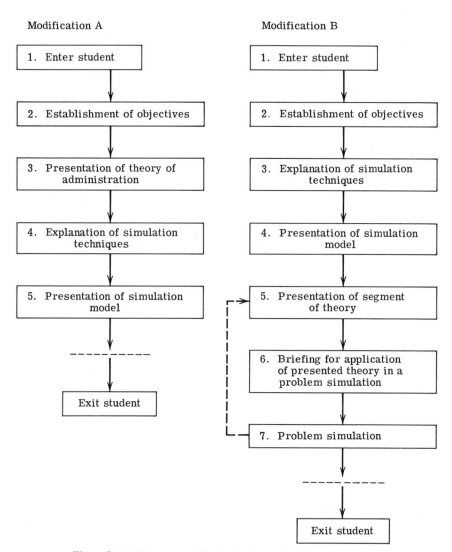

Figure 2. Modifications of the basic simulation learning system.

the cognitive learning required of the student consists of the intellectual understanding of theories of administration. The educational psychologist argues that cognitive learning does not go far enough to produce the true internalization of subject matter that becomes evident as long-lasting changes in the individual's daily behavior. What is lacking is literally the "feel" of living with the subject matter or, in the psychologist's term, "affective learning." Many students go through their academic careers without perceiving the relationship between cognitive and affective learning. Those who do perceive it, and who are articulate enough to verbalize the learning experience, agree with the educational psychologist: durable behavioral change grows out of a meaningful combination of cognitive and affective learning.

Before the beginning librarian is placed in the actual position of administrator at any level, he should experience how it feels to be faced with administrative problems. For some of these, available theory may be inadequate; and for most, he will have had no opportunity to try his hand at application of the theory to a particular problem. Similarly, the practicing librarian, in moving up the administrative ladder, needs to "try on" new administrative experiences and needs to gain new perceptions to assist in his fulfillment of daily responsibilities. The learner needs to know how it *feels* to make administrative decisions. He needs to ponder the choice between two candidates for a position, perhaps to make the wrong choice and to shrink from the wretchedness of having to fire a likeable, but ineffective, employee. The learner needs to labor over a floor plan or a budget, and then be told to do it over with a different set of conditions. No amount of theory, per se, teaches him the frustration, the pressure, the panic; he must *feel* it by experiencing it. Techniques used in simulation teaching emphasize learning through experience.

Roleplay is probably the best known of the experiential methods. It is the enactment of a situation in which learners play the parts, or roles, of—in our case—library staff, management, and users. Roleplay offers the learner insight into the thinking and emotions of various individuals in the library orbit as well as practice in human relations and communication skills. Another technique, the in-basket exercise, is especially useful for practicing communication skills along with decision-making. In these exercises each learner receives one or more communications of a type that might logically turn up in an administrator's in-basket. The learner must respond *in the role of the individual to whom the item is addressed* with an appropriate out-basket item. The in-basket technique is combined with narrative in a programmed text format called an "action maze" for teaching the effects of a sequence of decisions. The addition of competitive elements and scoring techniques converts roleplay exercises, in-basket exercises and action mazes into learning games, which learners play sometimes as individuals and sometimes in teams.

Although the classroom techniques described as "experiential" emphasize affective learning, in their reactions to simulation teaching students report that these techniques result in a combination of intellectual and emotional learning different from that of other teachning methods. Each of these techniques will be discussed in detail, with examples, in Part III of this book.

SIMULATION MATERIALS

It will be apparent to experienced teachers that simulation teaching requires somewhat different kinds of teaching materials than those used with more traditional methodologies. Library models have already been mentioned. These models—whether physical, verbal, mathematical, or of some other variety—represent real libraries in a controlled way. It is admitted that they are incomplete in that many details not relevant to the problems to be studied are omitted. It is important, however, that the models be accurate in the characteristics they do display.

In my own teaching I use a single model for the duration of a course, workshop, or institute. The model is presented to the learners in advance of any problem-solving, along with (1) a contextual statement to describe the on-going situation in the library which gives focus to the problems under study, and (2) a time frame for the action.

The problems to be considered are embedded in incidents in the daily life of the library, incidents which are illustrative of an administrator's responsibilities. In coursework at the master's level each problem is described to the students in writing, along with suggestions for personal preparation before participation. These kinds of materials are described more fully and illustrated in the following chapters.

CHAPTER HIGHLIGHTS

Simulation is
   . . . a representation of reality.

Simulation in the classroom is
   . . . low in risk to students,
   . . . high in student involvement.

The simulation learning system is
   . . . a problem-centered, experiential way of learning.

Simulation materials include
   . . . models,
   . . . contextual statements,
   . . . incident materials,
   . . . course management materials.

REFERENCES

1. For examples, see Paul A. Twelker, ed., *Instructional Simulation Systems: An Annotated Bibliography* (Corvallis, Oreg.: Oregon State University, 1969).

2. D. M. Garvey, "A Preliminary Evaluation of Simulation" (Paper read at the 46th annual meeting of the National Council for the Social Studies, Cleveland, Ohio, November 23–26, 1966).

3. Ibid.

4. Harry I. Wigderson, *The Name of the Game—Simulation* (Visalia, Calif.: ADAPT, A PACE Supplementary Education Center, 1968). Research Brief Number 4. (Available as ED 028 647)

5. Nancy G. McNulty, *Training Managers: The International Guide* (New York: Harper & Row, 1969), 13–21.

2.
Simulation Teaching Materials
• •

Just as other teaching methodologies have specialized materials that accompany them, so does simulation. In some traditional methodologies it is customary to use a textbook, occasionally written by the teacher who is using it, more often written by someone else. For some subjects additional materials, such as exercises, lab books, or audiovisual materials, are available in published form; in other subjects the instructor must produce his own. In library science we have long had textbooks and formbooks. More recently, programmed texts, audiovisual materials and casebooks have become generally available. Most teachers, when they use traditional methods, use published materials supplemented by their own. This book presents examples of simulation teaching materials in order to help library science teachers to understand the kinds of materials needed in simulation teaching, to offer materials that can themselves be used in administration classrooms, and, hopefully, to inspire teachers to produce more and better simulation materials through their own research.

The first of the simulation examples presented in this book, the Industrial Library Simulation, was designed for the master's-level course "Special Library Service" which I teach at Florida State University School of Library Science. I designed the second example, the Governmental Library Simulation, for use in continuing education situations; later, it was adapted for use in my master's-level course. Both simulations can be used, and in fact have been used, by other teachers. In a given teaching situation, any instructor would probably want to supplement these materials with additional items of his own.

Although the categories of materials as presented here are well established, there are few limits on what research might produce within these categories. Other forms, and indeed other categories, would derive from the objectives of a given teaching situation, the nature of the simulation, the needs of the students and the plans of the teacher.

The materials used in simulation teaching are described in four categories: models, contextual statements, incident materials, and course management materials. These various kinds of teaching materials fit into the teaching sequence as shown in Figure 3.

LEARNING SEQUENCE   RELATED KINDS OF
                                         MATERIALS

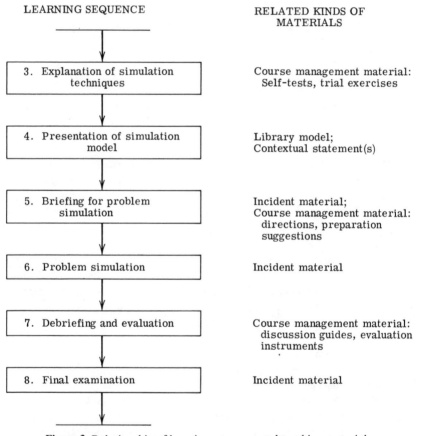

3. Explanation of simulation   Course management material:
   techniques   Self-tests, trial exercises

4. Presentation of simulation   Library model;
   model   Contextual statement(s)

5. Briefing for problem   Incident material;
   simulation   Course management material:
                                          directions, preparation
                                          suggestions

6. Problem simulation   Incident material

7. Debriefing and evaluation   Course management material:
                                          discussion guides, evaluation
                                          instruments

8. Final examination   Incident material

Figure 3. Relationship of learning sequence and teaching materials.

TWO SUSTAINED SIMULATION PACKAGES

The two sets of illustrative materials referred to throughout this book are found in Part VI. Each set might be described as selections from a "teaching/ learning package" which, in its entirety, comprises a library model, contextual statement(s), incident materials that apply to the model, and course management materials. Such a package, which embraces the objectives of an entire course and includes sufficient material for an academic term, provides the teaching/learning basis for a *sustained simulation*. An integrated system, the sustained simulation is characterized by movement of a model through time, by the incorporation of decisions in the problems that follow, and by feedback.

The Industrial Library Simulation was prepared initially in 1963–1964. It has been classroom tested with ten classes of master's-level library science students at Florida State University School of Library Science. The material included in this book has been extensively revised on the basis of the original trials. The Industrial Library Simulation package consists of:

1. Industrial Library Model.
2. A Contextual Statement.
3. Five Units of Study, each centering on an area of administrative responsibility and each including additional contextual statements, incident materials and course management materials.

The Governmental Library Simulation was prepared initially in 1970 as part of a research study conducted at the Catholic University of America of the educational needs of middle- and upper-level library personnel in the federal government of the United States. It has been classroom tested with two master's-level classes at Florida State University School of Library Science, two continuing education classes, and one continuing education institute at Catholic University Department of Library Science. The parts of the simulation included here consist of

1. The Federal Library Model, including contextual statements.
2. Selections from the Participant's Resource-Log, including additional contextual statements, incident materials and course management materials.
3. Selections from the Director's Guide, including suggestions for classroom management of the problems.

SIMULATION MODELS

The word "simulation" in present educational terminology is applied to teaching methodologies characterized by problem-solving in the contextual framework of a model. This model may be, in different subjects, a mathematical formula, a physical miniaturization, a visual image, or a verbal description. In every format the purpose of the model is to provide realistic parameters for the study of problems. Thus the presence or absence of a model makes the difference as to whether a given instructional technique is appropriately called a "simulation," or whether it is more appropriately classified as some other problem-solving *genre*, such as case study.[1,2]

Questions have been raised in conversations with library school faculty about the appropriateness of using the words "model" and "parameter" for library representations that are essentially nonmathematical. Aside from the fact that these terms are routinely used in this way in other fields, the library models for simulation teaching do meet the dictionary definitions for these words. According to *Webster's*, models are "miniature representations," and "descriptions used to help visualize something that cannot be directly observed." Simulation models provide "characteristic elements" and "constant factors" (*Webster's* definition of "parameter") for use by students in practising decision-making in libraries. A few writers about simulation teaching have begun to use the word "simulate" instead of model. It is certainly a possible alternative; however, it seems artificial and awkward. Its use with students (and others who are in early stages of familiarity with simulation teaching) seems to introduce a semantic hurdle. In the interests of accurate communication with teachers and educational researchers in other disciplines, from whom we can learn a great deal, it is suggested that the words "model" and "parameter" be accepted in library science with the definitions above.

The moon-shot simulations on television utilize scale mock-ups of vehicles and moon terrain as models. Other sophisticated simulations have used audiovisual productions and computer-produced realia. Pragmatic considerations prompted me to begin classroom simulation teaching with less sophisticated models, composed of words and simple diagrams (verbal/visual models) reproduced by mimeograph machine. If simulation teaching becomes widespread in library science, there is no reason why it should not utilize multimedia models.

The Industrial Library Model (Part VI, Example A) creates a hypothetical technical library, the library of the Field Research Laboratory, a component of the hypothetical Double XYZ Oil Company. The student gains knowledge of the company and the library from documents typical of those a library administrator would use in daily management of the library: organization charts of the parent company, the laboratory, and the library; floor plan of the library; statements of library policy; annual reports; and budget.

The Federal Library Model (Part VI, Example B) creates a hypothetical library for a hypothetical federal agency, the Department of Ecology. The student becomes acquainted with both the department and the library through descriptions in the *Government Organization Manual* and the *Department of Ecology Agency Manual*; departmental and library organization charts; the library's floor plan; budget; and annual reports.

In each model some documents are presented as completely as they would be in a real library; most, however, are sections of documents sufficient to convey the information needed in the simulation. Elimination of some peripheral detail (usually described as "noise" in learning situations) serves to focus the student's attention on the model's central features. Choice of specific information to be included is based on the administrative information that will be needed in the problems.

Many of the documents closely resemble existing ones normally used in real libraries of the type portrayed. This is true, for example, of the organization charts, which follow general practice in industry and government for presentation of hierarchical staff relationships. The Double XYZ Field Research Laboratory Library budget is also realistic, having been transcribed from an actual oil company research library budget in both format and substance. The Department of Ecology Library budget, on the other hand, is not realistic. Since government budgets are extremely complicated and the formats usually change with each administration, this budget is simplified in both substance and format, and is designed only to present a minimum of needed information in a way that is easy to understand.

At least one other document used in each model is unrealistic, the Library Professional Bookshelf. It is usually considered desirable (by teachers and curriculum committees) to present students with reading lists for courses, or in some way to point out to them good background material to which they can turn when necessary. Students, however, tend to resent such lists as either spoon-feeding or mickey-mouse. I have learned to relate the inevitable list to the given special library as a Professional Bookshelf—a device I have seen in many real special libraries as an actual group of materials, but which I have never seen as a real document.

In short, the only purpose of the simulation model is to carry selected information in a format that can be read and referred to easily. There is no implication that the model offers a standard of library practice to be emulated in real libraries. Nor is there any promise that the formats used in the various documents of the model are real formats used in existing libraries. Rather, the significance of the model is that it conveys information to students about the hypothetical library in which they will be making decisions and solving problems.

The model should be introduced to the students early in the learning system sequence. Each student studies the model in its entirety before the problem-solving begins, and is free to refer to it at any time during the course, just as an administrator might refer during a working day to his library's policy manual, prior annual reports, budget, or other documents.

CONTEXTUAL STATEMENTS

The simulation teaching materials must include, in addition to the library's background documents, one or more documents designed to define the operational situation in the library at the time the simulation incidents begin. Whatever documents are chosen to provide this operational setting comprise the *contextual statement*, which, in addition to defining the context for problem-solving, also sets the stage for the passage of time during the incidents.

In the Industrial Library Simulation the students are given a descriptive statement, as follows, along with the model:

> The Double XYZ Oil Company of Houston, Texas, after having operated in a single area of Texas for over sixty years, has decided to expand. Preliminary studies have indicated that a productive field lies under the Gulf of Mexico off

Collier County, Florida. A two-year lease for purposes of exploration and feasibility study has been obtained. Exploration will be carried on by a task force
which is viewed as a temporary operation to provide information needed to
make the company decision whether or not to attempt production from this
field.

Thus the student learns that the overall context in which he will be solving
specific problems of library administration is that of meeting the information
needs of the task force without completely disrupting on-going services in the
library at the home office. Planning must be done and problems must be
solved taking into account this context as well as all of the background information given in the model about the parent company and its research library.
It should be obvious to the student that problems generated for the home office library by the necessity of serving personnel at a remote location will be
included.

In the Governmental Library Simulation the context is presented in actual
documents, one of which is included in the model, and others which are
presented in the incident material accompanying the first problem. In this
simulation a small agency, the Office of Aerial Environmental Surveys in the
Department of Space, is being transferred to the Department of Ecology, and
the DOE Library has been directed to incorporate the OAES Library. The
DOE Library staff must plan and implement the transfer within certain
guidelines, meanwhile carrying on its regular responsibilities.

INCIDENT MATERIALS

The model and the contextual statements are supplemented by *incident
materials*, a term which embraces letters, memoranda, reports, minutes of
meetings, texts of phone calls, budget documents, personnel files, applications
for positions, service logs, performance evaluations, and/or any other type of
document used in libraries to convey management information. Some incident material is provided to the students in advance of each experiential
learning session. Other incident materials are generated by the students as
part of their group sessions or as assignments between class meetings. At
times it is necessary for the teacher to prepare additional incident materials
for a class in response to a decision the class has made.

To cite an example of incident material, in the first unit of the Industrial
Library Simulation (which deals with planning needed library service) one of
the roleplay situations calls for interaction between staff and users to identify
the services needed in the given context. When Unit I is scheduled for a class
session, students are expected to read the incident materials (see p. 17), which
accompany that unit.

It is possible to use a given model and contextual statement as the basis for
various levels of study by changing the incidents which form the basis for
problem-solving learning tasks. For example, since the Governmental Library Simulation was originally planned for use as a library school course for

MEMORANDUM

Double XYZ Oil Company
Field Research Laboratory
Administration and General
Services Division

To: Librarian, Field Research Laboratory

From: Head, Administration and General Services

The attached memo tells the story. Although we knew this was in the offing, we didn't realize how soon we'd be expected to implement the operation. And—since this will be the Company's first venture outside of Texas—we're feeling our way.

The Director tells me library services at the site are essential. Let me know as soon as you can what plan you will suggest for providing such services. If I can help, holler.

Attachment
cc: Director, Field Research Laboratory
    Head, Everglades City Exploration Project

. . . .

ATTACHMENT

MEMORANDUM

Double XYZ Oil Company
Field Research Laboratory
Director's Office

To: All Divisions and Departments

The Company has decided to lease off-shore exploration rights to a parcel of land in the Gulf of Mexico near Everglades City, Florida. Exploration activities at this site will begin six months from this date. Maximum exploration time is two years. The operation will be known as ECEP (Everglades City Exploration Project).

The exploration task force will consist of a maximum of thirty researchers plus necessary technical support personnel, approximately three to one. Some personnel will be transferred from FRL, Houston, to this project; others will be hired specifically for the project. The Director's Office will have overall responsibility for the selection and assignment of personnel, with implementation and assistance from AGS Division. Transportation and local housing arrangements will be made through AGS.

This memo will authorize division and department heads normally concerned with support of exploration activities to initiate planning. Extra-normal support deemed necessary should be requested directly from the Director's Office. Preliminary budget requests will be due in sixty days. The newly appointed ECEP Project Head and other key personnel are identified in a separate ECEP Personnel Memo.

working federal librarians who had a professional master's degree and some work experience, the incidents were based on the stated needs of working librarians in the federal government. Research preliminary to designing the Governmental Library Simulation showed that the self-perceived educational needs of federal librarians were closely related to their reported current job activities. These self-perceived needs were felt most keenly in the area of administration, with the highest ranking categories of activities being "planning library services," "directing library activities," and "staff management." The single most frequently cited current job activity of respondents in the survey was the direct supervision and guidance of subordinates.[3] The incidents originally designed for the Governmental Library Simulation, therefore, have as their major objective to give the working federal librarian direct experience, through simulation, in planning, directing and personnel management. The specific incidents related to personnel management, for example, are counseling an unsatisfactory employee, personal rights of employees *vis a vis* assigned library tasks, terminating an employee, and management of an internship program—all indicated as important middle-management personnel tasks. No incident was included about writing job descriptions or interviewing and selecting personnel since the research did not indicate that federal librarians felt a need for further instruction in those tasks.

When the Governmental Library Simulation is used as part of master's-level instruction, however, incidents related to job description, personnel selection and interviewing are routinely included. Although there is no research base to indicate exactly which administrative tasks are likely to be assigned to beginning professional librarians, it is assumed that writing job descriptions, interviewing prospective employees and selecting staff members are essential skills that should be included in introductory instruction. Variations are possible whenever the models are used with specific groups of learners whose needs have been identified through research or can be assumed.

Incident materials must include a time frame for the action that is to take place. It has been found that real dates quickly appear out-of-date to students; relative dates are necessary, however, for internal logic as the action moves the model through time. In the scheme that has been devised for the Industrial and Governmental Library Simulations, "19x0" is used as an initial date of significance in the life of the model library, for example, the date of founding. The first year of the library's existence is then 19x1, and so on. All communications in the model and the incident materials are dated in this fashion. If the date of a prior decade is needed (as in an early report, or in a comparison of statistics covering a long span of time), the date becomes 19–1. If projections into the next decade are to be made (as in a long-range planning document), the date becomes 19+1, and so on. Students are given a calendar showing the days of the week for the period of time to be covered by the action of the simulation. In the Industrial Library Simulation, the action covers six months of 19x7—the seventh year in the life of the Double XYZ Company's Field Research Laboratory Library. The Governmental Library Simulation begins in 19x5, the fifth year of existence of the Department of Ecology Library, and covers nine months in the life of the library.

COURSE MANAGEMENT MATERIALS

Course management materials are those that contribute to the operation of the course and its special techniques rather than to the substance of the simulation. Some of these materials are used only by the instructor, some only by the students, and some by both. In the Industrial Library Simulation the unit guide for each of the five units constitutes the basic course management document for students and instructor.

Industrial Library Simulation
Unit Guide
Unit I

UNIT I. PLANNING SPECIAL LIBRARY SERVICE

Unit Objectives:
1. To plan appropriate service to researchers at a location distant from the company's home office library;

2. To incorporate the plan in the policy manual of the Field Research Laboratory Library (FRLL) of the Double XYZ Oil Company;

3. To make the agreed-on plans known to the staff of the Field Research Laboratory.

Roleplay Activities:
1. Participating (through an assigned role) in a library/user planning meeting;

2. Reaching a consensus among library staff members about the nature of the service and the policies for providing the service.

Communication Activities:
1. Preparation of a call to a meeting;

2. Preparation of minutes of a meeting;

3. Stating the agreed-on policy for remote site service in a form suitable for inclusion in the library's staff manual;

4. Preparation of a publicity release to FRL personnel about the new plans.

Roleplay 1. A committee composed of Double XYZ Oil Company's Field Research Laboratory Library staff members, FRL management and researchers is convened to plan the information services to be offered Company personnel at the remote location.

Roles: FRLL Librarian, who calls the meeting and presides
        FRLL Reference Librarian
        FRL Director
        ECEP Director
        FRL Head, Administration and General Services Division
        FRL researchers, some of whom will be assigned to ECEP
        FRLL Secretary, who will prepare minutes of the meeting

Roleplay Time: 45 minutes maximum

Communications: Call to the meeting
                 Minutes of the meeting

Roleplay 2. The FRLL Librarian and department heads meet to incor-
             porate plans for the remote site information service in the
             existing library policy.

Roles: FRLL Librarian
        FRLL Reference Librarian
        FRLL Acquisitions Librarian

Roleplay Time: 30 minutes

Communication: Revised policy statement(s)

In-basket Exercise:

                                          Interoffice Memo
                                          ABC for Double XYZ
                                          Office of the Editor

To: FRLL Library Director

From: Editor, ABC for Double XYZ

Re: Story on plans for information service to ECEP

    An upcoming issue of ABC for Double XYZ will be devoted to inform-
ing company personnel about the new project "ECEP." Will you or one
of your staff write an article on the information services that will be
given to project personnel? If you anticipate that the article will exceed
1000 words, please call me for a redefinition of this assignment. I would
appreciate having your article in a week or ten days. If you need any
help, don't hesitate to call me. Many thanks.

Suggested Preparation: 1. Review how to preside at meetings.

                        2. Review how to take minutes.

                        3. Review how to write public relations re-
                           leases.

Suggested Readings: 1. Industrial Library Model

                        2. (As many up-to-date articles about planning
                           special library services as the leader feels
                           are needed.)

The Governmental Library Simulation is presented as a series of problems, rather than units, in order to emphasize to students the problem-solving orientation of a simulation course and in order to make the material more flexible for teachers in varying kinds of situations. The basic document for each problem differs from the unit guides of the Industrial Library Simulation because each problem relates to a single learning experience whereas a unit embodies two or more learning experiences. There is no significant difference between the two forms of presenting course materials; the semantic and format differences stem from the situations for which the two simulations were designed. Problem 1 in the Governmental Library Simulation follows:

PROBLEM 1

PLANNING LIBRARY CONSOLIDATION

Incorporation of the library of a hold-out agency into the departmental library has been ordered and must be accomplished in a given period of time. Resistance is evident at the planning meeting. It is the intention of the department administrative officer that two initial goals will be accomplished at this meeting: (1) the department library mission statement will be revised to include the mission of the incoming library; (2) at least the policy, if not the details, of assignment of personnel from the incoming library to the merged library staff will be agreed on.

Roles: Department of Ecology Assistant   DOE Personnel Officer
            Secretary for Administration   DOE Librarian
         Office of Aerial Environmental   OAES Librarian
            Surveys Administrative Officer   DOE Library Secretary

Roleplay Time: 30 minutes maximum

Suggested Preparation:

Review: 1. How to conduct a meeting

              2. How to take minutes

              3. Dynamics of participation in a group

              4. Statements relating to DOE Library (Model)

              5. Management of personnel reassignment

              6. Special library services

Sources: (References to appropriate part of the
              Federal Library Model)

             (Six to eight references from the literature of
              business administration)

Orientation games, exercises and pretests as well as discussion guides and evaluation forms are additional types of course management materials. Since

these fit directly into the discussion of classroom methodology which constitutes Part II of this book, further examples will be presented there.

CHAPTER HIGHLIGHTS

A sustained simulation is
> ... an integrated teaching/learning system.

A sustained simulation
> ... incorporates a large number of related teaching/learning objectives,
> ... moves a model through time.

A simulation model is
> ... a selection of the central features of reality to be used in teaching
> and learning.

A contextual statement is
> ... a group of simulated documents that provide the operational setting
> for problem-solving.

Additional teaching/learning materials include
> ... incident materials,
> ... a time frame,
> ... course management materials.

REFERENCES

1. Paul A. Twelker, *Simulation: An Overview*, 1968. (Available as ED 025 459)
2. Sarane B. Boocock and E.O. Schild, *Simulation and Gaming* (AMA Management Report No. 55; New York: American Management Association, 1961).
3. James J. Kortendick and Elizabeth W. Stone, *Post-Master's Education for Middle and Upper-Level Personnel in Libraries and Information Centers* (Washington, D.C.: Department of Library Science, The Catholic University of America, 1970). (USOE Project 8-0731, Final Report), pp. 193–194.

PART II.
The Teacher's Role in Simulation Teaching

3.
Orientation

· · · · · · · · · · · ·

Among the advantages claimed for experiential learning there is no hint that simulation is a substitute for the teacher. Neither is it a cure-all nor a guaranteed solution to teaching problems. It does eliminate—or virtually so—some of the components of the teacher's traditional role. There are few, if any, lectures to prepare, no syllabi to compile, no term papers to read far into the night. The teacher does continue, however, to direct the flow of the course in terms of scheduling specific learning tasks for each class session and assigning individual responsibility for specific participation in class activities. Thus the teacher continues in the role of course manager or coordinator, and he continues to be responsible for student evaluation.

Certain traditional aspects of the teacher's role are enhanced, however, and new roles are added. Orientation to a simulation course, for example, requires intensified teacher effort (and more classroom time) because experiential and group process techniques are unfamiliar to many, if not most, students. A good rule of thumb is to introduce students to the new style of teaching called "group process" during the first two or three hours of the course, or during a proportional period of initial time in a workshop or institute, leaving the specific experiential techniques to be introduced as they are to be used.

INITIATING GROUP PROCESS

Students have convinced me both verbally and by their behavior that they come to graduate library education with certain skills well in hand. They can sit through a lecture without interrupting; most can take notes sufficient unto the tests. They can ask questions designed to "psych out" the teacher. They can frame their own ideas as questions in order to reduce the risk of appearing to espouse ideas unacceptable to teacher or peers. They can identify real questions in areas they fail to understand so that they can ask these questions privately of the teacher (or friends) or look up answers on their own—again to reduce psychological risk to themselves. Graduate library students are usually highly skilled in independent academic work—reading, projects, bibliographies, term papers, essay exams. They are also skilled in participative academic work, although most such "participation" is hidden from the teacher and limited to "in-groups." Team projects are teacher-acceptable, but "cooperation" on lengthy reading assignments, dividing exercises among a group of friends, passing notes and assignments to roommates who will be taking the course in the future, mutual criticism of work in draft stages, tutoring among classmates—these participative activities do not usually receive the teacher's blessing. It is my firm conviction that these activities, real but covert, prepare students better for effective participation in library *staff* activities than do the traditional independent academic assignments. Group process teaching brings the participation out in the open and involves all students.

I have never understood why so many library schools emphasize personal skills almost exclusively when it is inherent in the very term "library service" that interaction is at the core of all library activity. The reading of any set of library objectives clearly shows that no achievement of their goals is possible without effective personal interaction and teamwork. It seems irrational to me, therefore, to devote almost one hundred percent of the student's education to perfecting personal academic skills and then expect him to perform immediately and effectively in the interactive situations that constitute the daily activity of administrators. Neither can the achievement of interactive skills be postponed on the excuse that few library school students begin their careers as top administrators or even as middle managers. The evidence is that most professional librarians begin their careers in positions in which they supervise one or more paraprofessionals; and supervision is one of the most troublesome and most under-taught of the interactive skills. The fact that simulation teaching is especially conducive to the development of interactive skills is a prime reason for choosing it as the mode for teaching administration. Every effort should be made to exploit this potential. Other courses emphasize the independent skills which are legitimately needed for individual intellectual tasks in many library jobs; but the administration course, leading to interactive tasks and team work, is primarily a group process course when it is taught by simulation. And it is incumbent on the teacher to lay the groundwork for this classroom style which is unfamiliar to most library science students.

The pedagogical task of developing interpersonal skills has environmental, cognitive and affective aspects which can be introduced to a group of learners in a variety of ways, some as simple as arranging chairs in a circle to allow complete eye-to-eye contact, others as complex as sensitivity training. The most complex must be left to special courses of instruction, either formal or informal, but many are easy to incorporate into graduate courses or continuing education workshops. The teacher who has not made a study of the relationships between classroom atmosphere and the development of interpersonal skills would do well to read such works as Herbert Kohl's *Open Classroom*,[1] Carl Rogers' *Freedom to Learn*,[2] and Malcolm Knowles' *Modern Practice of Adult Education*[3] until he feels himself accepting the important themes running through them:

> Adults are capable of participating in the planning of their own education and should therefore be offered choices as to ways and means of achieving their learning objectives.
>
> Adult learners need to be helped to identify and analyze their needs so they can choose and plan learning experiences that will be effective.
>
> All of those in a learning group—"teacher" and "students"—know more together than does any one separately; to achieve maximum learning, therefore, all must share in the learning process.
>
> To be effective, sharing must be built on honesty and credibility among the members of the learning group.

Once accepted and implemented, these concepts become part of the experience of the budding administrator and effect behavioral change in him. Through personal experience and practice among peers each individual learner develops a style of participative interaction which he can carry into group activities on the job.

The teacher's role is to facilitate all aspects of learning. Facilitation is such a different process from traditional chalk-and-talk teaching that the contrastive term "leader" is often used to replace the traditional "teacher," especially in nonacademic situations such as in-service workshops. It is the teacher/leader who provides the physical arrangements and the atmosphere of an open classroom. It is the teacher/leader who makes available cognitive input about group process in a variety of ways: taped mini-lectures, reading lists, small-group discussions, demonstrations, sometimes movies. Students are free to use whichever technique is most comfortable and convenient to them. It is the teacher/leader who plans effective orientation for group problem-solving using, among other devices, simple games designed for this purpose. Examples of such games can be found in education journals and manuals of human relations training methods.

The learner's introduction to interpersonal skills and group process begins at the first meeting of the learning group. The leader should be alert to return to the theme, however, in discussions of roleplay and debriefing behavior with individuals as well as with the group. Devices that can be used for reinforcement during subsequent sessions include:

Self-tests similar to those in popular magazines (I make up my own or adapt them from ones appearing in periodicals such as *Industry Week*, *SM/ Sales Meetings*, *Management Review*, and *Training and Development Journal*.)

Remedial mini-lectures (10–12-minute single-concept talks).

Roleplay "instant replays" to demonstrate differences of personal response to a given situation.

DEVELOPING RAPPORT AMONG LEARNERS

The atmosphere of openness and honesty so essential to skilled group process begins with the establishment of rapport during the first learning session. The opening order of business is to make certain that everyone knows everyone else by first name. Of course, name tags can—and sometimes should—be used, but they can't be read from more than a few feet away and they evoke memories of very formal occasions. Even in a one-day workshop, when time is at a premium, a few minutes spent getting acquainted will pay off. I make a point of arriving early and as soon as people begin to gather I introduce myself and begin to learn names. If the group is less than twenty-five, I try to introduce them—by first name—as each newcomer arrives. Since I'm very slow to learn names, the repetitive exercise helps me as well as the listening members of the group. I inevitably make mistakes, cover with a joke and everyone laughs with me. After I've performed the introductions a half dozen times, I ask someone in the group to try, thereby producing groans, more mistakes, more laughter and more repetition of the names. In workshop groups of over twenty-five introductions have to be performed after breaking into small groups. By birth month, by home town, by favorite color—any excuse to move people around, get them to exchange conversation and laugh together will help to establish rapport.

A formal class usually comes complete with roll, but to simply "call the roll" as an introduction is too rigid for a class that is to be characterized by freedom and interaction. There are always some students in my special libraries administration course whom I've taught in prior courses, but because our school is expanding rapidly to the multisection stage, there are usually some I don't know, too. I begin the patter with those I know and try to draw the others in. Sometimes students themselves unconsciously help:

> After setting up the room with chairs in a circle on one occasion, and before any members of the class had arrived, I returned to my office for some materials. I was delayed and was a few minutes late returning to the classroom. The class had gathered and all except one were in the circle. That one, who was unknown to me, had seated herself outside the circle behind some of the others.
>
> Dr. Zachert: It's good to see so many faces I know, and it's good to see some I don't know; I'll be able to make some new friends this quarter. I'm always surprised to be reminded that you don't all know everybody else in the library school. Look around. Do you know the people sitting beside you?
>
> Leslie: I do—because I always sit down beside people I know. It's the people on the other side of the room I don't know.
>
> Dr. Zachert: Is there someone on the other side of the room now whom you don't know?
>
> Leslie: Yes. (She indicated the girl sitting outside the circle.)
>
> Dr. Zachert: Come on, I'll introduce you. (I got up, and walked with Leslie over to the new girl, introduced myself, and asked her name—Eileen.) Leslie, this is Eileen; Eileen, this is Leslie. (To the class) Anyone else who hasn't met Eileen?

Since Eileen was new and a part-time student, no one had met her, so everyone got up and came to be introduced. I ducked back and Leslie introduced the next person to Eileen who was then "handed along" until she'd met everyone. By the time we sorted ourselves out and got back to our original chairs, the circle had magically added another chair and Eileen was "in." Ten minutes lost? No—a beautiful, spontaneous beginning for a course.

Games also set a stage that is different from that of the usual course, and they help to establish rapport. If you don't know any ice-breaker games, look for some in a handbook for group leaders. Or, if you want them to be games about libraries, make up your own.

One of my homemade games is a board game in which six to eight players work their way around the board and through typical experiences in a special library. Photocopy machine breaks down? Back up one space. A needed translation arrives quickly from the John Crerar Translations Center? Take an extra turn. Phone calls interrupt. Coffee breaks extend over lost turns. Crises arise in circulation, at the reference desk, and in the purchasing agent's office. Eventually somebody wins the key to the executive washroom!

After thirty minutes of this kind of introduction to special library words, ideas and happenings there are neither strangers nor enemies (except friendly ones) in the group. I usually allocate one third of the first class session to the specific objective of establishing rapport quickly in a new class, and I consider it a good investment.

UNDERSCORING THE
IMPORTANCE OF COMMUNICATION SKILL

The importance of both oral and written communication skill should be introduced as part of the orientation. Oral communication potentially includes feedback, a great advantage to both sender and receiver when it can be achieved. This potential is sometimes not realized, however, especially in administrative situations in which authority and hierarchy can interfere. A simple group experiment in communication can demonstrate the value of feedback in achieving mutual understanding. One such experiment (Exhibit 1) also demonstrates the affective responses of both senders and receivers to situations with and without feedback.

To introduce the importance of effective written communication in the simulation to come, I use a self-administered pre-test that gives each student the opportunity to evaluate his present ability privately (Exhibit 2). If he feels he needs to improve, the learner can take remedial action before he is called on to produce written communications for use in group situations. Low scorers on the pre-test are directed, at the conclusion of the test, to several remedial manuals. The leader should have copies of those referred to, or others, to hand out in response to requests for help. The leader should also have a file of communications that can be used for practice by learners who feel a need to have their work criticized by the leader. At the time of introduction, however, the leader should not force learners to submit work for criticism; he should criticize only if asked to do so. This pre-test also serves as an introduction to self-analysis and evaluation, and the point is made early that remedial action is at the learner's option and at his initiative.

ARRIVING AT OBJECTIVES

The objectives of a simulation course in administration might be stated (from the point of view of a curriculum committee or the course instructor) in broad terms of administrative behavior and the skills of teamwork, and they might be stated in such a way as to emphasize the experiential character of the course:

Learning Experiences to Develop Administrative Behavior:
Practice in the identification of alternative behaviors and/or solutions in response to administrative processes and problems
Practice in decision-making
Practice in following up the consequences of a decision

Learning Experiences to Develop Skill in Teamwork:
Practice in interpersonal skills
Practice in oral and written communication skills
Practice in group problem-solving skills

It is assumed in my course that the practice which constitutes the course learning experiences will be in the context of special libraries; that some descriptive background about special libraries, past and present, and their environments may be necessary as cognitive input during the course (if it is not conveyed to students elsewhere in the curriculum); and that this environment includes not only the *loci* of special libraries in industry, government, independent agencies, and academe, but also the professional environment of associations, supportive information agencies, a body of literature, and outstanding, contributing personalities. In administration courses related specifically to academic, public or school libraries similar assumptions would be made about the incorporation of background information on the specific type of library.

The learning experiences as stated above also assume that appropriate cognitive input of administrative theory is either a part of the course or that it has been studied previously by the students and therefore constitutes entry knowledge at the beginning of the simulation. A glance at the curricula of graduate library schools shows that administrative theory is taught in some as an introductory course followed by a separate course intended to provide some application of that theory, often in the context of a specific type of library. In other schools administrative theory and application are covered in the same course. Appropriate content for a course in administrative theory is discussed elsewhere in library literature. This book concentrates on a way of teaching the application of theory. Thus, to relate the objectives of the study of administration of libraries to Bloom's hierarchy of intellectual skills,[4] the study of administrative theory and of descriptive and historical background of specific types of libraries comprises skills of knowledge and comprehension; whereas the simulation course focuses primarily on application, analysis, synthesis and evaluation with reinforcement of knowledge and comprehension as a by-product (if student evaluations of simulation courses are to be believed).

A great deal has been written recently about behavioral objectives and their significance in teaching and learning.[5,6] Behavioral objectives state specific behaviors in which the learner is expected to become competent as a result of particularized learning experiences. They are correlated with evaluation criteria which specify the extent and conditions under which the behavior must be demonstrated in order to assure that the objectives have been achieved. This concept assumes that the knowledge or skills being taught can be so particularized and that a standard for performance can be precisely designated.

Very little has appeared in library literature, however, to show that administration courses are based on behavioral objectives. Since we do not have a research base that defines how administrators *should* act to obtain maximum results, or what constitutes optimum interpersonal skill for effective library staff work, it is virtually impossible to state behavioral objectives and criteria for administration courses at the present time.

Perhaps the objectives of library administration study should be labelled "expressive objectives," in Eisner's provocative phrase:[7]

> An expressive objective does not specify the behavior the student is to acquire after having engaged in one or more learning activities. An expressive objective describes an educational encounter: It identifies a situation in which [learners] are to work, a problem with which they are to cope, a task in which they are to engage; but it does not specify what from that encounter, situation, problem, or task they are to learn. An expressive objective provides both the teacher and the student with an invitation to explore, defer, or focus on issues that are of peculiar interest or import to the inquirer. An expressive objective is evocative rather than prescriptive.
>
> The expressive objective is intended to serve as a theme around which skills and understandings learned earlier can be brought to bear, but through which those skills and understandings can be expanded, elaborated, and made idiosyncratic. With an expressive objective what is desired is not homogeneity of response among studer ts but diversity.

In addition to the objective of providing students with learning experiences by which they can develop administrative behaviors and skills for teamwork, a course devoted to teaching the application of administrative theory should take into account the learners' own objectives. Some have their career goals set at the level of top management; most aspire at least to middle management; and virtually all have observed that supervision of paraprofessionals, student assistants or maintenance personnel will be required of them from the day they go to work as "professional" librarians. If time is allowed for learners to articulate specific objectives for simulation study (as a follow-up of their study of administrative theory) they typically arrive at such objectives as:

"To learn to interview someone for a job."

"To PERT a library operat .."

"To actually prepare a budget" (often, specifically "a PPBS budget").

"To learn how to handle complaints about personnel matters."

Frequently there are also statements of objectives which follow the general form, "I'd like to read more about . . . supervising . . . motivating employees . . . participative management . . . how to prepare forms . . . conduct a systems analysis of library operation . . . evaluate employees."

A significant part of the introduction to the simulation course consists of obtaining from learners statements of their personal objectives. Equally significant is a rigorous follow-up by the leader to make sure that each learner will be able to work towards his own objectives through specific assignments, directed personal projects, or open-ended learning time. If some learner objectives are inappropriate (because, for example, of misunderstanding of the scope and nature of the present course, or because the objective can be met more specifically by another course), a conference with the leader will help the learner understand why his objectives are not being incorporated in the present course. Openness about course objectives required by the curriculum will help create the atmosphere for simulation learning. Willingness to discuss learners' personal objectives and honesty in incorporating or emphasizing these objectives in the course are also significant factors in the group learning that evolves.

Open discussion of learner objectives and incorporation of these objectives in learning experiences are especially important in continuing education. The practical literature of adult education as well as the research literature of adult learning studies emphasizes the relationship between felt needs as objectives of learning and the success, in terms of valuation and durability, of that learning. Library science research such as Kortendick and Stone's study of educational needs of librarians[8] clearly shows that interest is closely related to job responsibility. Thus in any continuing education workshop, institute or seminar, membership in which is self-selected by the learners, it can be anticipated that each individual learner comes with his own personal objectives related to the announced topic. In the area of administration, many of these needs—and thus continuing education objectives—are very practical ones of improving expertise in administrative behavior and team skills. It is this important characteristic of adult learners—that they see their educational needs as very practical ones related to job responsibility—that makes experiential techniques so valuable for continuing education in administration.

THE AUTHORITY OF TRUST

The authority of trust is the only tenable authority in the open classroom. It is the authority that evolves as learners come to feel that "if the teacher asks them to do something, there is a sound educational objective behind his request, that they will find the experience useful to them, and that they will not be embarrassed by complying. In short, they must feel they can use the teacher's skill in reaching their goals."[9] The only way to replace the authority of position and the authority of knowledge—the usual classroom sovereignties—with the authority of trust is to be honest and open with learners at all times.

It is possible to set the stage, so to speak, during the period of orientation. To do so considerable care must be taken to make educational objectives explicit and relevant, to solicit learner opinion about details of the learning process and to incorporate that opinion in management of the class, to admit ignorance when in fact the teacher does not know the specific asked for. If at the same time that trust in the teacher is developing, the teacher is leading the group into making wise choices for itself, trust in the group will develop among the members of the group. Development of the authority of trust can rarely be completely achieved during the orientation period. It should, however, be initiated during the first meeting between leader and learners and thereafter cultivated in every possible way until the goal is realized.

CHAPTER HIGHLIGHTS

The teacher's role is
- ... more nontraditional than traditional;
- ... leadership;
- ... facilitation.

The task of orientation in simulation teaching is
- ... to initiate group process;
- ... to develop rapport among learners;
- ... to underscore the importance of oral and written communication;
- ... to arrive at group objectives;
- ... to establish the authority of trust.

REFERENCES

1. Herbert Kohl, *The Open Classroom* (New York: Random House, 1969).
2. Carl R. Rogers, *Freedom to Learn* (Columbus, Ohio: C. E. Merrill, 1969).
3. Malcolm S. Knowles, *Modern Practice of Adult Education* (New York: Association Press, 1970).
4. Benjamin S. Bloom, ed., et al., *Taxonomy of Educational Objectives: Handbook I, The Cognitive Domain* (New York: Longmans, Green, 1956).
5. Robert F. Mager, *Preparing Objectives for Programmed Instruction* (Palo Alto, Calif.: Fearon, 1962).

6. Miriam B. Kapfer, *Behavioral Objectives in Curriculum Development* (Englewood Cliffs, N.J.: Educational Technology Publications, 1972).

7. Elliot W. Eisner, "Instructional and Expressive Educational Objectives: Their Formulation and Use in Curriculum," in W. James Popham, et al., *Instructional Objectives* (Chicago: Rand, McNally, 1969), pp. 14–18. (American Educational Research Association Monograph Series on Curriculum Evaluation, No. 3.)

8. James J. Kortendick and Elizabeth W. Stone, *Job Dimensions and Educational Needs in Librarianship* (Chicago: American Library Association, 1971).

9. Allen A. Zoll, *Dynamic Management Education*, 2nd ed. (Reading, Mass.: Addison-Wesley Publishing Company, 1969), pp. 4–5.

EXHIBITS

EXHIBIT 1. AN EXPERIMENT IN COMMUNICATION

The Communication Experiment has been described in several places, with slight variations. Its purpose is to demonstrate the value of feedback in communication.

Give each member of the group an $8\frac{1}{2}$ " x 11 " piece of paper, a pen or pencil, and a domino. With these tools each person is to draw the diagrams in Figures 4 and 5 from directions given by a member of the group, without seeing the diagrams.

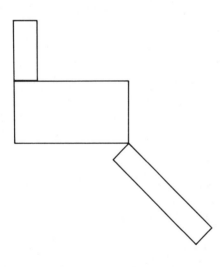

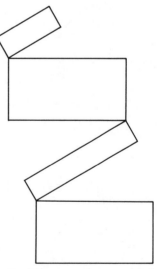

Figure 4. Communication experiment,
          diagram A

Figure 5. Communication experiment,
          diagram B

For Part 1 of the "experiment" the person giving the directions turns his back to the group, and the group is instructed not to talk, laugh, ask questions or, in fact, make any sound. The directions are given and the group members try to reproduce Figure 4. When the instructor has concluded, show the diagram to the group (use a transparency and an overhead projector for a large group). Usually very few, if any, people are able to reproduce the diagram from such limited directions.

For Part 2 of the "experiment" a different person describes Figure 5 but this time facing the group. He is able to respond to direct questions, as well as facial and body communication expressing confusion, frustration or misunderstanding. Instruct him to use any form of communication that will help the group. Instruct the group to ask any questions that will help them accomplish the task of reproducing the diagram. Usually at least half the group will be able to reproduce the diagram perfectly. Sometimes someone boldly asks, "Show us what you are talking about"—in which case the experiment ends because, for this kind of communication, visualization is the best instruction.

Follow the "experiment" with a discussion of communication with and without feedback, the inhibitors of communication, the facilitators of communication, the kinds of questions that resulted in the most helpful responses, and the feelings engendered in each individual in the two situations.

EXHIBIT 2. PRE-TEST ON WRITTEN COMMUNICATION ABILITY

<u>Objective:</u> To evaluate yourself on your written communication ability.

<u>Directions:</u> Read Communications A, B, C, D and E. Now write a response to each communication. Your response may be in the form of a memo or a letter. Head each response appropriately and write your message. (You may use scrap paper to draft your responses.) Next turn to the "Checklist for Effective Writing" which follows Communication E, and use it to evaluate your responses.

. . . .

<u>Communication A</u>

Interoffice Memo
Bureau of Community
Improvement
Finance Office

To: Head Librarian

From: Deputy Finance Officer

Re: United Fund Drive

Please send me the name of a responsible member of your staff to serve on the United Fund Drive Committee for the Bureau. State the individual's qualifications with emphasis on special capabilities useful in the forthcoming drive.

. . . .

Communication B

Interoffice Memo
Bureau of Community Improvement
Research Office

To: Head Librarian

From: Agnes Morrison

Re: Library hours

As a new researcher with the Bureau, I am spending quite a bit of overtime in the office trying to learn the ropes as quickly as possible. I have not needed to use the library as yet, but I forsee that I soon will. What are the hours the library is open? And how can I have access to it after the regular workday?

[Note: You have a pamphlet that tells hours, services, etc., that you can send if you wish. The rule is: nobody gets in after 5 P.M.]

. . . .

Communication C

Interoffice Memo
Bureau of Community Improvement
Personnel Office

To: Head Librarian

From: Administrative Assistant to the Chief, Personnel Office

Re: Meeting on revision of the dress code for non-exempt personnel

The Chief wants to be certain that you can attend the meeting scheduled for Wednesday at 2 P.M. because so many of your employees are in the non-exempt category. How about it?

[Note: At 2 P.M. on Wednesday you have an appointment with Sam McDonald, a representative from a microfilm equipment company for a demonstration of some equipment you are considering for purchase.]

Communication D

> 821 Juniper Street
> Lansing, Michigan
> September 10, 19x5

Head Librarian
Bureau of Community Improvement
P.O. Box 22935
Washington, D.C.

Dear Sir:

Thank you for notification of my appointment as an intern in your library beginning October 1, 19x5.

As I understand the terms of the appointment I will be expected to work twenty hours per week for one year on rotating assignment throughout the library under your direction. During this time I am permitted to take course work toward the masters degree in library science at nearby Central State University. At the end of the year I will be considered for permanent appointment to the Bureau library staff.

The Department of Library Science at CSU has informed me that, if I am working twenty hours per week, I will be permitted to register for only half the usual academic load and it will take me two years to complete my degree. Obviously, it is to my financial advantage to work less, carry a full academic load, and complete my degree in one year. This letter is to notify you, therefore, that I accept the internship appointment, but will work in the Bureau library for only ten hours per week.

Looking forward to seeing you October 1,

> Sincerely,
>
> *Kim B. Reese*
> Kim B. Reese

[Note: You are authorized for twenty-hour-per-week interns only and all plans have been made for a group of six interns on that basis. It is too late to revise plans. It is also too late, in all probability, to get another applicant screened and appointed by the beginning date. You need all six interns to carry out the plan and for future jobs in the library.]

. . . .

Communication E

> Interoffice Memo
> Bureau of Community Improvement
> Office of the Chief
> September 15, 19x5

Boss: This was hand delivered at 9:10 am today —Marge

To: Head Librarian

From: Chief, BCI

Subject: Attached letter [Communication E: Attachment]

Please draft a reply for my signature.

<u>Communication E: Attachment</u>

Commission on Interagency Mission Cooperation
Northwood Office Building A273
Bethesda, Maryland

September 14, 19x5

Chief, Bureau of Community Improvement
P.O. Box 22935
Washington, D.C.

Dear Sir:

    It is my understanding that federal libraries are required to cooper-
ate with each other. However, the library of the Bureau of Community
Improvement has been harassing the Commission Library and me personally for the past three weeks. They want me to return a book obtained from them on interlibrary loan. I am using this book in Commission
work and I cannot do without it.

    It is just such instances of **noncooperation among agencies whose
missions are complementary** that the Commission is seeking to identify
in order to eliminate waste in the federal complex.

Sincerely,

George Foster, Commissioner

. . . .

CHECKLIST FOR EFFECTIVE WRITING*

Directions: Read the checklist, then read the communication to be
            evaluated. Reread the checklist, marking each item
            "Yes" or "No" on the Evaluation Form following the
            checklist. Do this for each response that you have writ-
            ten to Communications A, B, C, D and E.

1. Is the communication <u>complete</u>?

    <u>Ask yourself</u>: What does the recipient already know about this
               subject? What does he need to know? What prob-
               lems will he encounter in following up on this
               communication? Where can he go for further in-
               formation?

---

*Based, in part, on: U.S. Department of Health, Education and Welfare,
Division of Personnel Management, <u>Getting Your Ideas Across Through
Writing</u> (Training Manual Number 7; Washington. Government Printing
Office, 1950), "Check Your Writing," pp. 4-14.

Now check for: Names
                Dates
                Places
                Background
                Purpose
                Source for further information

2. Is the communication <u>concise</u>?

    Ask yourself: What are the essentials of the message from the re-
                   cipient's point of view? Does the communication
                   state the essentials once? Are unessential words
                   and phrases avoided?

    Now check for: Redundancy
                    Long-windedness
                    Padding
                    Beating around the bush

3. Is the communication <u>clear</u>?

    Ask yourself: What kind of language will the recipient understand
                   best—casual, technical, professional jargon, legal or
                   some other? Are simple, direct words preferred to
                   unusual or vague ones? Is the sentence and para-
                   graph structure easy to follow? Is information pre-
                   sented logically?

    Then check for: Appropriate language
                     Simplicity of structure
                     Logical presentation

4. Is the communication <u>correct</u>?

    Ask yourself: Will the recipient actually get information that is fac-
                   tually correct, in accordance with policy from this
                   communication? Are all aspects of presentation of
                   the communication correct?

    Then check for: Facts
                     Figures
                     Names
                     Grammar
                     Spelling
                     Form

5. Is the communication <u>appropriate in tone</u>?

    Ask yourself: Will the recipient have friendly, cooperative feelings
                   toward you as a result of this communication or will
                   he be antagonistic, insulted or turned off?

    Then check for: Stilted phrases
                     Legalistic tone
                     Indifference or antagonism
                     Governmentese

EVALUATION FORM

Communication Identification	Checklist Question	Evaluation
A	1	Yes_____ No_____
	2	Yes_____ No_____
	3	Yes_____ No_____
	4	Yes_____ No_____
	5	Yes_____ No_____

Overall evaluation for response to Communication A (Check one below)

I really got the idea across	I almost made it	Stop! Look! Re-write necessary!	What was I thinking of?	I blew it!

Communication Identification	Checklist Question	Evaluation
B	1	Yes_____ No_____
	2	Yes_____ No_____
	3	Yes_____ No_____
	4	Yes_____ No_____
	5	Yes_____ No_____

Overall evaluation for response to Communication B (Check one below)

I really got the idea across	I almost made it	Stop! Look! Re-write necessary!	What was I thinking of?	I blew it!

Communication Identification	Checklist Question	Evaluation
C	1	Yes_____ No_____
	2	Yes_____ No_____
	3	Yes_____ No_____
	4	Yes_____ No_____
	5	Yes_____ No_____

Overall evaluation for response to Communication C (Check one below)

I really got the idea across	I almost made it	Stop! Look! Re-write necessary!	What was I thinking of?	I blew it!

Communication Identification	Checklist Question	Evaluation
D	1	Yes_____ No_____
	2	Yes_____ No_____
	3	Yes_____ No_____
	4	Yes_____ No_____
	5	Yes_____ No_____

Overall evaluation for response to Communication D (Check one below)

I really got the idea across	I almost made it	Stop! Look! Re-write necessary!	What was I thinking of?	I blew it!

Communication Identification	Checklist Question	Evaluation	
E	1	Yes_____	No_____
	2	Yes_____	No_____
	3	Yes_____	No_____
	4	Yes_____	No_____
	5	Yes_____	No_____

Overall evaluation for response to Communication E (Check one below)

I really got the idea across	I almost made it	Stop! Look! Re- write necessary!	What was I thinking of?	I blew it!

Criteria for this test: Four of the five communications should rate
    "Fully Satisfactory" or "A Good Try," on the following scale:

Fully Satisfactory	A Good Try	Passable	Needs a Patch Job	Toss in File 13

Your next step: If only two or three communications rated high, you
should formally review the art of written communication. You may ask the teacher to help you plan your
formal review. If none or only one of your communications rated "Fully Satisfactory" or "A Good Try",
arrange an interview with your teacher immediately.
Perhaps you should defer this course until you have
obtained intensive instruction in the art of written
communication.

If you did not meet the criteria for this test, what do you plan to do
about it?

Do you know where to get review information? Yes _____ No _____
If "No," ask your instructor for help.

4.
Coordination
• • • • • • • • • • • •

To devise the learning stimulus, to observe and analyze learner behavior, to respond to that behavior as critic, confidant, ally and further stimulus; to juggle all these hoops plus those of time, space, paperwork and other components of administrative hassle—this is the daily requirement of the teacher who elects an experiential classroom mode. All of which is encompassed in the word "coordination."

As Clark Abt expresses it in *Serious Games:*[1]

> In this kind of education, the teacher has a responsibility to be much more analytical and lucid in the presentation of the game mode and in the analysis of the game consequences than is usually required by the lecture system. In a class where games are used, the teacher must learn to give brief but very intensive analyses and explanations, interspersed with longer periods of observations of student experiments and occasional coaching remarks. This is entirely different from the continuous pattern of doctrinaire topical material transferred from textbooks to the teacher's mind to the teacher's mouth to the student's pencils. And it should be more rewarding and entertaining. The teacher is now an attendant, an audience at a drama in which student actors display their problem-solving capabilities in intellectual contests. There is suspense over the uncertainty of the outcome, and emotional identification with contesting actors. But the teacher is also the critic, evaluating each player's interpretation of his role.

BRIEFING

The heart of the simulation learning system (as was shown in Figure 1) is in the "Briefing⟶Problem⟶Debriefing" loop, which is repeated as often as needed to fulfill the objectives of the teaching/learning situation, be it academic course or in-service workshop. Briefing is the preparation of the learning group to participate in a given problem-solving experience; debriefing is a follow-up discussion characterized by analysis of the cognitive and affective content of the experiential problem-solving, reinforcement of specific learning objectives, and identification of need for further learning experiences in support of the immediate objectives.

Both briefing and debriefing are specialized forms of communication, some of which is necessarily teacher-centered, but much of which can be, and should be, learner-centered. A fine line of distinction for the leader's role in this communication has been described as "nonauthority with reference to the *content* of the sessions but . . . authority with reference to the *functions* of the group."[2] This is not to say that the leader is not *an* authority on the content of the learning, for indeed he should be such to direct learning; rather, it is to say that the leader is not *the* authority from which the communication of the content stems. The teacher's role in the communication process is that of initiator, helper or devil's advocate as the case requires, and referee—all of which is embodied in the term "leader."

Briefing includes preparation of the learner for the cognitive aspects of the problem to be studied, as well as for the experiential procedures to be used, and for the specifics of the incident in which the problem is embedded. Because of the importance for adults of participation in the planning of personal learning, I like to provide as many options for this preparation as possible.

For the learner's guidance in preparing the cognitive aspects of a problem in administration, I would provide (a) a general bibliography on administration from which the learner could choose readings, (b) a list of specific reading suggestions that relate closely to the problem under study, (c) a classroom lecture on the theory that is to be introduced at this point, or one or more mini-lectures on cassettes if the theory is being reviewed, and (d) films or videotapes related to the cognitive content, if such are available, for viewing on the learner's time and at his option.

The experiential techniques were introduced to learners during the general orientation: warm-up exercises for roleplay or a trial in-basket exercise for in-baskets. The action maze requires no special preparation, and games usually require only the instructions for their play. The specifics for each problem are presented in narrative form and in the incident materials (described in Chapter 2, with examples in Part VI, A and B).

In the sustained simulations that I use in teaching the administration of special libraries each model includes a "Professional Bookshelf" which comprises the general bibliography. The course management materials include specific reading suggestions and incident materials for each problem. When the problem is scheduled, all that is required is the assignment of roles to the participants. If cassettes or films are available, announcement can be made when a problem is scheduled; or this information could be included in the course management materials.

If initial emphasis on group process has resulted in cohesiveness, the group may perceive some common needs in addition to their individual needs for preparation. Again, I try to allow for some group choices: they may request additional documents relating to the problem situation; they may request a demonstration, or lecture review of relevant principles, or they may ask the teacher to play the role of library consultant in a roleplay of seeking information about the problem. On occasion I have invited experts such as architects and finance officers to play themselves in an information-seeking roleplay for specialized input before the group works on a specific problem.

Thus the briefing is at two levels: the preparation of the class as a group, and the preparation of each individual. These levels and the options are shown in Figure 6.

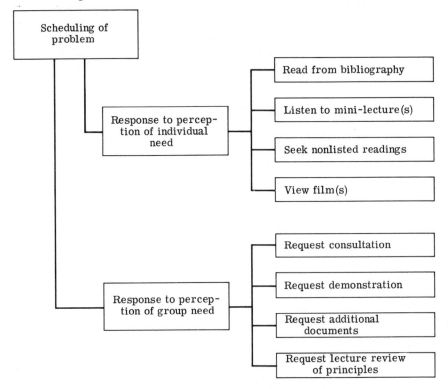

Figure 6. Preparation options in response to perceived needs.

The use of simulations and experiential methods in short continuing-education experiences, such as one-day workshops, raises special problems about briefing. How can the leader assure that the group has sufficient cognitive content to apply to the experiential problem-solving? If the major objective of the workshop is to provide participants with a problem-solving experience, little time can be taken for cognitive input and it is unrealistic to assume that everyone would prepare in advance even if reading materials or recorded lectures were made available. Also, the ability of a group to integrate large amounts of cognitive input in lecture form so as to be able to use it immediately in a problem-solving experience appears to be limited.

Recently I have been experimenting with a workshop model, represented in Figure 7, that appears in initial usage to have several advantages: (a) The tone of the workshop is set immediately in the opening experience, for which a game or an action maze seems to be easiest and most effective simulation to use. (b) It is crucial for learners to understand the technique of "experience

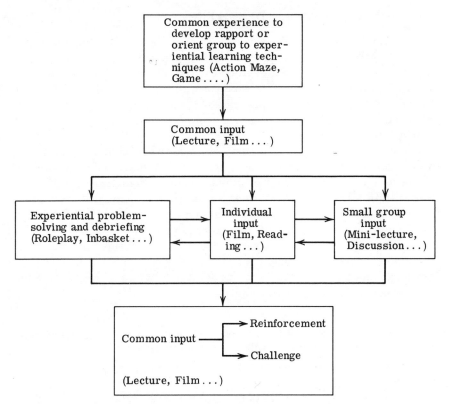

Figure 7. Sequence of briefing, problem-solving and debriefing modules for a one-day workshop.

followed by debriefing" since it is the major learning strategy used; its introduction as the first order of business is a clear demonstration. (c) A well-designed opening experience provides a setting of relevance for the cognitive input of the second module. (d) The active involvement of learners' minds early in the workshop seems to be a good psychological move; it helps to wake them up and to avoid the day-long passivity characteristic of many didactic "programs" masquerading as learning experiences. (e) Adults do learn differently from one another, and offering option modules acknowledges the fact. In some instances free choice can be allowed the learners. Under other circumstances the group is divided and each subgroup is routed to each alternative in turn. Variety, reinforcement and personal satisfaction result. (f) The final module of input to the total group is especially important for group cohesiveness if the group is to follow up the workshop by working together in a common circumstance or on a common problem (as would be the case for a library staff workshop); it seems to have learning reinforcement and psychological values in any case.

DEBRIEFING

Procedurally the debriefing begins as soon as the problem-solving experience ends, and embraces two phases. The first phase is one of self-analysis for each learner; the second is one of group analysis. During each phase both cognitive and affective aspects of the experience are analyzed and expanded. The leader's role is to stimulate and to reinforce in such a way that both the long-term and the immediate objectives are achieved; from time to time he might also have to arbitrate.

During the first weeks of an academic term, or with a continuing education group that is unaccustomed to these procedures, a questionnaire-type form can be used to direct each learner's thinking about his immediate experience and to train him in the process of self-analysis. For roleplay, it must be remembered that players and observers have different experiences and the form should provide for analysis from each point of view.

To illustrate, the "Self-Analysis and Evaluation" forms included in the Governmental Library Simulation *Resource-Log,* as seen in the following example, provide a focus for each learner to use in his personal preparation and at the outset of the group debriefing.

Self-Analysis and Evaluation Form for the Government Library Simulation, Problem 1, Planning Library Consolidation.

Directions: Answer A, and B or C.

A. Before roleplay:
　　1. What do you understand the immediate goals of the meeting to be?

　　2. If you were chairman, how would you attempt to accomplish these goals?

B. After roleplay: Roleplayers:
　　1. Were the goals of the meeting accomplished? Yes _____ No ___ If "No," why not?

　　2. Were you able to act as you think you would act in a similar situation? Yes _____ No _____ If "No," why not?

　　3. Thinking back over the roleplay, was there anything you feel you should have done differently? Yes _____ No _____ If "Yes," what? Explain.

C. After roleplay: Observers:
　　1. Were the goals of the meeting accomplished? Yes ____ No ____ If "No," why not?

　　2. Which roleplayers took leadership roles in accomplishing the business of the meeting?

　　3. Which roleplayers did little to accomplish the business of the meeting?
　　　　What could these roleplayers have done to improve their performances? Explain.

As learners become familiar with the debriefing procedure, the form can be shortened so that it serves only to initiate the process, as the following example shows. Eventually it can be dropped completely.

Self-Analysis and Evaluation Form for the Government Library Simulation, Problem 8, Response to Complaint

Directions: Answer A, and B or C.

A. Before roleplay:
   What are the real questions at issue? Have you prepared adequately to defend the library at any time? If not, why not?

B. After roleplay: Roleplayers:
   How would you rate your skill in thinking on your feet? Your communication of your own and the library's points of view? If these needed improvement, how could you try to improve?

C. After roleplay: Observers:
   What level of skill in the particular kind of communication involved was exhibited? If this level needs improvement, what would you prescribe for the roleplayers?

Following the few minutes allowed for learners to think silently about self-analysis, the group discussion of the learning experience takes place. It should be as detailed as possible, emphasizing possible alternatives to administrative decisions made in relation to the problem and the reasons for the choice of alternative that was arrived at, as well as exploring the affective responses of the learners to the problems they experienced. The leader might wish to prepare a question guide to help himself in leading the group discussion. If one of the objectives of the experience is to help learners become good discussion leaders, question guides could be given to them by the director or they could be assisted in preparing their own.

Suggested Discussion Questions for the Governmental Library Simulation, Problem 1, Planning Library Consolidation

1. Were the goals of the meeting accomplished? If so, could they have been better accomplished? How? If not, why not? What prevented the accomplishment? Could failure have been avoided?

2. How was the resistance of the Office of Aerial Environmental Surveys personnel evidenced? Was it well countered? Could it have been better countered?

3. Why were the OAES personnel resistant? What are some of the other ways (besides showing resistance) that people act when they are insecure and unwilling to change?
   What is the likelihood that the OAES Library staff will give lip service to the transfer, but try to sabotage the effort?
   How should the Department of Ecology Library Director watch for such sabotage and what measures can he take to counter it?

4. Did the chairman effect a smooth closure for the meeting? Did he assign jobs to be done as follow-up? Clearly? Does everyone understand what will happen next?
Were dates and/or places for follow-up activities clearly stated?

5. Do all students understand the official communications channels in large organizations? It may be necessary to refer to the organization charts (<u>Federal Library Model</u>, Document C) to review this point with the class.

Student perception, as reported in evaluations of debriefing as a process, indicates that the best debriefing sessions are those that (a) reinforce the linkage between the theory of administration and the application and interpretation of that theory in relation to the problem just experienced, (b) provide additional insight through the explicit statement of generalizations new to the learners, (c) provide common input for the peer discussions that inevitably continue after the group session, and (d) relate closely to the stated objectives of both the total learning experience and the immediate problem-solving. In the Industrial Library Simulation the objectives are stated unit by unit as decision-making and administrative tasks related to the model. Specific behavioral experiences desired for the learners are described as "activities."

Objectives and Activities from the Industrial Library Simulation, Unit I, Planning Special Library Service

<u>Unit Objectives:</u> 1. To plan appropriate service to researchers at a location distant from the company's home office library.

                  2. To incorporate the plan in the policy manual of the Field Research Laboratory Library (FRLL) of the Double XYZ Oil Company.

                  3. To make the agreed-on plans known to the staff of the Field Research Laboratory.

<u>Roleplay Activities:</u> 1. Participating (through an assigned role) in a library/user planning meeting.

                  2. Reaching a consensus among library staff members about the nature of the service and the policies for providing the service.

<u>Communication Activities:</u> 1. Preparation of a call to a meeting.

                  2. Preparation of minutes of a meeting.

                  3. Stating the agreed-on policy for remote site service in a form suitable for inclusion in the library's staff manual.

                  4. Preparation of a publicity release to FRL personnel about the new plans.

The specific objectives of each part of a course or continuing education workshop are based on the general objective that underlies simulation teaching of library education, i.e., to help an individual develop the following characteristics of an administrator:

1. The ability to identify various alternatives in a situation and to choose from among them, on the basis of well-articulated criteria, those which are most suitable for himself, his staff, and his library.
2. The ability to make decisions and to live with the results.
3. The ability to work with others in a participative way as well as to direct them in an authoritative way, and the ability to differentiate the situations in which each mode is most appropriate.
4. The ability to communicate with top management, with staff at all levels, with users and with all with whom he comes in contact in the course of conducting the library's business.

The learning experiences for simulation teaching are based on these desired characteristics of administrators and are designed to give the learner opportunities to practice various behaviors and to adapt them to himself. It is the leader's responsibility to ensure that sufficient and appropriate opportunities are in fact available, that the learner has whatever external resources he needs to take advantage of the opportunities, and that the learner becomes increasingly proficient in analyzing and evaluating his own knowledge and behavior, and in prescribing to meet his own needs.

The ultimate in professional behavior—prescribing to meet one's own needs— is usually the last experience of either course or workshop, a kind of debriefing of the total learning experience. Each learner, at the end of a course, is asked to project a self-development plan for his next three years of professional growth. At the end of a one-day workshop, the learner is asked to state what he believes is his own most immediate need in terms of a "next continuing education experience." Particularly with a class in which the leader has come to know the individuals over a period of time, response to each individual's plan should be made in terms of the leader's perception of the learner's needs.

In all of the aspects of group process implicit in experiential learning, none is more important than the development of group cohesiveness and its underlying prerequisite, the trust group members have in each other. The development of trust and cohesiveness within the learning group is, therefore, a prime responsibility of the leader. Trust and cohesiveness are displayed through the words and actions of group members, especially during debriefing. Although lack of trust and cohesiveness can inhibit ability to accomplish the tasks of roleplay, the very assumption of roles tends to mask the true state of the group. The relative lack of inhibition during debriefing, on the other hand, accentuates either the presence or the absence of these characteristics. In either event the debriefing words and actions provide the leader with evi-

Table 1
BEHAVIORS DEFINING TRUST
AND OPENNESS, AND COHESIVENESS[3]

A high frequency of:	A low frequency of:
Trust and Openness	
Making here-and-now statements	Anecdotes
Making self-disclosing statements	Making nonself-disclosing statements
Members request and reinforce self-disclosing statements	Self-disclosing statements cut off, rejected, ignored
Members make self-disclosing statements	Irrelevant talk about other people or things
	Members cut off or reject feedback
Members ask for and give feedback to other members	Members minimize problem
Members ask for help with problem	Silence
Spontaneous unprompted participation	Defensive statements
Members reinforce each other	
Cohesiveness	
"We" statements (referring to the whole group)	Negative statements about whole group with positive remarks about a subgroup (clique)
Statements expressing liking for group	
Statements expressing desire to continue group	Statements expressing dissatisfaction with group
Attention directed to speaker	Statements expressing desire to terminate group
Talk directed to other group members	
Equal participation of members	Absenteeism
Talk relevant to previous members' statements	Tardiness
	Distracting behavior (yawns, horseplay)
Cooperative statements ("Here's a way we could do this. . .")	Statements directed to leader only
	Time monopolized by leader or two or three members
	Statements cutting off others by referring to self prematurely ("The same thing happened to me. . .")
	Statements changing the subject
	Competitive statements ("That's nothing. . .")

dence for diagnosis of specific training needs. The behaviors listed in Table 1
have been identified as those defining trust (and openness) and cohesiveness.
The list is worth a leader's study in order to enhance his own behavior as well
as to study the behavior of a learning group.

PACING SIMULATION LEARNING

The time variations possible in briefing and debriefing give the leader control of the pace of the learning, a necessary component of course management. The leader can schedule more or less classroom briefing time, depend-

ing on his assessment of the needs of a particular learning group, and counting on individual preparation to supplement whatever is done in group sessions. If the group does not do the anticipated preparation, the leader must allow more time for briefing; as he must for continuing education workshops for which preparation cannot be done in advance. There are similar considerations about debriefings although they characteristically take more time than briefings and they should not be hurried. The time needed for debriefing is hard to predict. The leader neither wants to cut it off while it is productive nor drag it out when it is not. I have found it wise to allow close to maximum time, but to be prepared with supplementary plans for the group in case there is time for additional learning experiences. Follow-ups outside of scheduled learning sessions are possible with individuals or subgroups.

The time dimensions of the problem-solving experiences, on the other hand, are more nearly preset by the nature of the problem and the experiential methodology chosen. Roleplays can be planned for any length of time the leader desires, but ten minutes to forty-five minutes seem to be the limits of productive roleplay. Suggested time allowances, based on experience, are indicated in the course management materials. In-basket exercises, because they are individually carried out, are customarily used as between-session assignments during courses; otherwise, the number and complexity of the items to be dealt with determine the item required. The out-basket items generated by students can be critiqued individually by the leader, or can be debriefed in a group session. When the latter alternative is chosen, time must be allowed for everyone in the group to read all of the out-basket items, a process so time-consuming that I use it only for very special purposes.

A suggested schedule follows for using the Governmental Library Simulation as a sustained simulation during a fifteen-week semester with group meetings once a week for three hours. The basic pattern of the weekly meetings is a ninety-minute session followed by a fifteen-minute break and a second session of sixty minutes. This leaves unscheduled fifteen minutes of the three hours to provide flexibility. The schedule, as shown in Table 2, was planned for use by practicing librarians who gathered at the university as a group only once per week. It therefore allows time for roleplay committees to prepare together and for individual preparation.

The one-day workshop projected in Figure 7 can accommodate a time schedule in which the first and last modules are each one half hour in length, the second module is three quarters of an hour, and the three alternative modules are each one and a half hours. With two quarter-hour breaks and an hour and a half for lunch, the workshop requires seven and three quarter hours.

Alternating group and individual experiences, as well as alternating input, problem-solving and analytical segments of the workshop, is an important part of pacing. The projected schedule and workshop model take psychological, emotional, physical and intellectual needs into account.

Table 2
GOVERNMENTAL LIBRARY SIMULATION:
SUGGESTED SEMESTER SCHEDULE

Class Meeting	Session 1 90 Minutes	Session 2 60 Minutes
1.	Introduction and Orientation	Continue Orientation. *Alternative:* Pre-testing or personal study of model
2.	*Problem 1.* Planning Library Consolidation	Questions and Answers about model; Committee and individual preparation for Problem 2.
3.	*Problem 2.* Presentation and Justification of Space Recommendations	Critique documents from Problem 1. *Alternative:* Film on the management of change
4.	*Problem 3.* Coordination and Direction of an Internship Program	Critique final communications from Problem 2. *Alternative:* Film on persuasive communication, or personal preparation for Problem 4.
5.	*Problem 4.* Presentation and Justification of Budget Revision	Committee and/or individual revision of budget documents. *Alternative:* Committee and individual preparation for Problem 5.
6.	*Problem 5.* Quality Control of Library Operations	Critique final documents from Problem 4. *Alternative:* Film or lecture on quality control methods for library operations
7.	*Problem 6.* Counseling an Unsatisfactory Employee	Problem 5 group reports and class discussion.
8.	Mid-term evaluation	Film(s) on supervisory communication skills. *Alternative:* Personal follow-up of evaluation
9.	*Problem 7.* Coordination of Division Plans	Discussion of individual reports.
10.	*Problem 8.* Response to a Complaint	Critique of documents from Problem 7. *Alternative:* Film(s) on confrontation and/or supervisory communication skills (if not used previously)
11.	*Problem 9.* Initiating a Complaint	Critique of documents from Problem 8. *Alternative:* Group or individual preparation for Problem 10.
12.	*Problem 10.* Refusal of a Staff Member to Help a Library User	Critique of documents from Problem 9. *Alternative:* Group or individual preparation for Problem 11.
13.	*Problem 11.* Terminating a Probationary Employee	Further discussion of Problems 10 or 11. *Alternative:* In-basket exercise
14.	*Problem 12.* Allocation of New Equipment	In-basket exercise. *Alternative:* Discussion of in-basket exercise is used in Class Meeting 13
15.	Final Evaluation	Final debriefing on course.

Note: The scheduling of a problem automatically means that briefing time must be worked in in advance to prepare the class, and debriefing time must follow the learning experience. In general, all of this takes place during the first session of each weekly meeting. The alternatives noted above could be used as extra learning experiences on those occasions when the debriefing does not take all of the allowed time.

SELECTING APPROPRIATE EXPERIENTIAL TECHNIQUES

Both briefing and debriefing, as techniques, are closely related to traditional teacher-centered instruction. Where adult learning is concerned, it is important to find ways to disperse this focus on the teacher without diminishing the position of the leader as manager and as resource of the learning group.

The very nature of the experiential techniques is that they are learner-centered. But the leader inexperienced in their use is sometimes confused as to which specific technique is most appropriate in relation to a given learning need. After stating the specific learning objective as precisely as possible and determining that it can best be met by a group experience, the choice can be made by thinking through a series of questions:

1. Is a written record of the experience needed as part of an evaluation procedure?
   If Yes, prefer an action maze to an in-basket exercise.
   If No, any experiential technique can be used.

2. Does the problem central to the objective require that the learner seek a substantial amount of additional information?
   If Yes, prefer an in-basket exercise or roleplay with pre-assigned roles.
   If No, any experiential technique can be used.

3. Does the problem or process central to the objective include interaction in real life?
   If Yes, prefer roleplay or a game.
   If No, prefer in-basket exercise or an action maze.

4. Is the problem or process highly compressible?
   If Yes, prefer roleplay or a game.
   If No, prefer an in-basket exercise or an action maze.

5. Is the problem or process interactive, but *not* highly compressible?
   If Yes, prefer a game.
   If No, use either game or roleplay.

6. Does the objective relate closely to one or more specific professional roles?
   If Yes, prefer roleplay, an in-basket exercise or an action maze.
   If No, any experiential technique can be used.

CHAPTER HIGHLIGHTS

Coordination includes
>   ... briefing, debriefing, pacing and selecting appropriate techniques for objectives.

Briefing is
>   ... the preparation of learners for a problem-solving experience.

Debriefing is
>   ... the follow-up discussion after a learning experience—to analyze, to reinforce, and to identify further learning needs.

The leader is responsible to
>   ... make both briefing and debriefing as learner-centered as possible;
>   ... provide options for learner's use in briefing;
>   ... develop cohesiveness and trust in the learning group;
>   ... coordinate the learning through selecting techniques and pacing learning modules.

REFERENCES

1. Clark C. Abt, *Serious Games* (New York: Viking Press, 1970), p. 31.

2. Raymond J. Corsini et al., *Roleplaying in Business and Industry* (New York: Free Press of Glencoe, 1961), p. 71.

3. John D. Krumboltz and Beverly Potter, "Behavior Techniques for Developing Trust, Cohesiveness and Goal Accomplishment," *Educational Technology* 13 (January 1973): 27. The entire article (pp. 26–30) is valuable reading for leaders of any kind of experiential learning or group process.

5.
Evaluation

· · · · · · · · · · ·

Appraisal of learner performance is an essential component of the teacher's role whether course strategies are traditional or innovative. It is also one of the most troublesome aspects of the role. The difficulties spring from the difference between what teachers would like to achieve in measurement of growth and development and the methods that are available for doing so. The difficulties are compounded by the wide divergence among both professional educators and the public in regard to definitions and philosophies of education.

Controversy on the subject of evaluation of learners is characteristic of all levels of education, and the arguments are especially complicated for the teacher of adults. The long tradition that anyone who is seated in a classroom be treated like a child is under attack from many quarters. Psychologists, educational administrators, testing experts, proponents of students' rights, and students themselves all have their points of view. Teachers, at whose desks the buck stops, are more likely to feel frustration, guilt and ineptitude than advocacy for any theoretical point of view. Their inescapable responsibilities are to university registrars, whose demands are in terms of A, B, C, and D, and to the adults in their learning groups, whose demands are for more meaningful evaluation.

The literature of simulation teaching in fields other than library science clearly shows that simulation designers and teachers feel their prime responsibility is to the learners, leaving registrars to take what solace they can from the fact that "grades" for credit courses *are* submitted, albeit frequently with disclaimers as to their significance. My concern is also for the learners. The means I use to evaluate, rather than merely "grade," stem from the tenets of adult education: evaluations should lead the individual into new insights about himself and suggest new paths of learning rather than merely appraise episodic classroom performance. It is as important that the individual learn to evaluate his own performance as that a teacher should evaluate him; perhaps more so. The nature of simulation study offers opportunities for several nontraditional kinds of learner evaluation (both by self and by mentor), and a search for the means to meet these opportunities leads into appraisal methods of management and social psychology as well as adult education.

Let us admit at the outset that the means used are not those of tradition or of scientific data collection and rigorous statistical analysis. This is not to say that the means used are not intensive, focused or meaningful. It is my belief that these evaluation procedures are considerably *more* meaningful than traditional grading practices and that they are, in addition, more responsive to expressed learner needs, and rigorous in ways new and strange to many library science classrooms. Nor does my avoidance of more "scientifically" based evaluation indicate lack of knowledge that such techniques have, in fact, been suggested for the analysis of performance in roleplay, in-basket exercises and games. Virtually all of these techniques, however, in their present forms, seem to me more appropriate to the analysis of individual performance for research purposes than for personal evaluation.

Just as the essence of simulation learning is performance and involvement, so the core of the evaluation process is the observation of performance and evidence of involvement. The pace is lively; the involvement is multifaceted; and the learning director's ability to assimilate multiple stimuli is limited. Most of what follows, therefore, are suggestions for ways to focus and to capture the myriad observations of an on-going learning group.

AIDS TO OBSERVATION

The best aids to observation are additional sets of eyes and ears. Graduate assistants, other faculty, student and professional peers—all can help the leader by focusing their attention on assigned aspects of the group interaction and reporting their observations. Training learners to observe each other is not difficult. And they seem to appreciate the added learning that attaches to alternating between active involvement in experiential problem-solving and the more reflective mode of participation through observation. As many learners have pointed out, alternating between doing and observing is itself a simulation of the supervisor's lot in many library jobs. Add to observation the development of criteria for evaluation and the design of records for use with supervised personnel, and the relationship to job reality seems even more vivid.

Even with additional eyes and ears it is impossible for the leader to catch the nuances of verbal and facial expression and the body language of all participants. Further, analyzing cognitive and affective behavior for the entire learning group during the group session is extremely difficult. Making a record of exactly what is happening and being said while it's going on becomes essential. I have used audiotape and cassette recorders for years, and have recently begun to use a videorecorder. Learners have access to these records also, and use them to study themselves intensively, as well as to sharpen their skills of analyzing the behavior of others. The tapes, if preserved during an entire term of study, frequently show remarkable changes in behavior and have been used on more than one occasion to convince the learner who says, "Oh, no, I couldn't have done [or said] that!"

LEARNER INVOLVEMENT IN EVALUATION

Initially, I involve learners in evaluation of their own performances and those of others through a roleplay session, as described in Chapter 4. The next step is to involve them in establishing criteria for performance. Since the major learning experiences of a sustained simulation are in terms of job performance, the establishment of criteria is in the same terms. Both the Industrial Library Simulation and the Governmental Library Simulation begin to focus on personnel management early in the simulation. The idea of establishing criteria for job performance is, therefore, introduced during a briefing session. The objective, the group is told, is to prepare an evaluation instrument for use in the model library. This objective can be accomplished in one of several ways: (1) a leader-centered discussion about both the content and the form, with the group designing the instrument during the discussion; (2) the same kind of discussion led by one of the learners; (3) delegation of the task of instrument design to a committee, followed by group critique and formal acceptance or rejection of the instrument (if the instrument is rejected, the group must then determine how the task will be accomplished); (4) either (2) or (3) expanded into roleplay with roles appropriate to the model library. Exhibits 3, 4, 5, and 6 at the end of this chapter are examples of such evaluation instruments designed by students.

The learners are also told in advance that they will actually be evaluated by the instrument they design. With a small group I evaluate each member at the halfway and the three-quarter mark of the course. With a large group time limitations reduce this to a single evaluation. The process works this way: The learner completes the instrument with regard to his total performance in the course to date, and I complete a second copy as if I were his job supervisor (again, using his course performance as the "job"). He then schedules a Performance Review Interview with me. During the interview we compare the two evaluations and discuss the differences as well as any items which both of us evaluated negatively. We also discuss what the learner needs to do as the "next step" in his career progress. At the end of the interview I either recommend him for a raise (which is the equivalent of an A), retain him at his present salary (B), or place him on probation (C). These interviews are as much like the "real thing" as I can make them, and they tend to be very specific and surprisingly candid. There is every indication that the total evaluation process is taken seriously by the learners, and many really "sweat it" for a raise. On the course evaluations submitted at the conclusion of a term, the Performance Review Interview is often rated among the top three most valuable course experiences. (A word of caution: Allow a minimum of 30 minutes for this kind of interview and expect that it will take longer for most individuals.)

I have also experimented with having learners evaluate each other with the same, or similar instruments. This they do *not* like to do, and, in my experience, even a substantial amount of debriefing does not make them comfortable in the supervisory role of evaluating another person. In efforts to accustom them to this necessary task I have tried having learners roleplay performance review interviews and more generalized employee counseling or development interviews. I have also tried having them write their evaluations of each other in the forms of employee file reports and recommendations for other jobs. None of these ways completely relieves the individual's anxiety in making judgments about his peers, but most learners attest to a reduction of the level of discomfort.

Another device for helping learners to plan and to evaluate their participation in simulation study is an "Objectives–Performance–Evaluation Grid," an example of which is shown in Exhibit 7. Using the grid is more time-consuming than using an evaluation instrument that is essentially a checklist, but less time-consuming than keeping an anecdotal record of objectives and performance during a full-length course. It appears to me to be most useful with learners who have had little or no job experience, or those who are inclined to be rather undisciplined as students. It provides focus and a record of accomplishment for both learner and group leader or counselor.

With many groups it is easier to analyze and evaluate the content of the problems than the group process by which the problem-solving was achieved. "Stop Action" is a technique for improving a group's ability to focus on its own interpersonal processes.[1] The idea of "Stop Action" should be explained to the learning group during an orientation or briefing session, or the leader can introduce it by explaining it in a sentence or two. Basically, it is a parenthetical look at group action. As the group is working on a debriefing discussion, for example, the leader intervenes by saying, "Stop the action and discuss for five minutes *how* your group is working. Is everyone participating? If not, what are the inhibiting factors in individuals or the group? Whose ideas are gaining the audience? How is the originator achieving this? Have any expressed ideas been ignored? Why?" The group discusses its own activity in this way for the allotted time. Then, on another signal from the leader, the group reverts to its original activity and picks up where it left off, hopefully with more productive interaction. If the leader thinks it will be helpful to do so, he can return during the general debriefing to questions such as, "Why are some group members never satisfied with the reception granted their ideas? How do their feelings of nonsatisfaction affect their behavior, or the ability of the group to complete its task?" Judiciously used, "Stop Action" can be an insightful technique.

Fish-bowling can also be used to focus on group process during debriefing. Divide the group in half, placing one half in an inner circle, and the other half in an outer circle. Each person in the outer circle is assigned to observe one person in the inner circle. The inner circle begins the debriefing and continues until a signal from the leader or until an agreed time interval has passed. Then the outer circle describes the group process, pointing out facilitating and/or inhibiting actions and communications and, finally, making suggestions for improving the process. The subgroups then change places and the (new) inner circle picks up the debriefing, attempting to implement its own suggestions. (Caution: Be sure that during the second debriefing, no one is observing the individual who originally observed him.)

EVALUATION OF THE LEARNING GROUP

The learning director is constantly involved in a three-level process: (1) evaluation of the group process, in order to maintain a healthy, vigorous environment for learning; (2) evaluation of individuals in the group for personal feedback, individual counseling and institutional reporting; and (3) evaluation of the learning materials *vis a vis* the needs of the specific group and the improvement of the simulation. The first two levels of evaluation will be discussed in this chapter, the third will be deferred to Chapter 10 because of the role of the evaluation of materials as feedback in the design process.

Checklists and/or diaries can be used to record group process. Either can reflect process alone or can reflect both process and content of group interaction. A very simple scale related to process is shown here.

Checklist of Group Process[2]

———— Every member of the group participated frequently and enthusiastically.

———— The majority of the group participated at least once; nonparticipants paid attention.

———— A few members of the group participated actively; the remainder were inattentive much of the time.

———— Group response consisted primarily of token participation and resistance to participation.

Since this checklist, as it stands, does not aid the leader in either maintaining desired behavior or diagnosing undesired behavior, responses to the following questions, added to the checklist, will facilitate interpretation:

1. Describe in a sentence or two the learner behaviors that best represent the category checked above.
2. Which learners did not respond in the same way as the majority of the group? How did these individuals behave?

Such a simple form, completed after every group session, takes a minimum of time and creates a running record. Rejection of group process, whether it is passive or disruptive, can be identified and dealt with at the earliest possible time—a requisite for creation and maintenance of a healthful, energizing learning climate.

Since the interaction in experiential problem-solving relating to administration is basically group decision-making, a checklist of factors in the effectiveness of this process can provide a revealing focus for evaluation. The following checklist is based on Marchant's analysis of effectiveness factors.[3]

Checklist of Factors in Effective Group Decision-Making

Directions: If the statement is more true than false of the group under observation, mark it plus. If it is more false than true, mark it minus. Use the space between statements to note ways in which the group was especially effective or ineffective, and to describe behavior of outstanding facilitators or inhibitors of effective interaction.

———— 1. Numerous cues were available for testing and selecting proffered decisions (or solutions to problems).

———— 2. The group was self-correcting in providing its own feedback and recognizing certain decisions and solutions as potential mistakes.

———— 3. The group pooled ideas, selected some for building on and tested those selected without inhibition.

———— 4. The group acted with objectivity and cohesion.

The learning director can expand or add to these simple devices at will in support of his own specific objectives for the group. At least one additional facet seems indicated in a course dealing with the content of administration, that of monitoring the group's linkage of decisions made and actions taken to the theory of administration. A checklist for this purpose would be so closely related to specific objectives and content of a given course that it would have to be individually designed for that course. An excellent example of such custom-designed evaluative criteria for the study of library administration, related unit by unit to the overall course objectives, is contained in the *Leader's Handbook* of Goodman and Stone's *Human Resources in the Library System*, one example from which follows:[4]

Criteria for Evaluation Related Specifically to Unit Objectives

Objectives for the First Half of Unit: Management as System and The Librarian—Worker as a System

A. To examine some of the external forces and influences on the management system of the library.

B. To consider the sources of the management system's power and authority.

C. To examine the impact of management's power and authority on the worker.

D. To explore the meaning and implications of role behavior in organizations.

Evaluation: Participants will be considered to have understood these concepts when they have demonstrated that they are able to apply the learning they have accomplished to situations discussed in the meeting. In addition the degree to which these objectives are achieved will be judged by the following:

A. The ability of the participant to depict graphically the power structure of his own library situation.

B. The ability of the participant to define on paper his idea of his own role as an individual librarian and the role his library organization expects him to fill.

C. The ability of the participant to induce from situations arising during the meeting some general management concepts relative to power and authority structures influencing the library.

The ultimate, one might say, of record-keeping is a diary. While it is undoubtedly a useful record, it cannot be written during the learning session and, as a retrospective record, is subject to the usual errors of such records. I usually attempt to achieve the best of both worlds by keeping a checklist during the session, and by preparing a diary of the first several sessions retrospectively from the audio- or videotapes. The diary helps me most in analyzing the mode and the pace of the interaction and the behavior of those who are passive or disruptive, because during the session I concentrate on the content. Another leader would, obviously, adapt the means to his own needs.

Simple graphic descriptions of group interaction can help in focusing quickly on the process. Figure 8 shows a form I use either for roleplay involving more than three people, or for debriefing. Blanks are mimeographed in advance. Names are added as people take their places and the flow of conversation is plotted as it occurs. Each line connects a speaker to the individual to whom he directed remarks or questions. The arrow is at the receiver's end of the connecting line. Short arrows, not connected to another individual, show a remark or question directed at the whole group. Cross-hatches show a sharp exchange and are located close to the initiator.

Figure 8 shows a fifteen-minute discussion in which Morris was the most talkative member of the group as well as the one to whom most of the individual remarks were directed. He tried to provide leadership by addressing many remarks to the whole group and by directing at least one message to every other individual. He got into arguments with two other male students by an-

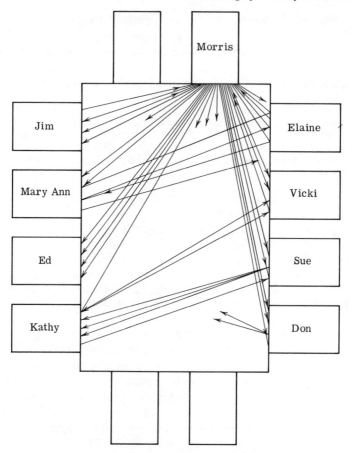

Figure 8. Group process diagram.

tagonizing them, and he had a lengthy exchange with a third. The women talked more to each other than to Morris or to the other men. Interchange among the men, other than with Morris, was virtually nonexistent. Since this was an open discussion and Morris had not been assigned a position of leadership, certain conclusions can be drawn. I usually ask a graduate assistant, seated at a distance from the group, to keep this kind of record, which is potentially valuable both to the learning director and to the group itself. After cognitive introduction to group process and some experience with its idiosyncracies, the record of a group's interaction can be placed before it for analysis and suggestions for corrective procedures. (Caution: Some groups do not need this kind of focus more than once or twice; for them, a reconstruction of the interaction, either mentally or with the help of the tapes, is meaningful and productive.)

There is a somewhat different measure that is especially helpful at the outset of work with a group. Originated by Moreno, it is called a "sociogram," and the technique has been described in numerous places. In any introduction to simulation methodology, as I point out the importance of the interaction we will be experiencing, I say, "Although each individual will work in various ways with every other individual, in the making of certain assignments I can respond to your preferences. I know that some of you live close to each other, or ride together, or have other classes that bring you into regular contact, or other reasons that make it easier for you to work together. Please write down for me the names of the two [or in a large group, three] other people with whom you would prefer to be assigned joint work. Be sure to sign your name." The choices are then tabulated.

This simple process quickly shows which individuals receive most choices, which individuals are mutually chosen, and which individuals are isolates. Initially, it is the isolates about whom I am concerned for I believe that the group process will be diminished by the extent to which they remain isolates. Often their failure to be chosen is unrelated to negative feelings toward them in the group. But for whatever reason they appear on the sociogram as isolates, I want to put them in a position of showing themselves to good advantage to the group as soon as possible. One favorite way of doing this in the Industrial Library Simulation is to assume that the model library has been asked by management to provide a briefing to the researchers who will be members of the task force about the place in which they will be working for two years. The "isolate" is to play the role of the reference librarian who prepares this report on Florida, Collier County and Everglades City, and to present it to the group. Virtually every graduate library school student can prepare such a report and my files and the FSU library have ample material on all aspects of coverage for such a briefing. Wearing my hat as "consultant" to the Double XYZ Oil Company Library, I work with the student to assure an excellent presentation. Several times I have seen the group attitude toward an individual change on the basis of this simple device. Other times, of course, it takes longer and more remedial measures. The sociogram gives the warning; the corrective measures are left to the ingenuity of the learning director. Needless to say, in subsequent assignments I honor the preferences people have indicated in the sociogram.

EVALUATION OF INDIVIDUALS

Given the objectives of creating a facilitative learning climate and helping each individual to new insights about himself as a learner, the group leader must evaluate each individual in the group in an on-going way. Traditional intermittent pencil and paper tests and the familiar products of individual activity (and, perhaps, learning) are inappropriate summations of learning that has been achieved through experiential group problem-solving. Evaluation is based, instead, on observation and analysis of behavior; it must be continued over a period of time in order to identify changes in that behavior and to assure that no single sample of behavior is overgeneralized in the analysis. It would help, of course, if we could verbalize precisely what constitutes excellent, effective administrative behavior and if there were no complicating variables. Since this is not the case, each teacher of administrative methods is free to choose the list of characteristics he personally espouses. I lean heavily toward a list of factors and indicators developed by a group of researchers from Teachers College, Columbia University, and Educational Testing Service, as reported by Norman Frederiksen.[5] These factors were identified as part of a research project, complete with scoring, and the originators do not claim that they can or should be used as I have used them. Nevertheless, the list has served me as the basis of a checklist and as cues for observations to be recorded in an anecdotal record. The list, modified and shortened, includes:[6]

A. Exchanging Information
   Asks subordinates for information, opinion or advice
   Gives information to subordinates
   Requires further information before deciding
B. Discussing before Acting
   Allows time for discussion
   Discusses with subordinates
   Communicates face-to-face
   Initiates a new structure (such as committee)
   Arrives at a procedure for deciding
C. Complying with Suggestions Made by Others
   Follows lead of subordinates
   Takes terminal action
   Follows lead by superiors
   Follows pre-established procedure
   Provides written follow-up
D. Analyzing the Situation
   Uses library values in arriving at decisions
   Displays broad conceptual understanding
E. Maintaining Organizational Relationships
   Involves superiors whenever appropriate
   Discusses with superiors, consultants and library users
   Avoids delay or postponement
F. Directing the Work of Others
   Specifies when work is to be done
   Gives directions or suggestions
   Communicates directions in writing
   Directs with courtesy

I prefer an anecdotal record for each member of the learning group, comprised of comments noted during roleplay and group discussions plus notes on the learner's communication style as evidenced in his in-basket work. No grades on performance are assigned in the traditional sense. The summation, for each individual, is recorded on a performance instrument and discussed with him in a Performance Review Interview, as described earlier in this chapter.

Occasionally there are reasons to include something more nearly resembling traditional grading. The institution may require a final examination of each student, for example. I use an in-basket test (described in Chapter 7) or an action maze (described in Chapter 8) with the added requirement that a written explanation be provided by the student to relate decisions and actions to administrative theory. ("*Why* did you do what you did?") Or—another example—a group may fail to coalesce in such a way that each learner has a real opportunity to demonstrate what he is learning. At other times the interruption of class sessions or the absence of learner or leader may prevent participation and observation. In these cases I use a variation of the traditional term paper or term project. The learner suggests a topic he would like to pursue in greater depth than he has so far, or a kind of project he would like to undertake. I cast his idea into a format consistent with the needs of the model library. For example, someone wants to prepare a procedure manual. I, as head librarian or as management supervisor, send him a memo requiring him to do so and setting the conditions. Exigencies of the academic situation and individual student interests have thus resulted in extensive reports (in a variety of formats) on topics such as library insurance, preparation of specification lists for library furnishings, physical modification of a library to accommodate handicapped users, role and problems of black administrators, library participation in affirmative action and "equal opportunity" employment, and training of paraprofessionals—to mention a few. The products of this individual work are, naturally, shared with the entire group. In spite of my preference for group interaction as the primary mode for the study of applying administrative theory in libraries, I would be the first to admit that such individual contributions to the group can add meaningful dimensions for many learners.

CHAPTER HIGHLIGHTS

Evaluation is
   ... the leader's responsibility to the learning group and to every individual learner;
   ... based on observation of learner performance and evidence of learner involvement;
   ... both a concurrent and a retrospective process;
   ... a difficult but rewarding process.

REFERENCES

1. Dorothy J. Mail and Stanley Jacobson, "Stop Action," *Today's Education* 58 (March 1969): 68.

2. The suggestion for this checklist, originally designed for elementary school use, came from Mark Chesler and Robert Fox, *Role-Playing Methods in the Classroom* (Chicago: Science Research Associates, 1966), p. 68.

3. Maurice P. Marchant, "Participative Management as Related to Personnel Development," *Library Trends* 20 (July 1971): 57.

4. Charles H. Goodman and Elizabeth W. Stone, *Human Resources in the Library System: Leader's Handbook* (Washington: HEW, Office of Education, Bureau of Research, 1971), "Part 1, Designs for Learning," pp. 145–146.

5. Norman Frederiksen, "In-Basket Tests and Factors in Administrative Performance," in *Simulation in Social Science*, ed. Harold Guetzkow (New York: Prentice-Hall, 1962), p. 130.

6. *Ibid.*

EXHIBITS

EXHIBIT 3. SAMPLE EVALUATION INSTRUMENT DESIGNED BY STUDENTS

Personnel Evaluation Rating Form

First Rating Period	Second Rating Period	Final Rating	Qualities to be Rated
_____	_____	_____	**I. Role acceptance** Is the individual generally participating in his assigned role? (Yes or No)
			II. Quantity of participation
_____	_____	_____	1. No participation
_____	_____	_____	2. Minimal participation without initiative
_____	_____	_____	3. Occasional participation with initiative
_____	_____	_____	4. Frequent participation
_____	_____	_____	5. Always participates
			III. Quality of participation
_____	_____	_____	1. Withdrawn, hostile
_____	_____	_____	2. Disinterested; reluctant to participate without urging; no initiative
_____	_____	_____	3. Interested, but seems unable to participate; lack of preparation, inexperience, immaturity, inappropriate responses
_____	_____	_____	4. Shows some initiative and competency; cooperative, mildly enthusiastic, interested, dependable, articulate
_____	_____	_____	5. Superior; exhibits considerable initiative, responsibility, foresight, creativity, resourcefulness and leadership

Anecdotal record:

EXHIBIT 4. SAMPLE EVALUATION INSTRUMENT DESIGNED BY STUDENTS

Directions: In the spaces provided below check the one of the four columns that most clearly indicates your evaluation of the employee during the work period since the last evaluation.

	Superior (1)	Fully Acceptable (2)	Borderline (3)	Unsatisfactory (4)
QUALITY OF WORK:				
Accuracy				
Speed				
Ability to organize				
Neatness				
SUPERVISORY ABILITY:				
Judgment in making decisions				
Anticipates work situations				
Discovers & develops ability of employees				
Delegates responsibilities				
JOB ATTITUDE:				
Interested in job				
Makes effort to progress				
Accepts suggestions				
Follows instructions				
Reacts well to authority				
Can work independently				
Profits by constructive criticism				
Promotes interest of the company				
INITIATIVE:				
Contributes new ideas or methods				
Develops new ideas or methods				
Plans work ahead				
DEPENDABILITY:				
Punctuality				
Low absenteeism				
Observes regulations				
Makes good use of time				
HUMAN RELATIONS:				
Works well with others				
Willing to take on added responsibilities in emergencies				
Flexibility				
PERSONAL:				
Appearance				
Integrity				
Overconcern with outside interests				

Dates of observation period: _____

Date of report to employee: _____

Signed: _____
        Supervisor

EXHIBIT 5. SAMPLE EVALUATION INSTRUMENT DESIGNED
             BY STUDENTS

DOUBLE XYZ OIL COMPANY

Employee Rating Sheet

NONE SOME REASONABLE GREAT VERY GREAT EXCESSIVE

1. ATTENTION TO APPEARANCE

2. ABILITY TO TAKE THE INITIATIVE

3. RESPONSE TO CRITICISM

4. ABILITY TO EXPRESS SELF

5. JOB PREPARATION

6. WILLINGNESS TO ADAPT

7. ABILITY TO ADMINISTER

8. JOB ATTITUDE

9. SELF-CONTROL

10. TACT

11. ACCEPTANCE OF RESPONSIBILITY

12. SELF-CONFIDENCE

13. AMBITION

Interviewer's Recommendation for Merit Raise:
   Highly Recommend___ Recommend___ Recommend with
   Reservation___ Doubtful___ Do Not Recommend___

Comments:

Signed: _____
                                    Supervisor

EXHIBIT 6. SAMPLE EVALUATION INSTRUMENT DESIGNED
BY STUDENTS

Department of Ecology
Employee Evaluation

Directions: Check those characteristics that describe employee

A. Relationships with other people
___ displays poise and self-confidence
___ is tactful—establishes rapport easily
___ participates fully in activities requiring social interchange
___ is sufficiently mature for his age
___ his general demeanor stimulates favorable reactions in
persons he meets
___ appears emotionally stable

B. Oral and written expression
___ enunciates clearly
___ has good command of language
___ organizes his thoughts logically
___ speaks convincingly for his point of view
___ writes convincingly for his point of view

C. Intellectual ability
___ applies common sense to the solution of problems
___ is good at reconciling diverse points of view
___ realizes basic issues involved in a problem, as apart from
incidentals
___ is quick to understand new, involved or difficult problems
___ recognizes his own limitations and asks for help when he
needs it
___ shows evidence of imaginative thinking in his approach to
problems

D. Motivation and initiative
___ can be depended upon to carry out assignments on his own
___ has made good use of the opportunities available to him in
the past
___ appears interested in new opportunities to further develop
his abilities
___ is ambitious—has high level of aspiration
___ shows evidence of interest in or aptitude for public service

E. Leadership qualities
___ assumes a major role in group activities
___ other activities (academic or work) give evidence of leadership promise
___ is able to organize and promote concerted action when
called for
___ associates tend to look to him for assistance or advice
___ his personal and intellectual integrity inspires trust and
esteem

If absence of checks indicates negative evaluation, explain, and recommend how employee can be helped to improve his performance.

Signed: _____

Date: _____

EXHIBIT 7. EXAMPLE OF AN OBJECTIVES-PERFORMANCE-EVALUATION GRID

Directions: Under A list the content units for which you have personal learning objectives and your objectives for each. Under B, C and D indicate your objectives in relation to each activity. Under "Description of Activities," briefly describe, in each column, your activity and your reaction to your own involvement and performance. In the space marked "Self-Evaluation" evaluate your learning in relation to your objectives.

A. Content Area	B. Briefing	C. Problem-solving		D. Debriefing
		Roleplay	In-basket	
I. Area: Financial Management				
Objectives:	1. Read about PPBS & "zero-base" budgeting systems	1. Budget planning with staff 2. Justify a budget to management	1. Prepare PPBS budget	1. Critique several budgets 2. Discuss PPBS
Description of Activities:	1. Read 4 items—o.k. 2. Mini-lecture— listened twice— good	1. Role: Head, TS— managed to get what I wanted into asking budget 2. Observer: supported criticism of asking budget & felt case was made for reducing it	1. O.K.	1. Saw 3 budgets— all different. Discussions revealing 2. Not enough discussion of nitty-gritty: ran out of time

Self-evaluation: Good unit. Got a lot out of it. PPBS budget very time-consuming on first trial. Would like to look at more examples and discuss in detail, especially means of justifying desired new services. Found it easier to plan with others than expected. Objectives achieved mostly.

II. Area:

Objectives:

Description of Activities:

Self-evaluation:

Note: The form can be continued or expanded to cover as many content areas as comprise the learning experience. (In this example underlined material represents the student's handwritten notes.)

PART III.
Experiential Techniques in Simulation Teaching

6.
Roleplay
· · · · · · · · · ·

The search for innovative methods of teaching library administration has coincided with a studied movement in other disciplines to test alternative instructional methods that emphasize student involvement. Thus recent advances in educational psychology and in education for other professions have provided librarianship with much experimental background and some well-tested models. These new instructional methods combine content (or cognitive) learning with emotional (or affective) learning. The techniques characteristic of this innovative instruction are called "experiential" because they stimulate students to learn in both ways *through first-person involvement.* In the study of administration, for example, the cognitive learning required of the student consists of the intellectual understanding of the theories of administration. The educational psychologist argues that cognitive learning does not go far enough to produce the true internalization of subject matter that becomes evident in long-lasting changes in the learner's daily behavior. What is lacking is literally the first-person "feel" of living with the subject matter.

Many people find that their own experiences in learning—and non-learning—support the psychologist's belief. Therefore, before the learner is placed in the actual position of an administrator (at any level), he should experience how it *feels* to be faced with administrative problems whose solution cannot be derived from theory alone. The neophyte needs to know how it *feels* to make administrative decisions. The methods that are used in simulation teaching emphasize learning through experience—experiential learning— without neglecting the usual cognitive aspects of academic learning.

Roleplay is probably the best known of the experiential methods. Its underlying concepts are based on contemporary "role theory." As it has developed through the research of social psychologists, role theory provides a theoretical explanation for one's own behavior, the behavior of others, and the interaction between oneself and others. Thus the better we understand role theory the greater insight we have into our own behavior and that of others, particularly behavior stemming from group relationships.

Some of the tenets of role theory are especially valuable in explaining the behavior of individuals as members of groups (such as library staffs or professional organizations), and in teaching people to work in such groups:

> The individual as a group member responds both in terms of his unique individuality and of past and present influences generated by the group(s) of which he is a member.

> A group of individuals is a subsystem of the total social organism. Thus the group, like society as a whole, is structured around positions or offices, each of which is invested with a status *vis a vis* the others, and each of which is designated by a term such as chairman, department head, reference librarian, library technical assistant or stack attendant.

> An individual shapes his behavior around his understanding of himself, his own position in the group and the status of that position. These factors together comprise his "role," and his behavior reflects his interpretation of his role.

> As part of his own process of maturation each individual evolves not only his own role but also certain expectations relating to individuals in positions tangential to his own. These expectations comprise stereotypes of roles other than his own and lead to modifications of his behavior in relation to others in his group(s).

> An individual occupying a certain position is influenced in his role by the expectations of others in the group. He may be supported by these expectations or he may find his own perception in conflict with the group's stereotypes (i.e., pattern of expectations) of his position.

> An individual is always, simultaneously, a member of several groups, such as family, work, ethnic, economic, social and religious group. It is possible that the expectations of these groups may differ for the same individual. If so, conflict within himself or within one or more of the groups may result.[1]

These tenets imply that a change in position or in status suggests the need for a change in behavior. A student, new staff member or staffer advancing into a new position will probably find himself faced with the necessity of responding in an unfamiliar role. Roleplay in library school or in continuing education offers valuable opportunities to explore new job roles without the risks inherent in "learning on the job."

WHAT IS ROLEPLAY?

To include all of its meanings "roleplay" would have to be defined in four ways. (1) In theatrical terms, words and actions presented repetitively in a predetermined manner at the direction of a playwright are roleplay. (2) In sociological terms, everyday words and actions constitute behavior in patterns (or roles) determined by a given culture. (3) Dissimulative roleplay is the use of words and actions to deceive or to create false impressions. (4) In educational usage, roleplay is the spontaneous use of words and action under contrived circumstances in order to diagnose, inform or train students.[2]

Only educational roleplay is relevant to this discussion. The spontaneous enactment of a situation in which learners play the parts has been described as "first person action in a learning situation."[3] It should be remembered, however, that classroom roleplay almost always includes an audience as well as those selected members of the class who are performing the enactment. It is the intention of educational roleplay that both players and audience will benefit from the experience, though in different ways.

WHAT IS THE PURPOSE OF ROLEPLAY?

A variety of purposes for roleplay have been identified by different writers, depending on the age of the students, the immediate objective of the learning experience, the subject matter involved and other factors.[4,5,6] Those that follow are the purposes that I have used most often, that have been most conducive to learning (judging from student feedback), or that are most consistent with the experience of other teachers of library science (as expressed, mostly, in informal conversation).

The purposes, as listed below, are not mutually exclusive. Nor is there a ranking implied in this list. The primary purpose in one learning experience is not necessarily the primary purpose in another. In fact, if roleplay is to be used at frequent intervals with an on-going class, the primary purpose should be varied from one experience to the next in order to keep learner interest at the peak.

1. *To stimulate discussion.* The first-person experience with audience participation through identification gives learners the feeling of being involved in the situation portrayed, and they will talk about it later very readily.
2. *To acquire insight and sensitivity to the feelings and actions of others.* "Body language" during personal interaction contributes especially to the achievement of this purpose. Another way to express this purpose is "to identify with the role of another person."
3. *To try out proposed or intended action.* Learning strategies for managing people and obtaining feedback on decisions are both risky procedures on the job. Roleplay for "trial balloon" purposes appears to be one of the most valuable uses of this technique in the teaching of administration.
4. *To understand points of view different from one's own.* Obviously related to both 2 and 3 above, this purpose serves specific objectives with either cognitive or affective attributes. That is, the learner is helped in understanding either another person's intellectual argument or his behavior or both, depending on the situation portrayed.
5. *To make concrete an abstract idea or process.* "When you are talking about such ideas as 'participation,' 'conflict,' or 'theory X and theory Y,' you can design exercises to illustrate, in a very involving way, what these ideas mean at a 'feeling' level, rather than treating them only at the intellectual level."[7]

6. *To train in skills.* With some instructors this purpose is reserved for manual skills, requiring dexterity, but roleplay can also be used to aid in learning such skills as handling a grievance, counseling an employee, or chairing a meeting.
7. *To detect situations that are potentially difficult.* This purpose appears to be achieved best by having students *design* roleplay situations. Thus learners with prior experience in administration can be expected to achieve this purpose more readily than can beginners.

TEACHER PREPARATION FOR ROLEPLAY

Teaching through roleplay is not a whole new ball game. You need discard nothing you have learned in the past about the administration of libraries; you merely use your knowledge in a different way. There are, however, some specific preparations that you can make.

First, prepare yourself cognitively by reading what several experienced leaders say about the direction of roleplay. The references for this chapter and the bibliography in Part V provide starting points. Chain-read until you feel you understand what the authors are saying.

Second, try to allay your fears by following several practical suggestions. Many teachers are fearful that the spontaneity of roleplay will result in clowning and eventual chaos in the class. Ask yourself honestly—are your students irresponsible? Mine have been grateful for the appearance of new methods in the classroom and in workshops and have been eager to carry out new learning designs; I have never encountered a "runaway" class. To be on the safe side, keep the warm-up exercises in library terms, with immediate follow-up discussions on the purpose of the exercise. If horseplay is attempted, nip it in the bud by asking why the roleplayer acted as he did and why the group responded to his behavioral invitation. This does not mean that laughter is ruled out, only that laughter-gone-wrong needs to be explored for its hidden meanings, which must then be resolved.

Some teachers lack confidence in their ability to give low-key direction to the give and take of the usual debriefing. A tape recorder, a small group of friendly, purposeful students, and a sympathetic peer are your best guides. I taped every experiential session during my first two years of using these methods, for personal follow-up study of my own performance. Every tape was critiqued by my husband, a "natural-born" listener and an experienced discussion leader. Any trusted friend can serve this purpose for you. As preparation for using the more difficult and more unusual techniques I invited friendly doctoral students and graduate assistants to my home in small groups. After dinner we tried out games, action mazes or whatever, roundly criticizing the teaching materials, the methods and our performances. Several of these students were already experienced teachers and were at the time enrolled in innovative classes in the Florida State University College of Education. Thus I built a store of valuable input, sound criticism and happy memories of Ferol Accola, Nancy Bush, Sister Laurine Cairns, Tom Downen, Don Foos, John Hall and Veronica Pantelidis. Another way to gain the needed experience and confidence is to attend courses or workshops, or to work with a consultant.

A third step, and a necessary one preceding each individual class session, is to provide yourself with appropriate cognitive input. Study directions for the roleplay at hand very carefully so that there will be no procedural hitches. Work out the relationships between the stated purpose of a given roleplay and the needs of the group so there will be no hesitancy in your leadership. Review all theoretical material which the roleplay is to exemplify or elucidate so that there will be no significant omissions or failure to relate cognitive and affective learning.

LEARNER PREPARATION FOR ROLEPLAY

Warm-up

If the learners have had little or no experience with roleplay, a warm-up period will help them get the swing of it. When roleplay is to be used regularly during a term, warm-up should be included in the general orientation and need not be repeated before each individual enactment. In a workshop setting, a ten- or fifteen-minute warm-up immediately preceding roleplay may be useful. Many learners are introduced to the technique in public school or college, however, and they readily transfer their ability to any given roleplay. If the learner group in continuing education is predominately young and outgoing, I rarely use any warm-up except the general orientation with, perhaps, some spontaneous open-ended conversation with several members of the group.

SAMPLE WARM-UP EXERCISES[8]

A. Exercises with Minimal Emotional Involvement and Expression
   1. Pretend you are . . . shelving books . . . reading shelves . . . browsing.
   2. Show the group what you would do if . . . the air-conditioning broke down and the temperature in the library reached 95° . . . both phones began ringing just as a troublesome patron walked up to the reference desk . . . you dropped a card catalog drawer in a room full of researchers working quietly.
   3. Without using any objects, show the group how you . . . open and sort the mail . . . check in serials . . . read an o.p. book dealer's catalog.
   4. Pretend you are walking . . . through tables and stacks in a quiet reference room . . . through an empty lobby after hours . . . around the sections of a card catalog at a busy time.

The leader may begin to help learners interpret feelings by asking what they thought the roleplayer was feeling as he performed his role.

Show how you feel when . . .
   1. . . . you get a phone call complaining about a service you performed.
   2. . . . your supervisor reprimands you sharply and for a prolonged time in front of your coworkers.

3. ... you see evidence that someone has been using your typewriter and the carriage return refuses to operate.
4. ... the reference volume that you need is not in its place on the shelf when you are trying to answer a phone question for a notoriously cantankerous patron.
5. ... you get the news that you're being promoted to department head at a minimal salary increase ... at a healthy salary increase.

Briefing

Briefing begins when the assignment is made to a class, and the general suggestions for briefing in Chapter 4 apply. In addition, for roleplay an abstract of the situation at the beginning of the action or a statement of the nature of the action that is to take place is given to each learner. The abstract is followed by a list of roles and an indication of the class time to be allotted to the roleplay.

For example, in the Industrial Library Simulation, unit descriptions are distributed to the class immediately preceding each unit. (See examples in Part VI.) A unit typically includes two or three roleplay descriptions, as, for example:

> In two time segments one or more applicants for the same position are interviewed by the FRLL Librarian and/or by two Department Heads; later these three individuals meet to make their selection.
> Roles: FRLL Librarian
>   FRLL Reference Librarian
>   FRLL Acquisition Librarian
>   Applicant(s)
> Roleplay Time: Segment 1. 20–30 minutes per interview
>   Segment 2. 20 minutes maximum

In the Governmental Library Simulation the *Participant's Resource-Log*, distributed to each learner at the beginning of the course, includes abstracts of twelve problems for roleplay.

> A proposal for an intern program to develop professional personnel for the DOE Library, submitted over a year ago, is funded rather suddenly. Three interns have been selected and have arrived for work. Their first two weeks on the job they spend in a training institute for new federal library employees. This institute is held at the department library of the Department of Space. During this time the DOE library staff must make specific plans for the utilization of the interns. The Library Director calls his four chiefs into a planning session for this purpose.
> Roles: Director, DOE Library
>   Chief, Bibliographic Services
>   Chief, Documentation Services
>   Chief, Circulation Services
>   Chief, Technical Services
> Roleplay Time: 40 minutes maximum

The briefing abstract used during a sustained simulation can be short because background material about the library and information relevant to the total situation is contained in the model which all learners have read. In a continuing-education experience there is usually less time for input and more information must be presented in the abstract. Following is one which I have used in several different workshops (administration of a reference department, techniques of supervision, and staff development).

> The Reference Department of the State Technical University Library has long prided itself on it participation in the State Personnel Development Plan, whereby the University exempts all tuition fees for employees who pursue job-related continuing education. The eight employees of this unusually stable staff have all availed themselves of this privilege more than once during the past five years. Several employees (from head reference librarian to the technical assistants) annually attend courses, conferences, workshops and other educational experiences.
>
> This enviable record came to a screeching halt two years ago when Vernell Myers joined the staff as a junior reference librarian. Fresh out of library school, with experience as a college library page as the only exposure to the "real world" of libraries, Vernell has been quick to learn and has blossomed into a valuable, responsible staff member in all areas of academic reference service. Two years have passed, however, and Vernell has been assigned new responsibilities for information retrieval, but has not requested funds or leave for study purposes.
>
> The head of the Reference Department, noting this exception to the department's record as the annual report is being prepared, decides that the time has come to push the matter. A memo is circulated to remind the staff of the general policy and to invite each staff member to apply now for tuition waivers for the next quarter, or to make an appointment with the department head to discuss individual development plans. The "long-time" staff responds, to a man, within two weeks. Two more weeks go by with no word from Vernell.
>
> The department head decides the time for confrontation has come and calls Vernell into the office for a conference, the purpose of which is
> > . . . to find out "why,"
> > . . . to convince,
> > . . . to plan.
>
> Roles: Head of the Reference Department
> Vernell Myers, Junior Reference Librarian
> Roleplay Time: 20 minutes maximum

Role Assignment

In classroom usage of roleplay, assignments are typically made one or two class sessions in advance, depending on the amount of cognitive preparation a roleplayer needs to make. For example, in roleplay centering on justification of space planning a longer time has to be allowed than on problems relating to supervision. Space planning usually requires searching literature for standards, precedents and ideas as well as drawing plans; a problem in supervision usually requires only a brief review of theory and of relevant policy statements in the model.

The general instruction for roleplay in my classes is: "Assume the library staff role assigned to you according to the expectation of behavior in that position that your library education has given you. Act as you think you would in the given situation and in the group interaction." The group is told during the initial orientation and at the briefing before the first roleplay that some assignments may be made *for specific learning objectives* that will require persons to display attitudes and behavior different from their usual patterns. It is stressed that this is done in order to create a needed learning climate and that the undesirable attitudes and behaviors are not to be held against the roleplayer after the session.

If part of the objective of the specific roleplay relates to affective learning accompanying surprise, or sudden change in plans, then the only assignment made in advance is to the individual who provides the "surprise." With a class of very inexperienced learners, for example, I would introduce such a roleplay by saying, "One of the important attributes of an administrator is flexibility, that is, the ability to shift gears quickly in order to meet an unexpected problem. Our assignment for this class was to have the staff committee that is developing a personnel evaluation form present their draft to the head librarian for criticism. Jay is playing the role of the head librarian. Just as the meeting gets underway, however, the librarian's secretary interrupts with apologies to say that one of the clerical staff is in the outer office, very upset, and insisting on talking with the head librarian that very minute. Jay, what will you do?"

Nine times out of ten Jay will ask the secretary to calm the employee and set up an appointment to follow the committee meeting. I accept this response and allow the group to begin the assigned roleplay. The person playing the part of the upset paraprofessional has been instructed in advance, however, that if the head librarian's response is a put-off through the secretary, he is to force his way into the committee meeting and insist on talking to the head librarian immediately. Approximately once in ten roleplays of this situation Jay will leave the committee to talk with the upset employee, who then initiates the real roleplay of the session. Jay, of course, must move spontaneously into the situation. With a more mature group I would skip the introduction, allow the assigned roleplay to get started and let the "surprise" occur as part of the enactment. In either case, the real roleplay is the response of the administrator to the emergency.

The instruction for the actor who provides the "surprise" is given on a 3" × 5" role card as secretly as possible. The written instruction is given, even though I may also ask the roleplayer to come to my office to talk about the implications of his assignment and how he is to carry it out. This is done so that the roleplayer will have the description of the role for personal reflection and preparation exactly as it was designed by the instructor.

I also use a role card for students assigned to roles that include such negative attitudes as hostility, obstinacy, obstructionism, or prejudice, even when the abstract clearly shows that such attitudes will be present and that dealing with them is one of the purposes of the roleplay. Experience has shown me that library school students and librarians usually will not give full breadth to such a role without special instruction. Further, I find that spelling out negative behavior and suggesting some reading about it in a psychology text puts the roleplayer in a better position later to discuss the behavior as a phenomenon. He is less personally involved with the specific behavior and serves as a resource about it for the group. An example of a role card is shown here:

> *Role: Vernell Myers, Junior Reference Librarian* In library school you were a complete student, routinely going beyond the minimum in assignments, following up on extra reading and generally trying to take full advantage of the professional library and faculty. You have confidence in your education and feel you arrived on the job better prepared than most employees. You are also scrupulous about doing the job in its entirety. The assignment of new responsibilities carried no fears; you feel more than adequate. In short, you carry your load and you don't mind an extra half hour now and then. You have no intention, however, of giving your entire life to the job; it isn't your life style. You have other interests and you volunteer chunks of your own time to them. Without lowrating what anyone else chooses to do, you refuse to attend meetings or to take courses. Stand pat. Be polite, but firm. Don't give in except to truly superior, convincing arguments.

ACTION

Getting the feel of roleplay takes longer in first experiences with the technique than in later ones. Some transfer to library science education can be expected with a group that has used roleplay in other kinds of learning, so the instructor will do well to find out in advance how much experience a given class has had. Allow sufficient time, but do have a timetable. This is the reason for the statement of roleplay time included in briefing information.

On the other hand, roleplay should not arbitrarily be stopped at the expiration of the given time. Perhaps it took these particular roleplayers an extra bit of "random activity" to get on the track. Perhaps an unusual number of productive ideas have come out and each must be explored. Perhaps the roleplayers have been on the track but, being inexperienced, are reacting slowly. A good rule of thumb is to stop the action by instructor intervention before the accomplishment of the roleplay objectives *only* if it loses its direction, or if it goes off in a direction clearly foreign to the objectives.

Initial roleplay for beginners should center on normal problem-solving situations without conflict. I have found staff planning meetings to be excellent. Conflict and sensitive issues should be introduced only after rapport has been established among the group members and after members of the group have become familiar with roleplay techniques. In continuing education, conflict can be introduced earlier provided proper groundwork has been laid for it in the specific objectives discussed with the group. In any use of roleplay it must be honestly admitted that this technique is a spontaneous activity and people may react in unexpected ways. No reaction is ruled out *per se* in advance, and all reactions can be discussed during debriefing with advantage to the group. At the same time it should be pointed out that an unexpected reaction may cause embarrassment to some roleplayers, or may appear to be harrassment of one player by others. A severe reaction by one roleplayer might cause another to founder in his role. The roleplay incidents suggested in this book have been designed carefully to avoid untoward reactions but, should one occur, it would constitute reason for the director to intervene in order to protect participants from experiences contrary to the objectives of the roleplay.

Whenever possible in my material, roles are described in terms of a position and learners use their own names during roleplay. For some problems, however, names must be given in the accompanying materials (e.g., in job applications) and these names are then used in the roleplay. Unless there is a reason to use a name ordinarily associated with one sex only I try to incorporate "either-sex" names in the materials. Some experienced group leaders claim that there is no problem in having learners fill other-sex roles. I have found with library science students that the use of other-sex names creates a distraction and I avoid such usage. I do often use table signs or nametags to show the position the person is playing. Especially if there are more than three or four roleplayers involved, this practice avoids digressions to find out "who's on first."

When sex-related attitudes are involved in the problem, I set up the roleplay one way and wait for a member of the group to point out that the situation would be different if the sexes in the given positions were reversed. At that point, we reassign the roles and replay the action. One example of this occurred when the library school students first began to wear "mod" or "hippy" clothing. A problem was introduced into the Industrial Library Simulation in which a library user complained in writing to the head librarian about the clothing of a young staff member and demanded that a dress code be instituted. The roleplay called for the head librarian to discuss the problem with the staff member and both roles were assigned to women. The action went well but during the debriefing someone pointed out that a much more sensitive situation would arise if the head librarian were a man and the young staffer a woman. We reassigned the role of head librarian to a man and replayed the situation in what turned out to be an insightful way. The young staffer had the last word, however, and used it to toss out a new problem, "If the company is going to insist by a dress code that I must wear dresses four inches longer than I wear at any other time, then long dresses are a uniform and the plant employees' union has established the precedent that the company buys workers' uniforms. I'll wear longer dresses, but I'll bill the company for them as uniforms!" *That* created a discussion!

Learner feedback tells us that roleplay is most meaningful to those most involved, so it is the leader's responsibility to involve as many people as possible. In my initial roleplay with a class I prefer to involve all learners as players. The first problem in the Industrial Library Simulation, for example, is expandable in terms of the number of players. It is a problem in planning services for users, and the inclusion of "researcher" among the roles permits involving all who are not assigned other roles. If the total number of role-players becomes too large, however, some will sit back and avoid participation. Four is an excellent number for a single roleplay and six is sometimes not too many. More than six and there will probably be several non-participants.

The most universally accepted way of involving everyone in the learning group in roleplay is to assign all those who are not players to be observers. As part of the preparation for roleplay, therefore, attention should be devoted to the nature of meaningful observation. Checklists and other guides to observation and analysis can be used. Designing such a checklist or guide can itself be a valuable learning experience. Sometimes the assignment of observers is a general one in that everyone tries to observe all the action. At other times it is better to assign specific learners to observe specific roleplayers or to observe in relation to specific objectives.[9] Apparently, only experience tells the leader when to utilize each kind of observation. Perhaps it doesn't really matter as long as every learner feels a specific responsibility in relation to the action.

Physical accoutrements for roleplay are minimal. No effort is made to provide stage scenery or realistic settings. Tables and chairs are usually all that are required. Some special problems, such as a demonstration of in-service training to paraprofessionals, might benefit from the presence of a typewriter, order forms, a bibliographic style manual or whatever. Common sense is the guide, remembering that learner imagination can supply almost anything.

DEBRIEFING

The general discussion in Chapter 4 applies to debriefing after roleplay as well as to the follow-up of other techniques. In addition, some specific suggestions apply.

Roleplay leaders agree that it is very important to bring the group sharply back to reality at the conclusion of the roleplay. It is important, first, in order to dissociate actors completely from the roles they have played. Some leaders advocate the use of role nametags with a ritual tearing of the tags at the end of the roleplay to symbolize the dissociation. Others advocate change of position, breaking up the "stage and audience" arrangement by having the role-players join the observers for the ensuing discussion. The entire group might even move to another part of the room and arrange itself in a circle. Complete dissociation is important, secondly, because the group must now analyze what has happened during roleplay in as detached and objective a way as possible. I have found a few minutes of quiet time for personal reflection and getting thoughts in order to be a good way to make the switch. At the outset of a class, especially with beginners, I use a formal questionnaire to focus attention on analysis; as the course proceeds, the questionnaire becomes more abbreviated, and may finally disappear. (See the two examples in Chapter 4).

Thus I try to instill a habit of self-analysis that is developed by using a form, but that does not ultimately depend on the presence of such a form.

The debriefing discussion may begin with the roleplayers; it may begin with the observers; or it may be a free-for-all. There appear to me to be advantages each way, and because roleplay is used so often in my classes, I deliberately try to vary the technique to retain interest and to bring the different points of view of players and observers into central focus regularly.

In the sustained simulations (as opposed to individual roleplay which has no cumulative implications) it is important to arrive at a decision for the model library because later problems depend on earlier decisions. In the Industrial Library Simulation, for example, several alternatives are possible in answer to the question, "How will service be provided to a task force at a location distant from the home base?" The obvious ones are (1) a library can be developed at the site; (2) service can be supplied from the home base; (3) service can be contracted for with a public or academic library at or near the site. Appropriateness of responses to later problems of staffing, building resources, physical planning and financing depend on which choice is made initially. The choice is entirely up to the learners; my responsibility as instructor is to see that the various alternatives are carefully considered and that the choice is justified. Thus debriefings focus on the substantive aspects of library science and their application within the environment of a specific kind of special library. Even the problems of interpersonal relationships are designed to bring out information about the industrial and governmental work environment as well as principles of supervision, personnel management and human relations.

"Instant replay" is a technique I have found useful to assure consideration of alternatives. During debriefing a suggested alternative is tried out by returning to a point in the roleplay and picking up the thread, substituting the alternative for the original idea or solution. Sometimes this is done with the same roleplayers, sometimes with others, spontaneously assigned. Two-person roleplays lend themselves to later pairing of the entire group, each pair then replaying the action with their own choice of the alternatives that have been discussed. Roleplay of a firing interview, for example, seems to be traumatic but very meaningful, judging by student feedback. It is an experience that all can have through pairing and replay.

"Role reversal" is another technique that often seems appropriate as part of debriefing. Especially after roleplay of conflict or negative attitudes, replay of the action with the participants in the opposite roles to those played initially helps each participant to understand the other's position. Feedback is emphatic on this point, with learners often expressing surprise that role reversal is so insightful an experience. This expression is itself valuable as the basis for a discussion about understanding other people's points of view.

Debriefing doesn't always end with the conclusion of the formal sessions. A certain amount of follow-up discussion continues privately between instructor and individual learners. The amazing thing to me is how much goes on between learners. Evaluations of the course typically include such statements as: "If you want to hear the real debriefing, Dr. Z—hours and hours of it—you should bug the student lounge." "We spent more time outside of class sessions debriefing than in them."

Some of the most meaningful continuations of learning with my classes have come from roleplay with linkage across out-of-class time, as well as between cognitive and affective learning.

VALUE AND LIMITATION OF ROLEPLAY[10]

> I hear, and I forget
> I see, and I remember
> I do, and I understand.[11]

The primary value of roleplay in professional education is in the linkage it provides between cognitive and affective learning. The dimensions of roleplay include the active nature of the technique, the impact of the first-person experience, the deliberate, objective analysis of alternative behaviors and solutions. All contribute to the learning experience. Some participants claim the greater value derives from actually playing a role, citing the personal "trying on" of certain behaviors and the "trying out" of suggested solutions to problems as the most meaningful part of the experience. Others claim the values of insight and peer instruction during analytic and objective discussion are at least as substantial. Whichever, it seems safe to assert that roleplay is valuable to learners-as-players and to learners-as-observers, admitting that in a given instance the experience may be different depending on the type of involvement. Especially in small groups the involvement tends to be total and the level of individual participation high. Therefore, as a technique for helping learners to forge ahead into the unknown world of professional reality, it seems singularly appropriate.

This is not to say that roleplay is a technique without limits. Caution and careful planning are in order, as with any other methodology. Perhaps the first specific is that roleplay as therapy belongs in the medical jurisdiction, not in that of the educator, notwithstanding its value in the re-education which is the therapeutic requisite in certain illnesses. To avoid roleplay as therapy, some guides for the instructor may be helpful. Emphasize normal work situations with normal patterns and problems, but avoid the specifics of libraries and personalities known to members of the learning group. Therapy for personal problems, if its need becomes apparent, should be turned over to medical practitioners. Therapy for the problems of specific libraries, should these be uppermost in the minds of some learners, should be turned over to qualified consultants. These ground rules should be laid out in advance and the roleplay leader should guard against being inveigled into a role as therapist or consultant not his by right of qualification, or into a situation beyond the bounds of teaching/learning objectives.

On the other hand, the leader may have to handle the intensive expression of personal points of view among group members, even occasional confrontation. In such situations he does not have to probe personal problems or idiosyncracies that may surface, nor should he. Rather he should maintain a nonjudgmental attitude himself and help the group focus as impersonally as possible on the management of similar problems in the work environment. The question, "What alternatives (of behavior, strategy or problem solutions) are available in this situation?" sets the stage for a discussion at a level of abstraction that can be managed. Usually those most intensely involved a moment before will themselves suggest alternatives and the discussion will be back on an even keel.

I anticipate that confrontations will occur more often during debriefing than during roleplay in my classrooms. After my introductory explanation that certain negative attitudes and behaviors may be "planted" in order to set up a specific roleplay situation, learners accept such behavior whether it was actually planted or not. They play up to it and the action moves along. The time interval before debriefing serves to put psychological distance between the confrontants. (Usually they don't sit beside each other during the debriefing either!) If the intensive involvement continues during the discussion, I focus away by directing impersonal, nonjudgmental questions to other members of the group. Sometimes learners turn up in my office later, concerned about their own behavior or that of others. I try to help them understand the possible causes and, if the climate seems conducive, I try to get the confrontants together away from other members of the group to resolve the problem. On rare occasions it has been possible to go back to the group and talk over the entire incident to everybody's benefit, but I would never push for this conclusion.

A caution of a different type is that the roleplay/debriefing sequence cannot be timed to the minute. Limits can be set for the enactment, but the debriefing must be carried to a natural conclusion if the complete potential in both cognitive and affective directions is to be achieved. My use of roleplay was, therefore, severely restricted when I had to teach my administration course on a fifty-minute schedule. The hour-and-twenty-minute class sessions that we had for a while were better, but the optimum schedule I have found is the three-hour session once a week. I plan the roleplay as the initial class activity and remain flexible about the rest of the plan for the session. This particular caution also applies to the use of roleplay in short continuing-education formats, such as one-day workshops. The danger is one of overcrowding. Roleplay, when it is used, should not be squeezed into too little time, or else its potential cannot be realized.

There are other cautions relating to the use of roleplay in continuing education: (1) It does not lend itself to immediate use in groups in which learners do not know each other and time must be spent in establishing rapport. The time may be well spent, especially if there are adjunct reasons why members of the group should get to know each other well, but the time must be allowed for in planning. (2) It is not roleplay to stage an enactment in front of a large group and then break into small groups for discussion. This technique often serves well as a valuable discussion-starter, but since it is not a first-person experience for the audience, it is not roleplay. (3) Roleplay for training in skill development or problem-solving should not include workers and their supervisors in the same learning group. No one wants to make a mistake, expose his weaknesses, or appear at even a slight disadvantage in front of his boss. The result is that a learner who feels no embarrassment or guilt in front of other learners on his own level may feel quite differently when his boss is present, and the psychological climate for learning from roleplay will be adversely affected.

A final caution for roleplay leaders is to avoid falling (or being shoved by lazy learners) into habits of traditional teacher-centered learning. Don't confuse the debriefing with extra lecture time, not even for mini-lecturers; resist telling the learners how they should have handled the situation; refuse to demonstrate "how you would do it on the basis of your experience." The trap may be either obvious or very, very subtle, but beware. And be firm. The learner learns from his own experience, aided and directed by the leader to be sure, but his own experience nevertheless.

On balance, in spite of the cautions (and the criticism from some quarters), roleplay is a valuable technique, worthy of conscientious planning and judicious use along with other techniques in professional education for library administrators.

REFERENCES

1. Summarization of role theory is available in many textbooks of social psychology and its applications. See, for example, Paul F. Secord and Carl W. Backman, *Social Psychology* (New York: McGraw-Hill, 1964). A valuable discussion in the context of roleplay as an instructional technique is in Fannie R. Shaftel and George Shaftel, *Role-playing for Social Values* (Englewood Cliffs, N.J.: Prentice-Hall, 1967), Chapter 7, "Role Theory," pp. 111-128.

2. Raymond J. Corsini et al., *Roleplaying in Business and Industry* (New York: Free Press of Glencoe, 1961), p. viii.

3. Allen A. Zoll, *Dynamic Management Education*, 2nd ed. (Reading, Mass.: Addison-Wesley Publishing Company, 1969), p. 47.

4. For example, see Alan F. Klein, *Role Playing in Leadership Training and Group Problem Solving* (New York: Association Press, 1956), pp. 130-164.

5. Alvar O. Elbing, Jr., "The Influence of Prior Attitudes on Role Playing Results," *Personnel Psychology* 20 (Autumn 1967): 309.

6. Corsini, *op. cit.*, pp. 17-34.

7. Zoll, *op cit.*, p. 48.

8. The suggestion for this kind of warm-up exercise came from Mark Chesler and Robert Fox, *Role-Playing Methods in the Classroom* (Chicago: Science Research Associates, 1966), pp. 64-65.

9. Elbing, *op. cit.*, pp. 315, 318.

10. For more extended discussions of values and limitations of roleplay, see Chesler, *op. cit.*, v.p., and Klein, *op. cit.*, pp. 165–176.

11. Chinese proverb quoted in T. L. Aldrich, "Elimināte Role-Playing Boredom," *SM/Sales Meetings Magazine*, May 1970, p. 60.

7.
The In-Basket Exercise

• •

The familiar multi-tiered in-basket might well be the heraldic device of the administrator. Plastic, metal or grained leather, it seems to personify the unending flow of paper coming within his purview. Some of this paper carries information he needs and wants, some carries information he needs but would rather not have, some carries irrelevant information that he neither needs nor wants. This paper comes from all around him in the organization—above, below and from lateral sources—as well as from outside the organization. Some of it is simply input to be read and filed or "bucked" on, some can be delegated to employees whom he supervises, some requires action on his part, and some is consigned to the "circular file." The action may be as minor as initialing and forwarding; it may be far-reaching enough to result in a firing or a new policy. Whatever the in-basket contains is the daily reality of the administrator's world. It has been said that "The ability to weigh the relative importance of individual bits of information, to recognize their interrelationships, and to formulate a decisive action from them often determines the final impact of a manager's decision."[1] A simulation in-basket exercise is the representation of that reality.

The in-basket exercise, as a training technique, is dedicated to the twin propositions that the skillfull use of the out-basket can increase managerial effectiveness and that communication is the name of the game. Essentially an in-basket exercise is a group or series of communications appropriate to the particular managerial environment being simulated. The items can represent a "moment in time" for a particular administrator, or they can represent a chronological sequence. The moment-in-time exercise, with a limitation on the response time allowed the learner, simulates the pressure of time in a work situation. The sequential exercise, which allows for feedback between the various in-basket items, simulates the interrelatedness of the demands on an administrator. The moment-in-time in-basket exercise is noninteractive, each learner dealing individually with the items. The sequential in-basket exercise can be made interactive by weaving it into roleplay enactments and their follow-up, or by computerizing it so that feedback is received by the learner immediately following his decision on each item. In either form of the in-basket technique the learner must assimilate each incoming communication and decide how to handle it. For moment-in-time exercises and for non-computerized sequential exercises, the learner follows his decision-making by preparing an appropriate outgoing communication (out-basket item). In the computerized sequential in-basket exercises designed to date, the emphasis is on the decision and its result and the learner does not prepare out-basket items. In every in-basket exercise the learner reacts in the first person, as the individual to whom the in-basket item is addressed.

An in-basket exercise can be designed in such a way that each learner must explain his reasons for the decisions he has made and for the actions he is taking. He can be specifically instructed to relate his reasoning to administrative theory. Or the exercise can be designed so that the learners prepare their out-basket items without stating their reasons, leaving explanation and defense to the debriefing discussion. The choice would depend on the purpose of the particular exercise, as do other elements in the design of an exercise.

USES OF IN-BASKET EXERCISES

Orientation, or Establishing Rapport

A short in-basket exercise can be used to orient a learning group to experiential techniques, or to establish rapport quickly at the beginning of a course or a workshop. For this use I would choose or design a moment-in-time exercise of five or six in-basket items. The exercise should be capable of completion in no more than twenty minutes, and simple enough that the debriefing would take only about another twenty minutes. The exercise should be relevant to the general purposes of the training, however, and it should be involving for each learner. It should illustrate characteristics of the learning experiences to follow, for example:

1. Some administrative problems require an immediate search for information before action can be taken.
2. Administrators are constantly involved in setting priorities.
3. General policies issued by top management may put a particular unit of an organization in a bind so that the administrator has to initiate explanation and/or complaint, or seek exception.
4. Middle managers are frequently asked to supply information or explanation for top managers to pass on as public relations. These requests are not low-priority items.

5. Decisions often generate a series of related actions and/or communications.

Exhibit 8 at the end of the chapter is an example of an in-basket exercise that could be used for orientation to the Industrial Library Simulation. The organization chart of the agency of which the library is a part is included in the model for the simulation. For use in a workshop, an organizational chart and perhaps other minimal information about the parent agency and/or the library might have to be supplied, but supplementary documents should be kept simple and to a minimum.

During orientation the director should give an introduction of a sentence or two and distribute a copy of the exercise to each learner. Each in-basket item should be presented on a separate piece of appropriate paper, that is, a letter should be typed on a letterhead, a phone call should be represented on a phone message form, and so on. Each learner should have a supply of paper, pen or pencil and perhaps paper clips. Those who complete their handling of the messages early might be invited to take a coffee break in order to keep the work area quiet until all have completed the exercise.

Sustained Simulation

In-basket items are an integral part of a sustained simulation. Both the Industrial Library Simulation and the Governmental Library Simulation in Part VI show that in each unit or problem in-basket items are part of the course management materials. They are used to set the stage for a roleplay, to convey background and supplementary information, and to give top management's point of view and directions to the library. They are used to move the model in time by telling what happens between roleplays; sometimes they are used to precipitate crises. Most of the in-basket items are included in the material given to learners at the beginning of the simulation; some items, however, serve as surprise elements during the life of the model library.

In-basket items can also be used to present out-of-class assignments in addition to those that stem from the roleplays. In fact, I try to make every communication with the learners an in-basket item, addressed to each one as the head librarian of the model library. I use buck slips on routed material and general distributions (and I'm always surprised how many young people have never seen one). In short, every effort is made to carry the simulation into all aspects of class management. Students even place their responses in an in-basket in my office. Examples of some of the kinds of in-basket items not included in the initial distribution of materials are presented on pages 92 and 93.

There are eight kinds of communications which I think beginning students of special librarianship should have at least one experience in preparing. The necessity for doing so during a sustained simulation is either written into the course management materials distributed initially to the entire group, or is

Example:
"Surprise" In-basket Item

Note:
Unit V in the Industrial Library Simulation requires the learners
to submit an "opening-day budget" or "make-ready budget" and
a first-year operating budget for the service to the company task
force at a distant location. As soon as these have been received
from each individual, complete with transmittal memo, each operating budget goes back to its originator with the following
cover memo. In the instance cited, the group had decided to establish a branch library for the Everglades City Exploration
Project.

> Interoffice Memo
> Double XYZ Oil Company
> Everglades City Exploration
> Project
> December 3, 19x5

To: Librarian, ECEP Branch Library

From: Director, ECEP

Re: First Year Operating Budget

Due to an overall cutback for the task force, it is necessary to
request revision of your estimated operating budget for the first
year of operation. Please cut your previous figure by 7 percent
and submit a revised comparison budget by December 6, 19x5.

cc: Librarian, FRLL

Example:
An Out-of-Class Assignment on the Evaluation of a Currently
Advertised Service, Reference Tool or Piece of Equipment for
Special Libraries

Note:
In advance of this assignment I choose something currently being
advertised in Special Libraries and request from the vendor
enough brochures to distribute to the class. Each brochure is
attached to a copy of the following memo.

> Interoffice Memo
> Double XYZ Oil Company
> Director's Office
> November 5, 19x5

To: Librarian, FRLL

At a meeting I attended last week, I picked up the attached brochure at an exhibit booth. Don't you think we ought to have this

in the library? If you feel strongly enough about it, we could probably make a budget adjustment to include it immediately.

Attachment: 1

Example:
An Out-of-Class Assignment to Accompany the Unit on Personnel

> Interoffice Memo
> Double XYZ Oil Company
> Employee Relations Office
> November 12, 19x5

To: Library Director, FRLL

From: Director, ERO

About that opening for an acquisition clerk that you mentioned to me recently—Joe Henderson in Plant Operations tells me that his niece has just come back home from UT and will be out of college for the remainder of the academic year. He'd like her to have a job with us and I'd like to oblige him. I've set up a tentative appointment for her to come talk with you Thursday at 10 A.M. Let me know if that's not o.k.

P.S. Don't worry about her being out of college. No academic problems;. she's a bright one. It was a disciplinary matter.

Example:
An "Extra" Reading Assignment

Note:
In this case the reference is highly relevant and I want to put some pressure on every student to read it.

> Interoffice Memo
> Double XYZ Oil Company
> November 19, 19x5

To: Library Director, FRLL

From: Head, Administration and General Services Division

Since you are good enough to send me notice of material that comes to your attention in which you think I might have an interest, I would like to return the favor. The attached item crossed my desk a few days ago. It is the best one-page description of PERT that I have seen. Although the company has not adopted a PERT system in toto, it is used frequently in relation to special projects. Would it be useful to you in preparing for ECEP? I'll be glad to talk it over with you at your convenience.

Attachment: 1

engendered by a special in-basket item. These eight kinds of communications, in no order of priority, are: (1) an information-carrying memo or letter; (2) communications about meetings (call to a meeting, agenda, or minutes); (3) a transmittal memo or letter; (4) an explanation to a supervisor of something that has happened or an action that has been taken in the library; (5) a library form; (6) a public relations communication (to an individual, an in-house group, or to the profession); (7) an evaluation of an employee (in-house or letter of recommendation); (8) a request to management (for an exception from a policy or for a favor). Each learner writes at least one of each during a sustained simulation and he critiques many of those written by his classmates. Whenever possible learners prepare their communications in response to different immediate needs of the model library in order to provide a wide range of examples for criticism. For example, in preparing forms three students might work individually on an application form, three on an interview evaluation form, and three on an orientation checklist for a new employee.

Testing

When the inevitable evaluation becomes necessary, an in-basket exercise can be given as a "take-home" exam. Individual items are chosen for specific purposes with specific classes, as in any other kind of examination. Examples of items that have been used with the Industrial Library Simulation are presented in Exhibit 9.

The evaluation of out-basket items is not easy. A few general criteria can be applied, for example: (1) the learner uses correctly the channels and operating procedures provided in the model; (2) the learner refrains from inappropriate actions; (3) the learner uses the tone appropriate to the type of communication; (4) the learner considers alternatives before making his choice; (5) the learner takes important special factors into consideration, such as humanistic factors, technological capability of the library, costing of alternatives (if you have asked him to explain the rationale for his response). In general, these criteria have to be applied in a subjective way. Such criteria as (1) the learner understands the underlying theory, and (2) the learner can locate factual information related to the problem, are more objective, but you must remember, in giving directions, to require the learner to link his response to theory or to present the sources of his information.

The originators of the in-basket exercise have reported ways to evaluate it,[2,3,4] but these seem more appropriate to a research use of the technique than to an instructional one. My efforts to adapt their methods proved too cumbersome to be feasible for small groups or in the limited time available for end-of-term evaluation. When I use an in-basket exercise as a final exam, I critique each learner's out-basket items for him personally and assign grades in much the same way as if they were traditional essay examinations.

DEBRIEFING

Debriefing begins with self-analysis, as usual. Here is an example of a questionnaire-type form for the learner's personal use after an in-basket exercise.

Example:
Self-Analysis and Evaluation Form[5]

Directions:
Check "Yes" or "No" beside each question as you review your responses to the in-basket items.

	Yes	No
Organizational Skill		
1. Did you take action on each item as you read it?	___	___
2. Did you read all items and plan your responses in terms of priorities?	___	___
3. Did you note an exact time and/or date for accomplishment of items postponed for the future?	___	___
4. Did you defer some items indefinitely?	___	___
5. Did you correctly identify others in the organization who would be affected by your responses or who should be informed of them?	___	___
Decision-making Skill		
6. Did you consign inconsequential items to the round file immediately on reading them?	___	___
7. Did you initiate action in some cases?	___	___
8. Did you relay problems about which you have no authority to the individual in the organization who is designated to deal with them?	___	___
9. Did you leave any items without action of some kind? (Other than the inconsequential ones.)	___	___
10. Did you "buck" an item that you should have dealt with yourself?	___	___
Communication Skill		
11. On rereading, did all of your out-basket items convey the tone you wished to convey?	___	___
12. Was each out-basket item concise, but complete?	___	___
13. Was all information, as you conveyed it, correct?	___	___
14. Did you include unnecessary details in any out-basket communication?	___	___
15. Did you direct carbon copies to everyone else in the organization who would be affected by your responses or who should be informed of them firsthand?	___	___

Preferred Responses: Yes: 2, 3, 5, 6, 7, 8, 11, 12, 13, 15; No: 1, 4, 9,
10, 14. If there was a difference of four or more between your score
and the preferred responses, you need to analyze your skills in
greater depth. If your score in a single section differed by three or
more from the preferred responses, you should consider asking your
instructor for special help in relation to that skill.

> Note:
> Some of the questions above would have to be changed, depending
> on the items used in a given in-basket exercise. It is sometimes
> useful to suggest that learners repeat their self-analysis after
> the debriefing to see whether they perceive their original re-
> sponses differently after the group discussion and why. The
> reasons can be very self-revealing: my group came up with
> many alternatives not thought of by individuals: failure to take
> humanistic factors into account, some relevant information over-
> looked, false assumptions, etc.

The debriefing discussion should, as usual, emphasize alternative actions
and reasons for actions taken, as well as how learners feel about their decisions. In addition, the form and tone of the out-basket communications
should be reviewed carefully. When the general discussion dies down the
learners can be divided into pairs to exchange communications written during
the exercise, each learner to critique the other's communications. Use the
Checklist for Effective Writing (in Exhibit 2), which provides criteria for criticism and discussion, as a guide. During the paired critique the leader should
circulate around the room ready to assist, but slow to give opinions. Keep the
critique session student-centered rather than teacher-centered. If two learners
cannot resolve their differences of opinion, call on another pair to read the
controversial communications, to listen to the arguments and to resolve the
problem. Pairs that conclude their discussions early should be directed to join
those still discussing so that everyone stays involved and no one is sitting
around doing nothing. The in-basket exercise, carried out in this way, takes
forty-five minutes to an hour.

In the study of administration, especially that in which participative management is emphasized, developing the learners as effective discussion leaders
is oftentimes an objective of the learning experience. Usually the debriefing
following an in-basket exercise is good training ground for learners as discussion leaders. The problem in each in-basket item is rather narrow in focus
(although the implications may be far-reaching). and the items are closely related to the roleplay in sustained simulations. The exercise is task-oriented
with specific criteria available for the communications, though not always for
the actions. Further, the in-basket exercise debriefing is usually shorter than
the roleplay debriefing.

Debriefing of an in-basket exercise used for orientation to experiential
techniques is usually led by the director rather than by a learner because the
debriefing is a demonstration of the technique. If the group is large, however,

it should be broken into smaller groups of three, five or seven (an uneven number in case a vote has to be taken for consensus) with a learner as the leader in each subgroup. Each small group can report its consensus on priorities and handling of items to the large group reassembled. The director might or might not choose to extend the discussion at that point as well as to summarize explicitly the principles involved in the exercise. The director would make his decision about how to handle the discussion on the basis of the complexity of the exercise, the sophistication of the group, and his own plans for the remainder of the learning experience, be it course or workshop.

It has been pointed out that, by varying the emphasis of the debriefing, the same in-basket exercise "can be used to focus on the particular solutions achieved, the method of attack, or the consequences of actions. The design permits concentration on limited aspects or balanced coverage of a broad, complex problem."[6]

VARIATIONS OF THE BASIC IN-BASKET TECHNIQUE

Multimedia Techniques

The criticism is sometimes made that the pressures of reality are not adequately portrayed merely by limiting the response time in an in-basket exercise, and it is true that the learner is usually protected during the exercise from interruptions that would normally occur at work. Harvard Business School faculty designed a 16mm motion picture to be used with printed in-basket material to overcome this criticism.

> Several days before the class session for which the "Hope Electronics" has been scheduled, the students are given copies of the general instructions and the printed data on the company to study at their leisure. When they arrive in class, they are then given the package representing the contents of the in-basket and are allowed several minutes to glance over it. The discussion leader then signals the projectionist, and the first part of the film is screened. For most of the students, who up to this point are deep in the correspondence, the first sign that another element is being added to the case is the sound of a door being shut. When they look up at the screen, they see a personnel director's office, shown from the perspective of the occupant when seated at his desk. In the background, a woman stands looking directly at the students, each of whom is roleplaying the personnel director, Mr. Estabrooke. Her first words, "Are you Mr. Estabrooke?" are addressed to the viewers.

> The film continues until Mr. Estabrooke is called to make a decision on the problem raised by the woman. The screen then goes blank and the leader begins the discussion in the usual way by asking one of the students to say how he would handle the situation.

> When the class has reached a "solution" to the problem or has explored it to the discussion leader's satisfaction, the projector is started again and another sequence is shown. Once more the screen goes blank and the class discussion continues. In the course of the discussion, the leader may suddenly switch from the problem just presented by the film to ask a question about one of the problems awaiting action in the printed in-basket material.

By this time, the students may well have forgotten all about their in-basket material. As a result, they find themselves having to quickly reorient their thinking to deal with it. Now they have to cope with two different sets of chronologically and subjectively related problems almost simultaneously, and a realistic pressure builds up. The degree to which this pressure can be applied is entirely at the discussion leader's discretion. Whenever he chooses he can add new elements to the educational mix, either by running more of the film or by referring at random to related situations outlined in the printed material.[7]

In this usage the screen action is seen as if through the eyes of Mr. Estabrooke, with the camera simulating leaning forward, standing, moving. Mr. Estabrooke is never seen; only his voice identifies him. The technique practically guarantees that each learner will identify with the voice, and the impact is intense. Evaluation of the augmented technique indicated that (1) people do not usually observe accurately, but can become more expert with practice; (2) "those involved in making spontaneous decisions . . . seem to react first emotionally and then rationally, depending upon how closely the situation affects them personally"; (3) the technique *does* increase the pressure and learners may react differently than under other classroom conditions; (4) the dual media presentation of a problem situation "results in a high degree of personal involvement and individual participation in the group discussion."[8]

Multimedia were used for a different purpose in "Sister Monica's In-Basket," an in-basket exercise designed to help prepare administrators of Catholic elementary schools for the problems they would meet.[9] Sister Monica is a newly appointed principal who must pick up the reins in the absence of both her predecessor and her secretary. The briefing—for each Sister in the workshop and for the learning group as a whole—is composed of

an array of written materials, slides and tape recordings. Sister Monica begins with a tape-recorded interview with Mother General about her new assignment. Through a series of slides and an accompanying tape recording provided by her predecessor, Sister Magdeline, Sister Monica tours St. Stephen's School and looks at the physical plant and the many classrooms of children and teachers, In this "guided tour" she also visits the church and the convent, and drives around the parish to become acquainted with the school and community setting. After this pictorial tour, she meets each teacher through a series of slides and learns something about each of them. Finally, she meets her new pastor, Father Schneider, and listens to his perception of her new position as principal.[10]

Sequential Techniques

Another criticism, especially of the moment-in-time exercise, is that it is static and does not portray the "movement" of decision-making, the volleying from listening or input mode on the part of the administrator to a mode of inquiry, analysis of new information, feedback or decision. The sequencing of related in-basket items throughout a sustained simulation is an attempt to meet this criticism, as is the computerized Sequential In-Basket Exercise (SIBE).[11]

The SIBE technique presents a three-layered problem in such a way that the learner makes a series of related decisions and deals with the consequences of these decisions. The conclusion of an SIBE exercise in the present computer-assisted format does not resolve the problem; rather, it moves an entire class individually through stages of a problem and provides the instructor with a record of the individual decision pathways. The record of each student's decision pathway and the cumulative record of the individual decisions provide the basis for classroom discussion of administrative theory and behavior.

For the developmental study of the SIBE technique four typical library administrator in-basket problems were designed. These problems were then programmed in Coursewriter II for presentation in the computer-assisted instruction (CAI) mode using teletype terminals for learner input and to provide hard-copy printout. This printout serves as a record for the learners of their individual responses to the problems, as well as for reference during the debriefing.

The basic configuration of SIBE is shown in Figure 9. For each problem sequence, the learner is presented with the initial in-basket item, designated a Seminal Problem (rectangle in the upper left corner of the figure) followed by four action choices and a "comment response" choice (first line of circles in the figure). The learner, in the role of an administrator, makes his choice of the action he would take by entering the designation of that choice (A, B, C, or D) via the teletype keyboard. Alternately, the learner can make the comment response choice (E) and enter a statement of his intended action via the keyboard.

A choice of action by the learner is followed immediately by the display of a follow-up communication (represented by the second line of rectangles in the figure) and five more choices (the second line of circles). All stages of the problem after the initial presentation are designated Derived Problems, and these may continue until the ingenuity of the designer runs out. In the first SIBE each Seminal Problem was followed by two Derived Problems, each complete with four action choices and a comment response choice. All learners receive the same Seminal Problem and its choices. Figure 10 is an example of an opening display. The Derived Problems that each individual receives depend on his own choices of action. Thus each learner determines his own decision pathway (represented in Figure 9 by running arrows). When the learner makes his third action choice, he has completed the computer-assisted part of the problem-solving exercise; debriefing is initiated at that point. As SIBE has been used to date, each computer-assisted session presents the learners with four Seminal Problems.

In order to accommodate any possible decision pathway that the learner might take, a total of thirty Derived Problems, with their action choices, must be stored in the computer with each Seminal Problem. However, in the course of working each exercise, a learner actually sees only the Seminal Problem

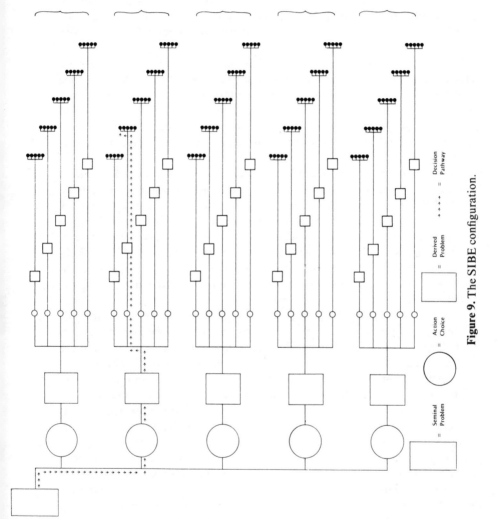

Figure 9. The SIBE configuration.

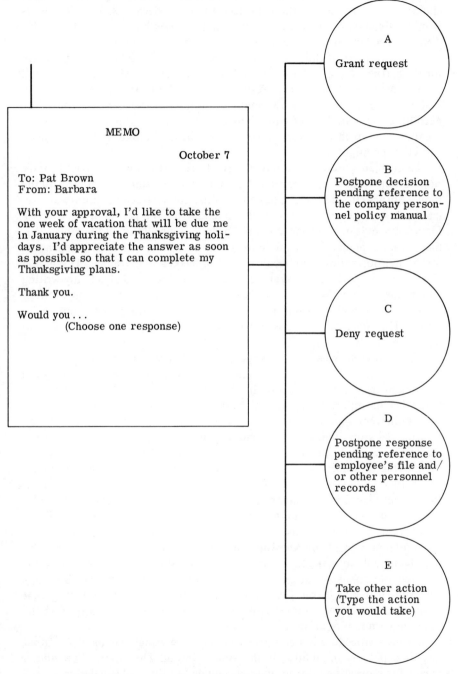

MEMO

October 7

To: Pat Brown
From: Barbara

With your approval, I'd like to take the one week of vacation that will be due me in January during the Thanksgiving holidays. I'd appreciate the answer as soon as possible so that I can complete my Thanksgiving plans.

Thank you.

Would you ...
(Choose one response)

A
Grant request

B
Postpone decision pending reference to the company personnel policy manual

C
Deny request

D
Postpone response pending reference to employee's file and/or other personnel records

E
Take other action (Type the action you would take)

Figure 10. Example of a Seminal Problem and its action choices.

and its five action choices plus two Derived Problems and their action choices, as determined by the sequence of his own decisions. Thus in a four-Seminal-Problem-exercise each learner must deal with and respond to twelve distinct decision-forcing situations, eight of which are contingent on his own decisions. In none of the problems is there a clear-cut right or wrong choice for the learner to make. However, some choices are less wise than others and these choices elicit unexpected results, causing the learner to be faced with major or minor crises of his own making. In this way the learner is shown the need for careful analysis of a problem, and the need for thinking through the possible consequences of various actions that he might take, and various decisions that he might make.

The problems presently stored in SIBE 1 are part of the Industrial Library Simulation. Each learner participating in that simulation is familiar with the model library. In addition, he has an organization chart of the library and related parts of the organization and a calendar for the period of the exercise for reference during his participation in the exercise. It should be noted that there is no explanatory narrative in SIBE; each administrator is dependent for both information and feedback on in-basket items alone. His action choices represent his out-basket; he simply omits the stage of actually writing an out-basket item. Whereas the usual manual in-basket exercise is a format for practice in both decision-making and in the preparation of communications, SIBE focuses on decision-making and has no communication component.

SIBE is presently used as a discussion stimulant and to initiate learners to the experience of "unfolding problems." Just when they think they've solved a problem by a decisive action, another in-basket item arrives to let them know they haven't reached any such happy conclusion.

In a different approach to the problem of portraying the movement of dicision-related communications around an administrator, Bessent developed a feedback procedure to simulate the searching for information that precedes the making of a decision.[12] The information search includes "discussing, investigating, and asking for opinions and advice from others," and it is a natural response from an administrator whenever an in-basket message provides him with insufficient information on which to base decisions or actions. There is, however, another dimension: "The successful handling of an administrative problem depends on knowing what information is relevant to the solution, being able to make the correct assessment of the information when it is received and doing this as efficiently as possible." The objective of Bessent's procedure is to help learners to develop "an information-seeking strategy that would optimize chances for selecting the most acceptable alternative with the minimum amount of information searching."[13]

Bessent's procedure is a computerized one with visual and auditory output display capability in addition to the usual printout. The program provides a means for requesting information not included in the package design as well as a means for requesting stored information. The program also provides the learner with diagnostic or corrective statements or clues if these are indicated by premature decisions or misinterpretation of information. A set of criteria for meeting the basic objective has been devised and a computer-managed scoring system is keyed to it. The procedure has the advantage of simulating the *inquiry* stage of response to a problem posed as an in-basket communication. Thus it meets the important criticism made by learners who have been exposed to SIBE that no inquiry for additional information is possible. Technical constraints within the program design for the Bessent procedure result in the inability to use situations characterized by high uncertainty. This probably means that the problem situations are simplistic for all except the least sophisticated learners.

The objectives of SIBE and the Bessent feedback design are different, though related. Both procedures were in developmental stages when reported, and no later information is available. Learner feedback from trial runs of SIBE was very positive. It confirmed the designers' opinion that the fast in-basket/out-basket communication, without additive or interpretive narrative, appeared realistic to the learners. The apparent realism of the simulation is also obvious to observers of SIBE in action. Learners respond vigorously to the teletyped communications with moans, groans and giggles as their mischoices become apparent to them. As the problems and decisions become more agonizing, tensions are expressed in body language. Almost every learner hunches, backs away, tears his hair, or lurches at the keyboard in an effort to get his decision "in" faster and to find out what happens next. Virtually all express regret that SIBE is over "so soon," and perceive the elapsed time of the exercise as much shorter than it really was.

Debriefing comments made after SIBE runs have highlighted advantageous by-products of the CAI experience, and some potentially valuable suggestions for future development and use of SIBE have been made.

> I think a familiarity with the computer was, in my case, a valuable by-product of this experience. The responses in SIBE seemed somehow to have more than one level or something—I would like one part of a given response and would object rather strongly to another part. This made me choose the comment response as a way out. As I chose so many of these [i.e., comment responses], SIBE lost some of its effectiveness for me.

> SIBE made me feel more close to a real life situation, and I lost less time in making decisions than in other in-basket exercises.

> I would have liked an SIBE program, perhaps weekly or at least at intervals, that progressed in difficulty.

> SIBE is a way of measuring decision-making abilities, quickly and correctly. The wrong decisions bring many difficulties which you can't solve. It is difficult to turn back after a wrong decision. [Note: Nothing is said to students in my classes about measuring decision-making ability with SIBE or any other technique.]

Perhaps part of my enjoyment of SIBE was in manipulating the gadgetry.

I felt under pressure with the machine [i.e., teletypewriter]; probably this was more from the novelty than anything else. It was a *good* experience.

Somehow the environment of the computer and seeing your choice of answers and the results being printed out was very much like real life. In both the results of one's actions are clearly and immediately visible. I liked the idea of being able to choose the comment response and type in a different action from those offered.

SIBE should include some way for the administrator to get additional information. On several of the problems it was obvious what information was needed, but there was no opportunity to get it. [Note: Information was offered in many of the action choices; obviously, it was not the information this student wanted. His point is well-taken, but it's a difficult design problem.]

SIBE has the psychological advantage of creating a feeling of urgency due to the rapidity of the teletypewriter. It seemed to force me to make more rapid decisions.

VALUE AND LIMITATION OF IN-BASKET EXERCISES

In the opinion of many teachers of administration, in-basket exercises have highly desirable values. From the leader's viewpoint, they are flexible in relation to specific objectives and time requirements, and they can be designed to focus on problems the learners are having at the time. With their emphasis on written communications and linking communications with decisions, they serve to balance roleplay. Learners feel that in-basket exercises are interesting, involving, and realistic, and that they provide desired feedback. Computerized exercises are preferable to manual ones for fast feedback. Teachers, learners and industrial personnel managers realize that in-basket exercises provide a way of sampling an individual's behavior in relation to various managerial skills. They have, therefore, been used in the military and in industry for the selection of individuals for management responsibilities.[14, 15, 16] Zoll suggests the following list of types of problems which can be appropriately included in in-basket exercises:

1. Relations with: the public, customers, suppliers, subordinates, superiors, other organizational groups, peers, etc.
2. Organizational difficulties in: control, planning, delegating, ethics, human relations, line and staff, etc.
3. Work habits as in: organizing own work, scheduling, communicating, delegating appropriately, getting beneath symptoms, etc.
4. Specific decision areas such as: credit approvals, policy decisions, developing subordinates, etc.[17]

There is not as much agreement about the limitations of the technique as about its advantages. Some feel that designing in-baskets is a simple, easy procedure; others feel that it is too time-consuming. Gilson finds that "the face validity makes it easier to assume that it measures what it is supposed to" when it is used in making judgments about individuals.[18] By analogy it might be suggested that it is easy to assume that it teaches what it is supposed to. In truth, it is difficult to measure what any experiential technique teaches, or, for that matter, what any other technique teaches.

There is little or no risk attached to in-basket exercises, yet there is emotional reaction, especially with sequential exercises. If learner opinion is positive, in-basket exercises are insightful and provocative as well.

REFERENCES

1. Thomas Q. Gilson, "A Look at the In-basket: A Realistic Technique for Selection and Training," *Management of Personnel Quarterly* 1:5 (Winter 1962): 3.

2. Norman Frederiksen, "Factors in In-Basket Performance," *Psychological Monographs* 76:22 (1962): 1–25.

3. Norman Frederiksen, D.R. Saunders, and Barbara Wand, "The In-Basket Test," *Psychological Monographs* 71:9 (1957): 1–28.

4. Norman Frederiksen, "In-Basket Tests and Factors in Administrative Performance," in *Simulation in Social Science*, ed. Harold Guetzkow (New York: Prentice-Hall, 1962), pp. 124–137.

5. This form was modified from one in Elizabeth Iannizzi, "Through Experience in Making Decisions," *Business Education Forum* 21 (February 1967): 13. Scoring added.

6. *Ibid.*, p. 7.

7. George W. Gibson, "A New Dimension for 'In-Basket' Training," *Personnel* 38 (July–August 1961): 77–78.

8. *Ibid.*, p. 79.

9. Glenn L. Immegart and Rev. Daniel Brent, "Sister Monica's In-Basket," *Catholic School Journal* (May 1968): 34–38.

10. *Ibid.*, p. 36.

11. Martha Jane K. Zachert and Veronica Pantelidis, *SIBE: A Sequential In-Basket Technique, The Pilot Study* (Tallahassee, Fla.: Computer Assisted Instruction Center, Florida State University, 1971).

12. Wailand Bessent, "A Feedback Procedure for Simulation of Administrative In-Basket Problems" (Paper presented at the AERA Symposium on Feedback in Simulation Techniques, New York, 1967).

13. *Ibid.*, pp. 5–6.

14. Gilson, *op. cit.*, p. 3.

15. Allen A. Zoll, *Dynamic Management Education*, 2nd ed. (Reading, Mass.: Addison-Wesley Publishing Company, 1969), p. 133.

16. Andrew A. Daly, "In-Basket Business Game," *American Society of Training Directors Journal* 14 (August 1960): 8.

17. Zoll, *op. cit.*, p. 135.

18. Gilson, *op. cit.*, p. 7.

EXHIBITS

EXHIBIT 8. SAMPLE IN-BASKET EXERCISE FOR USE IN
ORIENTATION

Directions:

You are Head Librarian of the Field Research Laboratory Library of the Double XYZ Oil Company of Houston, Texas. You have been attending a two-hour business conference-luncheon and have just returned to your office. At 2:30 you have a meeting scheduled with the head of Employee Relations in the FRL Administration Building, a short distance from the building which houses the library. This is a routine, but important, meeting with all unit chiefs. Your secretary, Suzi, has gone to lunch leaving the following items on your desk. It is now 2:15 P.M.

Read Communications A, B, C, D, E, F, and G. Rearrange them in the order in which you will act on them. List below your order of priority by placing the communication identification letters as you have rearranged them beside the numbers.

> 1.____
> 2.____
> 3.____
> 4.____
> 5.____
> 6.____
> 7.____

Take each communication in the order in which you have listed it and write your response on a separate piece of paper. If your response will be a phone call, head it "Phone Call" and write the message. If your response will be action, head the paper "Action" and write what you would do. If your response will be a memo or a letter, head the paper "Memo" or "Letter" and write the message in appropriate form. Do not omit any communication that requires a response.

. . . .

Communication A

Boss—

Don't forget your 2:30 appointment with Alice Mankin.

Suzi

Communication B

Interoffice Memo
Double XYZ Oil Company
Field Research Laboratory
Director's Office

To: Lee Capriano, Library Director

From: Donald Brooks

Can you explain the second paragraph in the accompanying letter?

D. B.

. . . .

Communication B: Attachment

Double XYZ Oil Company
Executive Offices
New York, N.Y.

Dr. Donald Brooks, Director
Field Research Laboratory
Double XYZ Oil Company
Houston, Texas

Dear Don:

Thanks again for the hospitality on my recent trip. You'll be glad to know I've completed my report on your request for an expansion lab and it will be ready for distribution to the Board of Directors early next week. A copy will be sent to you automatically.

One incident marred my trip. That last afternoon I saw an item in the library that I've been looking for for quite a while. My request for a photocopy to read on the plane was turned down rather rudely. I think your policy on photocopies could include visiting staff from HDQ.

My best to Marge and the family. See you at the quarterly meeting in about a month.

Sincerely,

Gerald Heffner
Staff Assistant to the President

GH:na

Communication C

> Interoffice Memo
> FRLL
> Reference Office
> 1 p.m.

To: Lee

From: Wayne

I've just received word that my wife's mother is critically ill
and I'm leaving immediately to drive her and the children to
Galveston. Can't tell when I'll be able to get back. Sorry to
leave without talking to you but Suzi's gone to lunch and nobody
seems to know when you'll be back. There are a couple of things
in process on my desk. Please take a look at them. I've jotted
down a few notes on each one to help you get rolling on them.
The search for Ken Walters in Applied Math is almost finished
and he wants it today if at all possible.

Sorry to run out like this. I'll call you as soon as I can size up
the situation.

Wayne

. . . .

Communication D

> Interoffice Memo
> FRLL
> Librarian's Office

To: Lee

From: Suzi

You ought to know that Mr. Richey from Production Research
fell off of a step-stool about 12:15 and cut his head pretty badly.
Jim went with him to the nurse's office when he refused to wait
for a stretcher. It made me wonder if we have any insurance.

Note: Jim is the Xerox machine operator, messenger, and man-
of-all work around the library—except that he is not now
around the library!

. . . .

Communication E

PHONE MESSAGE

While you were out *Alice Mankin* phoned.

Time: *11:15 am*

Message: *Please bring all your current job
description for nonexempt personnel
to the meeting.*   *Suzi*

Communication F

Interoffice Memo
Double XYZ Oil Company
Sheffield Refinery
Library

To: Librarians of all Double XYZ Company Libraries

From: Marguerite Atkinson, Librarian, Sheffield Refinery

Re: Exchange of technical reports

Do you have as much trouble getting tech reports from company units other than your own as I do? I have reason to believe that, if you will work with me on a policy and a procedure, top management will help us implement it company-wide.

Could we all get together during the upcoming meeting of SLA to talk about it? I suggest either Wednesday breakfast or Thursday lunch. Please let me know how many are interested and I'll reserve space for us and let you know when and where. Hope to see you soon.

. . . .

Communication G

Interoffice Memo
Double XYZ Oil Company
Field Research Laboratory
Training Section

To: Library
Materials Transport
Safety
Employee Relations

From: Joe Gonzalez

Re: Summer affirmative action program

In line with company policy and in cooperation with a local service club, FRL has agreed to provide an eight-week internship for 25 minority high school juniors. Each of the units to which this memo is directed will be assigned six internees; the extra one will work with me. We do not yet know the male/female distribution. All of the internees are enrolled in business or vocational programs in high school. The purpose of the internship is to give these young people some skill training and to persuade them to return to high school in the fall.

Please formulate some ideas for working with these young people to our mutual benefit and bring your plans to a meeting on Thursday of next week. We only have about three weeks to put this worthwhile community program in shape.

Note: A look at the organization chart of the FRL Library (Part VI, Industrial Library Model) shows that the library has a total of eight employees, of whom four are librarians.

EXHIBIT 9. SAMPLE IN-BASKET TEST ITEMS

Directions:
> You are to prepare an out-basket communication in response to
> each in-basket test item. The response may be in the form of
> a letter, memo, or the substance of a phone call. If additional
> action would be taken, this action should be described on a sepa-
> rate piece of paper. The response must show evidence of appli-
> cation of principles demonstrated and discussed during the
> course.
>
> Each communication must be interpreted and responded to from
> the viewpoint of the staff member to whom it is addressed, and
> in the context of the Industrial Library Model. Any material in
> the library or from an other appropriate source may be used.
>
> Hand in the in-basket items plus your responses.
>
> [Note: This test was planned to cover the following areas of admin-
> istration: Personnel Management, Public Relations, Coordi-
> nating Library Activities, Professional Involvement, Plan-
> ning, and Supplying Management Intelligence. The establish-
> ment of priorities was not a part of the test, nor was expla-
> nation of actions taken. Obviously, tests could be con-
> structed to include other topics and other objectives.]

. . . .

Communication A

WESTERN PERIODICALS
13000 North Rayner
North Hollywood, California

June 15, 19x7

Librarian
Field Research Library
Double XYZ Oil Company
Houston, Texas

Dear Sir:

Reference is made to your purchase order number 02266 of October 1, 19x6.

In this purchase order you ordered 160 magazines to start with
the October issues. We still don't have our check for this order
even though we have sent reminders each week for the last two
months.

We placed these orders promptly and even bought back issues in
a few cases and have given good service generally. If we don't

receive prompt payment for this account we will put the matter in the hands of our attorney.

Very truly yours,

Sol Grossman

Sol Grossman
President

. . . .

Communication B

Interoffice Memo
Double XYZ Oil Company
June 14, 19x7

To: Director, FRL Library

From: Head, Administration and General Services

Re: Library insurance

At the approaching management meeting in NYC of all Double XYZ affiliates the subject of insurance for company libraries is on the agenda for discussion by Administration heads. The policy under consideration is described in the attached folder. Please brief me on your professional thinking on the need for insurance and on this specific policy.

Attach.: "The Hartford's Special Library Policy," The Hartford Insurance Group (A brochure)

. . . .

Communication C

Interoffice Memo
Double XYZ Oil Company
June 16, 19x7

To: Library Director, FRL Library

From: Head, Employee Relations

Re: Your open position for a Clerk II in cataloging

Al Hatfield in Materials Transport has requested transfer of one of his clerks, Barbara Baker. She has been with the company three years and has been generally satisfactory from our standpoint. We would like to keep her if possible. Her latest evaluation form, completed three months ago, is attached. Can you use her in your open position for a Clerk II in cataloging?

If I can help in any other way, let me know.

Attach.: Evaluation form for Barbara Baker

[Note: The evaluation form would include some red herrings as well as a valid eyebrow-raiser.]

Communication D

COUNCIL ON WORLD HOUSING NEEDS
New York, New York

Research Library
June 10, 19x7

Mr. Andrew Morrison, Librarian*
ECEP Library
Double XYZ Oil Company
Everglades City, Florida

Dear Mr. Morrison:

The time has come for the SLA Education Committee to plan the
Continuing Education Seminars for the annual meeting next year.
As you know, you were asked to be a member of this Committee
in order that we might have the opinions of a recent graduate, an
individual working in a first professional position. We were delighted that you came to SLA this year and that you volunteered
for this committee. From your point of view, then, what are
some of the topics you would like to have presented for your own
continuing education?

Any help that you can give us will be much appreciated. We are
particularly interested in the "why" of each of your suggestions
because we will have the problem of deciding which ones would
be valuable to other recent graduates and which ones might possibly be the result of your own unique situation.

Looking forward to seeing you at SLA again next year,

Sincerely yours,
Shirley Newsome
Shirley Newsome
Chairman, SLA Education
Committee

*(Note: A female name is used for women recipients of the test.)

. . . .

Communication E

Interoffice Memo
Double XYZ Oil Company
Production Research
June 10, 19x7

To: Director, FRL Library

From: Ted Sparks, Head, Production Research

Twice in the last three weeks I have seen Roman Vallasandro, a
researcher in my department, lounging in the library.

I won't stand for that kind of goofing-off. Kindly call me the
next time you see him there.

Communication F

Interoffice Memo
Double XYZ Oil Company
Administration and
General Services

To: Director, FRL Library

From: Andy Andersen, Head

Two firms have submitted plans for custom-built trailers to house the ECEP Library. Drawings are in my office. Please study these plans and criticize them so that one plan can be chosen and any necessary revisions can be written into it before it goes out for bids.

(Note: This class had decided to house a branch library in trailers and two teams had submitted floor plans. Instead of a class critique, this memo was included in the final exam.)

8

The Action Maze

• • • • • • • • • • • • • • • •

An action maze is a printed description of an incident for analysis, followed by a list of alternative actions. Each action choice directs the learner to a new page which gives him the results of his action and a new set of alternatives to choose from. The results the learner receives after each step may give him more information as well as giving a reaction to his action. His selection may also lead to a dead end and send him back to make another choice from among the previous ones.[1]

The action maze is thus described by Allen A. Zoll in his provocative text for designers of experiential teaching materials, *Dynamic Management Education.* The learner responds in a first-person role to a programmed sequence of action choices scattered through a booklet of scrambled pages. (See Exhibit 10 at the end of this chapter.) Like SIBE, an action maze demonstrates the effects of a sequence of decisions; unlike SIBE, it allows for the inclusion of narrative, comment and replay loops along with in-basket items.

Depending on the instructor's specific purpose in using an action maze the response can be limited to action choices, or it can include the learner's narrative explanation of his choices. A fast run-through of an action maze with each individual learner recording his own decisions leads to animated discussion with emphasis on the reasons of different learners for making different choices, a process of justification. Having the learning group respond to a maze with group decisions also leads to discussion, but the emphasis will focus on arguments for and against the action alternatives, a process of convincing one's peers. When the instructor wants to evaluate learners individually on their ability to link theory with action choices, a third kind of use is possible. For this purpose the maze is worked individually, and each learner writes explanations for his actions in terms of his understanding of administrative theory.

Although an action maze is presented in a programmed format, Zoll contends that "it is *not* programmed instruction. The latter involves the teaching of a correct response both through reinforcement when the correct response occurs and by reteaching when an incorrect one occurs. The 'facts' of management can be taught by means of programmed instruction, but, in my opinion, complex attitudes and behavior patterns cannot be so taught."[2] There is no need in an action maze to have a single, predetermined correct decision pathway. Indeed, it is a better teaching device when all choices offered are feasible. Some student will make every choice offered in such a design, and the debriefing can be concentrated on subtleties of choices and decision paths.

One of the most valuable aspects of realism made possible by the action maze is its step-by-step quality. Confronted by a problem, the administrator makes tentative conclusions, looks for new evidence and/or takes initial action. The action choice brings a revelation of additional information, a reevaluation of the prior conclusion and possibly coming to a new conclusion; or the action choice brings a reaction to the administrator's action. The problem continues in this lifelike fashion to some conclusion.

The designer obviously has the choice with both in-basket exercises and action mazes to allow for student write-in to explain choices if such a provision is desired. Since the SIBE design allows for a comment response, I have used action mazes that do not include that option. Both SIBE and action mazes require considerable advance work on the part of the instructor (if originals are used), and I usually prefer to use learning devices that complement each other. With manual in-basket exercises it is easy to change the rules as you move through a course because the instruction to write an explanation can be given orally and no change in the design of the printed material is necessary. Pencil-paper in-basket exercises are the most flexible from this standpoint.

In their evaluation of action mazes as learning experiences, students find other values. Typical comments include:

> I like the fact that the action maze has a conclusion. It is also helpful that if you make a choice that is out of line, you get a direction to 'rethink' and the chance for another choice. At the time when it makes the most impression, the wrong turn is noted.

> The action maze is reassuring since we were told at various points 'good decision,' 'poor decision.' Thus the student gets a better idea of the correct procedure, or at least the procedure the professor thinks is correct! There was also a definite end to the action maze, and the student was shown the result of his decisions, although I suspect that all decisions led to the same final conclusion. [Note: This evaluation was written before the debriefing when the student learned, of course, that his guess was incorrect. Many students are surprised to find that more than one conclusion is possible and that what happens really does depend on his own choices.]

> There was a psychological advantage in that I could go back to a page already used to see the evolution and the results of my decisions.

In comparing the action maze and SIBE as alternative learning experiences, students say:

> An action maze is a simple type of SIBE, but in the action maze you don't get any further choice than those listed. For this reason SIBE is more useful than the action maze. If one uses the action maze as an introduction to SIBE, then it would be much easier to understand SIBE and get desired results.

> The action maze did not provide for open end questions, and this proved frustrating. I don't feel the amount of learning in either exercise differs that much although in the closed end action maze one can see definitely where a course of action will lead.

I did not experience that feeling of tension with the action maze which I recall was present in the SIBE exercise. It was easier to identify myself in my position as head librarian in the action maze. I certainly like the opportunity with both to explore alternate choices in the debriefing.

The psychomotor skills required in the action maze are much less demanding than those required in SIBE. I like the 'award' type statement at the beginning of some of the pages in the action maze.

Technical problems are fewer with the action maze. People who don't type do not have that barrier with the action maze. There's little chance for interruptions that occur with hardware. [This statement obviously came from one of the classes with which we did have hardware problems. They were not usual.]

The action maze presented more information to use in making decisions. I like to think that, as an administrator, I would have lots of information.

Not having any place for comments on the action maze results in having to make a choice and face the consequences of it. By typing in a comment in SIBE you could get 'off the hook.' Therefore, being made to select an action from the maze forces you to keep going until you have resolved the situation satisfactorily enough to get it over with. Very realistic.

Both methods are good for getting the student into the decision-making habit.

SIBE and the action maze involve the same presentation of a multifaceted situation with several alternatives and follow-up reports. I found the machinery [i.e., teletypewriter] much less distracting than page searching, especially on a long exercise.

SIBE offered the advantage of writing in an alternative or an explanation, and that was extremely important. However, the action maze seemed to 'cover' the problem better with more explanation and longer reactions. The machine noise was more distracting than reading your own copy of the action maze booklet. You can handle it, re-read preliminary pages, etc. I think I learned more from the maze because the situation was fuller. I enjoyed both.

Both of these methods were good experiences in that they portrayed the consequences of an action. I feel I learned equally from both.

Both were non-painful learning experiences; however, I felt more confident with the paper than with the computer. As for learning, I'm not sure of what I have learned other than to make decisions positively, take the good advice of others, take problems that concern more than just the library to the right people higher up and don't be afraid to go to them, and take care of the problem as quickly and completely as possible. [!]

When roleplay is brought into the comparison, typical comments include:

Concerning my learning from each technique, I would have to say that until the field of management is refined enough to be able to predict 'correct' decisions with accuracy, the action maze and SIBE can only cause the student to think about a decision before making a choice. With roleplay, however, the student can tell whether or not his views influence his fellow students.

Roleplay is the most difficult, but I preferred it for the non-decision-making aspects of administration [e.g., interviewing and planning] and for quick-thinking-on-your-feet exercises. I like and enjoyed SIBE and the action maze more, but perhaps roleplay was most beneficial.

One of the major reasons, a very simple one, why I felt roleplay was the most effective learning method for me was because it was the method we used most frequently. I think that once you become familiar and comfortable with a particular method you learn more from it. I can remember distinctly certain aspects of each roleplay situation, thinking what I would or would not have done, and what I should or should not have done as the administrator.

DEBRIEFING

Debriefing following an action maze is so similar to that following SIBE that no special comment is necessary. On occasion an experienced group of roleplayers will suggest roleplaying part of the action maze. This can be done to try out alternatives other than those used in the maze, for further exploration of the interpersonal relations of the maze. In fact, roleplay after an action maze is like instant replay of the kind so often used in roleplay debriefing. It can be an effective way to follow the individual use of the action maze with group interaction in the problem-solving.

VALUE AND LIMITATION OF ACTION MAZES

Zoll claims the value of action mazes to be the involvement of each learner in a first-person situation marked by a sequence of decisions, actions and reactions. Learners acknowledge this value and also note the reinforcement effect of instructional comments that are included in the maze. Some teachers especially value the potential for having a learner write into his responses explanations of his decisions in terms of administrative theory. The provision of many alternative decisions and actions in a maze introduces the possibility that some will be highly unrealistic. The designer's skill is put to a crucial test in providing feasible options whenever there is a choice to be made. As Zoll points out, "If a learner is forced to make a choice between actions, none of which he would actually take, it becomes an unreal experience."[3] Efforts to offset this particular characteristic might well be a specific part of debriefing.

Zoll also points out that we may be teaching "the learner only how to use an action maze in a classroom, with little or no change in his behavior in the real work situation."[4] The same point might be made about other experiential techniques, except that there is a body of research on each of the others which is lacking to date for the action maze.

The action maze has special values in continuing education situations because it is a quick way to give a large group of learners a common experience at the beginning of a workshop. "The Ann Davis Situation" (Exhibit 10) has taken, among my students, a minimum of 12 minutes working time and a maximum of 25 minutes. Other mazes I have designed take from 5 to 12 minutes of individual work before discussion can begin. I find that a short action maze focuses attention, generates individual involvement, and prepares the group for cognitive input better than do the other techniques. With a large group the action maze involves everyone more directly than does roleplay, and the controlled responses make charting decision pathways easier to comprehend quickly for debriefing than do open-end responses in in-basket exercises.

REFERENCES

1. Allen A. Zoll III, *Dynamic Management Education*, 2nd ed. (Reading, Mass.: Addison-Wesley Publishing Company, 1969), p. 249.

2. Ibid.

3. Ibid., pp. 250–251.

4. Ibid.

EXHIBIT 10. THE ANN DAVIS SITUATION: AN ACTION MAZE

The form used for recording a learner's decision path through an action maze is called a Path Record. A copy of the form, separate from the action maze booklet, is given to each learner. A sample is shown here.*

PATH RECORD: As you turn to each new page in your booklet, write the number of the new page in the next circle below. (Disregard the total number of circles. You will not use all of them.)

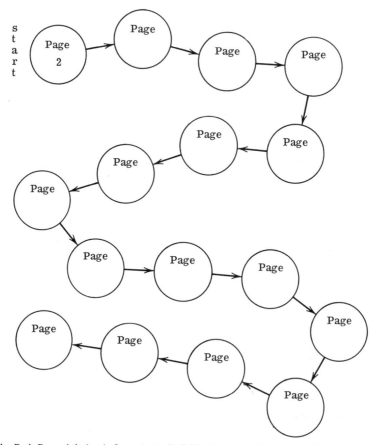

*The Path Record design is from A. A. Zoll III, *Dynamic Management Education*, 2nd ed. (Reading, Mass.: Addison-Wesley, 1969), used by permission.

"The Ann Davis Situation"

This is an experiment in a new way of thinking about how you act as a supervisor.

It begins with the statement of a situation which has the potential for undesirable consequences. Your course of action can and will differ from that of others. There is no one path to follow, just as there is no one clear-cut path in real life. Which path you take at any point in the developing problem will depend on your attitudes and action at each point, and you have certain choices.

This booklet is to be used differently from most, perhaps all, books that you have seen in the past.

Instead of looking at each page in sequence (page 1, 2, 3, 4, etc.), you are to decide on page 1 what action you would take, and then follow the instructions given following that choice. Other action choices will refer you to other pages, back and forth, as you go along. Follow the instructions without thought of usual procedures in book reading.

True preliminary pages follow this one. Read these pages before you begin the problem. You may refer to these preliminary pages at any time during the problem, but to no other pages. Follow the instructions.

Note: In an actual action maze booklet each page of text is a right-hand page, so that the learner has in view only the material that he is working on at the moment. The left-hand pages of the booklet can be blank or they can be used as available space in which the learner can write his explanations of his decisions and actions.

The Background

You are the head librarian of the Double XYZ Oil Company in Houston,
Texas. You have had, until recently, the following eight employees in
the company library:

Reference librarian: John Rogers, master's degrees in geology and
library science, has been with the company for five years. An
outgoing type, he is valuable in public relations and professional
matters both for his personality and his expertise. He is, however, a perfectionist and, at 35, beginning to show signs of advancing conservatism (=generation gap). This characteristic
sometimes causes problems with the young subprofessionals on
the staff.

Acquisition librarian: Earl Boardman, teacher turned librarian, received his master's degree in library science three years ago as
the result of company personnel development policies. He has
been with the library 11 years, as acquisitions clerk, technician
and librarian. At 45 he is a nonmilitant black, very much a
company man, and very secure in his own baliwick—which he
generally sticks to.

Catalog technician: Mary Stone, conservative, motherly, 55, began
as a clerk, took extension courses and in-service training opportunities to advance to technician responsible for cataloging,
catalog maintenance, and other duties relating to bibliographic
control of materials. Has been with the company 22 years.

Secretary: Marcia Rosenberg, 32 and still something of a swinger,
has been with the company 12 years since graduation from business college, with the library 8 years. Knows everybody in the
company, all the latest info without being a gossip. Invaluable
in public relations. A trusted friend of the head librarian.

Clerks: Betty Fellows, 22, does a good day's work in cataloging but
is something of a loner. With the company two years.

Jane Gordon, 19, still excited about her first adult job, idol-
izes Marcia and imitates her constantly. Being everybody's
friend sometimes interferes with work, but Earl has the situation under control.

Tom Jamison, an ambitious 22-year-old black, would like to
be an anti-establishment type, but is very much aware that the
company's equal opportunity policies are more than pages in a
book. He is availing himself of company help in completing a
college degree. Happy-go-lucky on the surface, the conflict is
underneath. Easily meets John's demands for quality work and
John is beginning to give him some technician-type tasks, as
time from other duties permits.

Sue Marshall, high school senior and part-time typist, has
ambition to become a professional librarian, does her work
carefully and quietly, but with her eyes open to learn all she can.

Recently, the company has approved a position for a patent librarian. This position is under the supervision of the reference librarian and carries the responsibility for acquiring, organizing and servicing the expanding patent collection. The collection is housed separately from the main collection, but adjacent to both the reference area and the literature searching (or bibliographic) alcove.

The library was fortunate to be able to hire an August graduate of an accredited library school. It is even more fortunate in that this person, Ann Davis, began college as an engineering major and followed that course of study for three years before deciding that engineering offers too few opportunities for women. She switched to math intending to go into computer programming but learned of computer opportunities in libraries and got herself a scholarship to library school. In her job interview she seemed determined to come to Texas (after being an Easterner all her life) and was willing to settle for the patent library job, unautomated though it is. Ann is bright, friendly, serious about her career and has gotten off to a good start with the staff. She has, at this point in time, been with the library five weeks.

CALENDAR

October						
S	M	T	W	T	F	S
				1	2	3
4	5	6	7	8	9	10
11	12	13	14	15	16	17
18	19	20	21	22	23	24
25	26	27	28	29	30	31

November						
S	M	T	W	T	F	S
1	2	3	4	5	6	7
8	9	10	11	12	13	14
15	16	17	18	19	20	21
22	23	24	25	26	27	28
29	30					

FIELD RESEARCH LABORATORY

Abbreviated Organization Chart

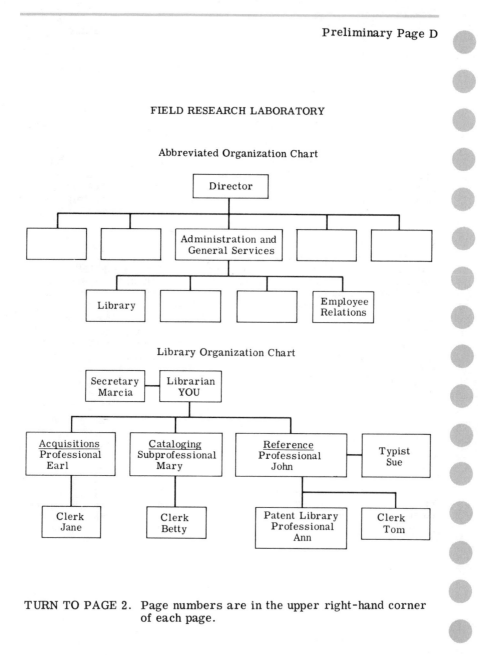

Library Organization Chart

TURN TO PAGE 2. Page numbers are in the upper right-hand corner of each page.

YOU ARE NOT FOLLOWING INSTRUCTIONS!

Nowhere are you instructed to turn to this page.

Remember, we said that this would not be like any regular book, in which you follow the pages in sequence. Instead, you will skip around following instructions based on the action you decide to take.

Now turn back to Preliminary Page D and follow the instructions.

The Situation

On Tuesday morning, October 6, Jane Gordon asks for, and receives, an interview with you. She seems somewhat nervous but eager to please you, as she says:

> "I don't want to be a tattle-tale, but there's something I think you should know. On Friday afternoon Ann Davis left at one o'clock without telling anybody. She wasn't supposed to be off because she told me not to tell anyone."

In response to the obvious question of how Jane knows this, it comes out that she had slipped away from her desk and was walking through the building lobby where she saw Ann heading for the front door. When Ann saw Jane, she stopped to speak but did not say where she was going. Instead, she said, "Forget you saw me," and went out the door.

Which of the four steps listed below would you take first?

A. Thank Jane, tell her to keep quiet and send her back to work. (Turn to page 5)

B. Reprimand Jane for carrying tales and send her back to work. (Turn to page 9)

C. Send Jane back to work without comment and call in Marcia to see what she knows about it. (Turn to page 12)

D. Call in Earl (since he needs to know Jane was off duty without permission) and John and make Jane repeat her story to them. (Turn to page 11)

YOU ARE NOT FOLLOWING INSTRUCTIONS!

Nowhere are you instructed to turn to this page.

Remember, we said that this would not be like any regular book, in which you follow the pages in sequence. Instead, you will skip around following instructions based on the action you decide to take.

Now turn back to page 2 and follow the instructions.

As good as his word, John returned to his desk and next morning made an opportunity to talk with Ann about her disappearance on Friday afternoon. About 9:30 a.m. you get a phone call from an annoyed John saying that Ann refused to tell him anything, told him off about interfering in her private business and that she is on her way to talk with you. You ask Marcia to show her in as soon as she arrives.

No doubt about it. Ann is mad and gives you her full opinion of John for checking up on her "behind my back." She maintains:

"For forty hours a week he can supervise me, but outside of that time what I do is my business. Please tell him I don't have to explain my actions to him."

"First, I'd like to get my facts straight. Did you leave early on Friday afternoon?"

"Yes, I did. I have some personal business that I plan to take care of on Friday afternoons, and I worked an extra hour each day, Monday through Thursday, so that I could take the time off."

"Well, that isn't exactly the way we go about getting time off." And you explain the procedure of getting permission from her supervisor.

"That's very cumbersome. I'm going to be doing this every week and I think it will be easier just to get a blanket permission."

"I'm afraid it will be impossible for you to have every Friday afternoon off. You came to work with the understanding that the work day is from 8 a.m. until 5 p.m., and those are the hours we need you here."

"I really don't see what difference it makes. I've been keeping a record of the requests in the patent library ever since I've been here and these statistics show you that in the past four weeks only one request was received between 1 and 5 p m. on Friday. The men do their main patent searching on Tuesdays and Wednesdays. Actually, by staying until 6 p.m. on Mondays and Tuesdays I can have more of the incoming patents filed for Tuesdays and Wednesdays when the demand is the heaviest. It doesn't hurt anyone on the staff for me to be off on Friday afternoon; it doesn't inconvenience the researchers since they don't use the patent files then anyway; and the longer hours on Monday and Tuesday give me quiet filing time to get patents ready for the midweek rush. What's wrong with that?"

At this point would you:

A. Deny her request, explaining why. (Turn to page 13)

B. Grant her request. (Turn to page 8)

C. Put her off a week in order to talk it over with the head of the Employee Relations Department. (Turn to page 15)

You didn't want to set a precedent, but you did want to maintain your dignity and courtesy with employees, so you chose the lesser of two evils, thanked Jane, asked her to keep the matter confidential, and sent her back to work.

Your first thought now is to ignore the matter, but it stays in the back of your mind. By noon you have decided to:

A. Call in Marcia and talk it over with her. (Turn to page 12)

B. Call in John to find out whether he gave Ann permission to leave early. (Turn to page 7)

C. Call in Ann and ask her about the matter without revealing your source of information. (Turn to page 6)

D. Discipline yourself into ignoring it. (Turn to page 17)

You have chosen to talk with Ann and send her a memo asking her to come to your office on Wednesday afternoon, October 7. You open by talking to her about her new job, how she likes it, whether she's getting settled, etc. Finally, you broach the matter of last Friday afternoon. Ann replies, very straightforwardly:

> "Yes, I did leave early. I have some personal business that I plan to take care of on Friday afternoons, and I worked an extra hour each day, Monday through Thursday, so that I could take the time off."

"Well, that isn't exactly the way we go about getting time off." And you explain the procedure of getting permission from her supervisor.

> "That's very cumbersome. I'm going to be doing this every week and I think it will be easier just to get a blanket permission."

"Im afraid it will be impossible for you to have every Friday afternoon off. You came to work with the understanding that the work day is from 8 a.m. until 5 p.m., and those are the hours we need you here."

> "I really don't see what difference it makes. I've been keeping a record of the requests in the patent library ever since I've been here and these statistics show that in the past four weeks only one request was received between 1 and 5 p.m. on Friday. The men do their main patent searching on Tuesdays and Wednesdays. Actually, by staying until 6 p.m. on Mondays and Tuesdays I can have more of the incoming patents filed for Tuesdays and Wednesdays when the demand is the heaviest. It doesn't hurt anyone on the staff for me to be off on Friday afternoon; it doesn't inconvenience the researchers since they don't use the patent files then anyway; and the longer hours on Monday and Tuesday give me quiet filing time to get patents ready for the midweek rush. What's wrong with that?"

At this point would you:

A. Deny her request, explaining why. (Turn to page 13)

B. Grant her request. (Turn to page 8)

C. Put her off a week in order to talk it over with the head of the Employee Relations Department. (Turn to page 15)

You have called John into your office, repeated Jane's story and asked him what he knows about it.

John tells you he was unaware of Ann's early departure and will speak to her about it.

(Turn to page 4)

October 7:

> You granted Ann's request that she be allowed to work until 6 p.m. Monday through Friday and be off at 1 p.m. on Friday each week.
>
> In the afternoon mail you get a memo from John reminding you of a regional SLA meeting on Saturday. He wants permission to place Ann in charge of the reference desk on Friday afternoon so that he can leave at noon to make the drive of several hundred miles.

October 8:

> Jane corners you in the elevator on the way to coffee break and tells you that Ann is still working until 6 p.m. each day.
>
> Mary Stone comes to your office in the afternoon to tell you that her married daughter will be in town for the weekend and she'd like to have Friday afternoon off in order to spend more time with her, and that she will make up the time next week. You tell her she may have the time, but it will have to be counted as annual leave.
>
> You write a memo to John telling him Ann will be away Friday, but that you will take the reference desk, and sending greetings to your SLA friends.

October 9:

> Marcia tells you that everyone on the staff knows you have granted Ann's request, that discussion and criticism are rampant, and that you should expect repercussions.

October 12:

> The morning mail brings you: a request from Betty for Friday, October 30, off, time to be worked in advance, no reason stated; a request from Tom to reschedule his week so that he can leave at 4 p.m. every Tuesday because he has a Tuesday night class and needs time to study; a memo from John reporting on the SLA meeting and requesting an interview about "scheduling"; and a memo from Employee Relations stating that Mary Stone has requested a transfer and they would like to talk with you about it.

At this point, would you:

A. Make an appointment with the head of Employee Relations to discuss the entire situation. (Turn to page 16)

B. Call Ann in and regretfully reverse your decision to her. (Turn to page 13)

C. Call a staff meeting to hold an open discussion and get everyone's opinion. (Turn to page 14)

Page 9

Although you do need to know when things are amiss, you do not want to encourage tattling and you prefer to find out through channels. So you sadly decide to reprimand Jane—after all, she's young and hasn't been here very long.

Your first thought now is to ignore the matter, but it stays in the back of your mind. By noon you have decided to:

A. Call in Marcia and talk it over with her. (Turn to page 12)

B. Call in John to find out whether he gave Ann permission to leave early. (Turn to page 7)

C. Call in Ann and ask her about the matter without revealing your source of information. (Turn to page 6)

D. Discipline yourself into ignoring it. (Turn to page 17)

Because of several incidents, the head of Employee Relations has just issued a new policy stating that no employee may reschedule his working hours to participate in personal activities without first submitting a written request giving detailed reasons for the change to his supervisor, this request to be approved by the supervisor upon consultation with the head of Employee Relations.

After the receipt of the new policy statement, you called in each employee for a conference about its implications for him. There was slight grumbling in some quarters, but the dust settled and things have been "normal" again for about two weeks.

On November 2 you have no more than arrived in your office when you receive a phone call from John, who tells you about a disturbing phone call he received the night before at his home:

"It was about 9 p.m. when this man called. I didn't recognize his voice and I've forgotten the name he gave me. But he said he is a lawyer and that he represents a group of concerned citizens who are trying to help Mexican farm laborers over near Amarillo. Apparently Ann Davis went along with a group of these people this weekend—about 25 altogether—and they were all arrested for demonstrating. The only way any of them can get out of jail is to come up with $100, each, for bail. He didn't ask me for any money, just told me the situation and asked me to report to the company where Ann is."

You thank John for letting you know, and then:

A. Call the staff together to tell them and to make arrangements about covering Ann's work. (Turn to page 24)

B. Phone the head of Employee Relations to inform him of the situation and request procedures. (Turn to page 22)

C. Phone the company lawyer for advice. (Turn to page 20)

D. Call the Director to inform him of the situation. (Turn to page 18)

You should have recognized that Jane is doing what she thinks Marcia does and that she wants to get into your good graces. Why put her down harshly by making her tell her boss of her own indiscretion? This would scarcely help her or get you closer to the facts. And why get John and Earl into the picture with Ann at this point? Perhaps John gave Ann permission sincerely; then you'd be in the position of checking up on his management of his staff. In short, why start this kind of a bruhaha?

Turn to page 2 and select another course of action.

You have called Marcia into your office, repeated Jane's story and asked her what she knows about it.

Marcia tells you that her friend at the information desk in the lobby mentioned it to her, but she presumed Ann had permission to go apartment hunting or some other good excuse and forgot it.

Together you decide to wait a week and watch Ann discreetly but closely.

(Turn to page 17)

You have decided to deny Ann's request and explain your reasons to her, mentioning the relationship of her request to supervision, security, morale, her status with the company, etc. You suggest that if she wishes to explain her reasons for wanting Friday afternoons off, there might be extenuating circumstances that would influence you to change your mind.

Ann listens quietly, makes no effort to explain, finally says ''Thank you'' and leaves.

The week after the interview she works a regular 8-to-5 schedule. The following Monday several members of the staff mention to you that Ann brought a suitcase to work on Friday and that she was picked up after work by a young man in an old beat-up car.

(Turn to page 10)

Democracy is great, but you are asking for a knock-down, drag-out fight. People are feeling envious, mad, ambitious, opportunistic, and hardly likely to see anyone else's point of view.

Turn to page 8 and select another course of action.

You have given Ann an appointment in a week, for October 14, and explained to her that you wish to discuss her request with the head of the
Employee Relations Department. You point out to her that, if there
are extenuating circumstances, you will be in a better position to help
her if you know what they are. She merely says:

"It's personal business on my own time. I don't care to go into it."

You and the head of the Employee Relations Department talk over the
situation. There is no stated policy against what Ann is proposing, but
you—and the personnel head—see lots of problems if she is granted
this request. After thorough discussion of her status, the effect of her
having dictated a personal schedule on library staff morale, the possible question of security in her working alone in the library an hour
each day, and her need, as a new staff member, for supervision, you
jointly agree that her request cannot be granted.

At your interview on the fourteenth Ann listens quietly, makes no effort to argue or explain further, finally says "Thank you" and leaves
the office.

The week of the interview Ann works 8 to 5 each day. On the following
Monday several members of the staff mention to you that Ann brought
a suitcase to work last Friday and that she was picked up after work
by a young man in an old beat-up car.

(Turn to page 10)

Thorough discussion of the present situation and its antecedents shows clearly that there is no alternative but to cancel Ann's request for a "personal schedule." Your friend in Employee Relations offers to help you out of a jam by initiating a clearer statement of company policy and circulating this to all employees.

You call Ann in to explain the reversal and she is bright enough to understand the problems involved. She listens quietly, makes no effort to argue or explain her request further, finally says "Thank you" and leaves the office.

Thereafter Ann works 8 to 5 each day. On the following Monday several members of the staff mention to you that Ann brought a suitcase to work last Friday and that she was picked up after work by a young man in an old beat-up car.

(Turn to page 10)

Page 17

The next morning, October 7, you get a phone call from an annoyed John. He tells you he "heard" that Ann had left early the previous Friday without his permission and that he had called her to his office and asked her about it. Ann refused to tell him anything, told him off about interfering in her private business and said she was going to talk to you. John thinks she is on her way now. You ask Marcia to show her in immediately if she appears—which she does.

No doubt about it. Ann is mad and gives you her full opinion of John for checking up on her "behind my back." She maintains:

"For forty hours a week he can supervise me, but when those forty hours have been worked what I do is my business. Please tell him I don't have to explain my actions to him."

"First, I'd like to get my facts straight. Did you leave early on Friday afternoon?"

"Yes, I did. I have some personal business that I plan to take care of on Friday afternoons, and I worked an extra hour each day, Monday through Thursday, so that I could take the time off."

"Well, that isn't exactly the way we go about getting time off." And you explain the procedure of getting permission from her supervisor.

"That's very cumbersome. I'm going to be doing this every week and I think it will be easier just to get a blanket permission."

"I'm afraid it will be impossible for you to have every Friday afternoon off. You came to work with the understanding that the work day is from 8 a.m. until 5 p.m., and those are the hours we need you here."

"I really don't see what difference it makes. I've been keeping a record of the requests in the patent office ever since I've been here and these statistics show that in the past four weeks only one request was received between 1 and 5 p.m. on Friday. The men do their main patent searching on Tuesdays and Wednesdays. Actually, by staying until 6 p.m. on Mondays and Tuesdays I can have more of the incoming patents filed for Tuesdays and Wednesdays when the demand is the heaviest. It doesn't hurt anyone on the staff for me to be off on Friday afternoon; it doesn't inconvenience the researchers since they don't use the patent files then anyway; and the longer hours on Mondays and Tuesdays give me quiet filing time to get patents ready for the midweek rush. What's wrong with that?"

At this point you:

A. Deny her request, explaining why. (Turn to page 13)

B. Grant her request. (Turn to page 8)

C. Put her off a week in order to talk it over with the head of the Employee Relations Department. (Turn to page 15)

You have decided to call the Director and talk with him confidentially
before doing anything else. This is a wise move because of the very
real possibility of newspaper and other publicity involving Ann's name
and company affiliation, and because of the delicacy of a situation involving unions and minority groups.

Unfortunately, the Director is out of his office for the morning and will
not be available until after lunch. You explain the situation very
briefly to his secretary and solicit her help in reaching him at the
earliest possible moment. Then you:

A. Write a confidential memo to the Director explaining the situation
   in case you are tied up and don't get to talk with him as soon as he
   returns to his office. (Turn to page 21)

B. Phone the Head of Employee Relations and inform him of the situation and request procedures. (Turn to page 22)

C. Phone the company lawyer for advice. (Turn to page 31)

D. Call the staff together and inform them of the situation. (Turn to
   page 24)

You have belatedly decided to tell your troubles to the Head of Employee Relations. By the time you get the problem explained, he has:

> signalled his secretary to contact the company lawyer;

> made himself a note to take care of public relations aspects;

> reached for his list of emergency phone numbers to call Ann's mother;

> reassured you that she'll be back on the job in a day or two at the most; warned you that she'll have to have additional time off to attend the trial; told you to sit tight; and reminded you that under these circumstances the employee must return through the head of his unit who must file a report with Employee Relations.

On November 5 Ann returns to work. About midmorning you:

A. Send for her to have a conference with you. (Turn to page 25)

B. Call John and ask him to talk with her about her responsibilities to the company and then to send her on to you. (Turn to page 23)

C. Call Employee Relations and tell them you have decided to fire her. (Turn to page 30)

Did you really mean to go over the head of Employee Relations? To do so is usually inadvisable and may result in repercussions you don't want. Think over the implications.

Before you call out the big guns, wouldn't a fact-finding foray be in order? Employee Relations just may have encountered similar problems before and they may—oh, joy—have a policy.

Return to page 10 and make another choice.

Perhaps you should reconsider. This is a ticklish situation and could probably be best handled in a personal report. The better path might well be to take other action now.

Return to page 18 and make another choice.

You decided to tell your troubles to the head of Employee Relations. By the time you can get the problem explained, he has:

    signalled his secretary to contact the company lawyer;

    made himself a note to take care of public relations aspects;

    reached for his list of emergency phone numbers to call Ann's mother;

    reassured you that she'll be back on the job in a day or two at the most; warned you that she'll have to have additional time off to attend the trial; told you to sit tight; and reminded you that under these circumstances the employee must return through the head of his unit who must file a report with Employee Relations.

On November 5 Ann returns to work. About midmorning you:

A. Send for her to have a conference with you. (Turn to page 27)

B. Call John and ask him to talk with her about her responsibilities to the company and then to send her on to you. (Turn to page 26)

C. Decide to send Ann to Everglades City as librarian for the company's project there (which needs a librarian). She already knows a good bit about the work in the home library and in another month she could be ready for more responsibility. Call Employee Relations and tell them to pull the ads for a librarian for Everglades City and to prepare some new ads for a patent librarian. (Turn to page 28)

In about ten minutes John calls you back excitedly. "Ann is on her way to your office, and she's mad." Before you can tell Marcia to show her right in, she's in.

"Fine thing! Not only do you have a staff meeting to discuss my private affairs, but you tell that over-age boy scout to teach me responsibility. I know more about responsibility to what counts—people—than either of you. I've had it will all of you. I quit!"

You begin to write an ad for a replacement for Ann.

THE END

You wait until the staff has gathered, then succinctly inform them of Ann's predicament. As you begin to discuss the reassignment of her duties temporarily:

Jane: Oh . . . and I thought she was eloping.

John: This will get us behind on the patents filing. I'll have to have extra help. She should know better than to get involved in that stuff.

Tom: Beautiful! Let's take up a collection for her bail.

Marcia: We should call Employee Relations right away and have them contact the company's legal consultant in Amarillo.

Mary: She told me her mother's name once. If I can find it, we ought to let her know.

Marcia: Her mother's name was on her application as "nearest relative." I have it in her file.

Earl: Maybe she doesn't want to be bailed out. Call her lawyer and ask him.

Betty: I could cover the Patent Desk for her; she's been teaching me to file the patents.

Mary: So that's where you've been disappearing to!

Earl: Anyway, she has some salary due her; Employee Relations should give her an advance for bail.

John: It's probably in the morning paper—company name and all. I'll go look.

Jane: I could drive over to Amarillo this afternoon and take her some food; they probably aren't feeding them.

Tom: Yeah! I'll ride along in case you have a flat tire.

Earl: The company ought to send her a plane ticket back.

John: The company ought to fire her for getting their name in the papers like that. You ought to call the director.

Now see what you've done. Get them back to work if you can.

Take Marcia's advice and call Employee Relations. (Turn to page 19)

You have asked Ann to come to your office and you are waiting at the door to greet her:

"Hello Ann. I'm so glad you're back. Are you okay?"

"Certainly. Why wouldn't I be okay?"

"I'm very interested in your concern for the Mexican farm laborers. Was this why you wanted so badly to come to work in Texas?"

"What if it was? It's my personal business."

"Yes, in a way it is. In another way, however, you want other people to make it their business, too, don't you? And so you must be willing to talk about it. Where, exactly, is the group you were working with? You know, I grew up in Amarillo and I know the area very well."

"I didn't know that. Well, it's a big farm to the northeast on state road 1032—it's called the Lonesome Pine Ranch. There are almost three hundred Mexicans there and the only quarters for them to live in are abandoned motel units that have been hauled in and a falling-down barn. They have to get their water from open pipes and they have no ice or refrigeration. So many of the children are feverish and sick, and they act retarded but there's no school for them. There's no commissary and they have to drive almost to Amarillo to buy food and the prices are exorbitant. Nobody up there wants to help them, and I just have to go. If I can't go back every weekend, I'll just have to quit."

"I understand how you feel. Of course, you do have to support yourself, too, don't you? Have you considered that there might be some ways you could help even more, ways that would allow you to work a regular schedule also? For example, you talk about the situation graphically and convincingly. Have you tried writing for small newspapers that might print a good story, even from a beginner? Or talking to civic and church groups to give them information and perhaps to raise money? Actually, there are groups of people here in Houston who are concerned about the problem. You just haven't found them yet. I belong to such a civic club and we're always looking for speakers. I could help you find others, too."

"Oh, would you? I hadn't thought of those things, but they are good ideas and I'd be willing to try."

"The company wants its employees to be socially conscious and I feel we could help you arrange time off at less frequent intervals, if you would work a regular schedule the rest of the time."

"I don't know. I do have to go back and help the women and children. But—if I could get there at least once a month I'd be willing to try the writing and speaking in between."

So you lose an opportunity to preach a sermon on the importance of the job and you gain another chance for Ann. Only time will tell whether she can modify her approach to social responsibilities. She's very young and needs direction for her idealism. At least now she knows you're on her side.

THE END

In about ten minutes John calls you back excitedly. "Ann is on her way to your office, and she's mad." Before you can tell Marcia to show her right in, she's in.

"Fine thing! You tell that over-age boy scout to teach me responsibility. All he cares about are his indexes and his bibliographies. I know more about responsibility to what counts—people—than either of you. I've had it with this outfit. I quit!"

You begin to write an ad for a replacement for Ann.

THE END

When Ann arrives, you begin your talk with a statement about understanding perfectly her feelings towards the farm laborers. You then tell her that sometimes on every job one must submerge his own natural inclinations in order to effectively perform the job in a responsible manner. But Ann breaks in on you:

> "You're a fine one to talk to me about responsibility! Don't you feel any responsibility to me? You knew I didn't want to bring my private affairs into the office; I deliberately didn't tell you where I was going or why. So what do you do? Call the whole staff in and make me sound like some kind of a criminal. I wouldn't work for you if you gave me all day off every Friday! I quit!"

Realizing that Ann is in a highly emotional state, you wait for her outburst to subside and then tell her that you will not accept her resignation until she has taken a week's leave of absence to think this action over. You outline the opportunities and advantages to her if she continues in the employment of Double XYZ Oil Company. Ann agrees to give this alternative some consideration and leaves in a somewhat less agitated state. You have bought a little time and may be able to keep her if you can convince her of your sincere concern for her rights as an employee.

THE END

So you decided to send Ann to Everglades City. Certainly, she will soon be ready, professionally, for more responsibilities. She might even get interested in the Seminoles. But . . . .

You should realize that Ann will interpret this as punative action. At the moment she couldn't care less about the Seminoles; it's the Mexicans she's interested in. She is a good employee in many ways. Why not help her give direction to her energy and idealism?

Why not return to page 22 and chose another action?

YOU ARE NOT FOLLOWING INSTRUCTIONS!

Nowhere are you instructed to turn to this page.

Remember, we said that this would not be like any regular book, in which you follow the pages in sequence. Instead, you will skip around following instructions based on the action you decide to take.

Now go back to where you were and follow the instructions.

In response to their inquiry you admit that her work has been better than usual for a new employee. She has learned quickly, kept her work up-to-date, drawn compliments from several researchers, and shown initiative (!). No wonder they hesitate to fire her. Furthermore, the company has now provided her with free legal advice, paid her bail, and given her a plane ticket back from Amarillo. If her energies and humanistic interests can be channeled, she should make a very loyal employee. Employee Relations suggests tactfully that you reconsider.

Return to page 19 and choose another action.

Did you really mean to go over the head of Employee Relations? To do so is usually inadvisable and may result in repercussions you don't want. Think over the implications.

Before you call out the big guns, wouldn't a fact-finding foray be in order? Employee Relations just may have encountered similar problems before and they may—oh, joy—have a policy.

Return to page 18 and make another choice.

9.
Games
· · · · · · ·

All learning games are simulations, but not all simulations are learning games. Learning games, like simulations, are representations of real life, more or less selective and more or less abstract depending on the immediate objectives of the learning. In order to meet the definition of "game," the learning play must incorporate (either explicitly or implicitly) a model of the segment of real life to which the learning is related. On the other hand, games, as one species of the genus "simulations," have some distinctive characteristics not associated with other subcategories. The major differences between games and other simulations are that (1) games have scoring systems that result in wins and losses for players, and (2) each game has a set of rules fixed for the duration of the game.

The long history of games for both recreational and serious purposes has been delineated by several qualified scholars and we need not repeat it here. The current crop of educational games, as a related but rather distinct subgroup of games of all kinds, stems primarily from the 1960s. Comprehensive overviews of educational or learning games are hard to come by. Progress in the development of learning games has been from a stage of uncritical design of games to a stage of struggle to find ways to evaluate learning-through-games. The decade closed on a note called "realistic optimism" by its advocates,[1] but regarded as unrealistic by its critics in terms of unchallenged assumptions, unreplicated game evaluations, untested hypotheses and lack of demonstrable relationships with social and behavioral theory.[2,3] It is only fair to point out that the criticism is from within, for the most cogent critics are themselves game designers and, in other contexts, they are game advocates. They seem to agree that the next period, already underway, will be one of field testing and data gathering, followed by the integration of new knowledge into game learning theory.[4]

Most of the educational games designed to date have pre-college learners as their target audience. Available games designed for adult learning are based on models that, for the most part, preclude their usefulness for teaching library science. For example, there are hundreds of business games, but their frame of reference, as models of commercial enterprises, requires that players make decisions and simulate processes in terms of profit and loss. This value system does not lend itself—as yet—to use in teaching library administration. Some of the available sociological games might have limited usefulness without stretching a point.[5]

James Coleman's concept of "social simulation games" offers what is possibly the greatest potential for games to dramatize the overall functions and relationships of libraries. The crucial role of social environment in Coleman's concept is analogous to the significance for libraries of their social environments. Further, this aspect of librarianship, though rich in connotations for current library goals and activities, is not easy for neophytes to understand or to integrate into their study of professional functions and processes. As Coleman explains it, "A social simulation game . . . is concerned principally with that part of an individual's environment that consists of other people, groups and organizations." The play of such a game constitutes interaction between the player and his environment, and the environment is incorporated into the structure of the game in one of two ways:

> One [way] is to let each player in the game act as a portion of the social environment of each other player. The rules of the game establish the obligations upon each role, and the players, each acting within the rules governing his role, interact with one another. The resulting configuration constitutes a social subsystem, and each player's environment consists of that subsystem, excluding himself. . . .
>
> A second way in which the social environment is embodied in a social simulation game is in the rules themselves. The rules may contain contingent responses of the environment, representing the actions of persons who are not players, but nevertheless [are] relevant to the individual's action.[6]

The research about educational games indicates that physical skills, intellectual skills, interaction with symbolic environments, behavioral strategies and social relationships can be learned through games.[7] Another way of saying it is that games have a positive impact on "factual knowledge, on attitudes, and on strategies."[8] Though the researchers cannot tell us exactly how this learning takes place, they tend to be consistent in claiming that it does. If so, a variety of special-purpose games related to everything from filing to user/staff relationships might be suggested for students of librarianship. Some of these games would probably not be worth the cost of development; others would be extremely valuable. If there is one advantage that is certain from the research to date, it is that games arouse and sustain interest and motivation for most players. This characteristic of educational games in general has been apparent in the few trials of library science games to date.

CHARACTERISTICS OF LEARNING GAMES

Several game designers and researchers have written generalized descriptions of the characteristics of learning games. Although they are subjective statements, an overview of some of their observations might be helpful in thinking about games for library science education.

1. *Learning games are fun, but because their basic purpose is to educate, entertainment "becomes an instrumental value, rather than the design objective."* [9] At first glance, this might seem self-evident, but it is easy to get caught up in group play. Designing an educational game is, therefore, more a matter of disciplining oneself within the limits of educational objectives, available analyses of the life situation, and institutional constraints, than a process of spontaneous, unrestricted creativity. The fun is in the playing of the game; background research and design are hard work.

2. *Models are the most salient components of games.* Factual information is conveyed by them, and through their manipulation both cognitive and affective knowledge is "generated" for learners. Logical models help to show relationships between assumptions and consequences in non-quantitative processes. Mathematical models facilitate the manipulation (especially by computer) of large bodies of data related to quantitative processes. Models also embody knowledge of environmental relationships and thus frequently provide the learner with a rationale for the game rules. [10]

3. *Games incorporate pay-off or rewards, the distribution of which determines who wins and who loses.* Mathematical game theory provides the concept of "zero sum," and "non-zero sum" games. In a zero sum game the winner's pay-off totals the loser's losses. Thus, if I win a certain amount you (or you and other players together) must lose that amount. A non-zero sum game does not have this condition, and the winner does not necessarily win at the loser's cost. Zero sum games maximize the competitive aspect of games, but are least lifelike. Non-zero sum games tend to result in a cooperation "which by necessity has to be a mixture of competitive or conflicting interests," [11] or a coalition—that is, a lifelike strategy. [12] In fact, some advocates claim that the personal responsibility for players to develop and to test problem-solving strategies is the valuable contribution of educational games.

4. *"Serious games combine the analytic and questioning concentration of scientific viewpoint with the intuitive freedom and rewards of imaginative, artistic acts."* [13] The task, for players, is a real one. Identification and evaluation of alternatives contribute to solutions; but so do strategy and, in many games, interpersonal relationships. Freedom stems from the absence of a predetermined solution known only to the teacher. Intellectual

work and social strategies pay off; second-guessing the teacher doesn't count.

5. *Games are governed by rules.* All simulations include rules that are closely related to the model by logic and that govern its manipulation during the game. In addition, games must have procedural rules to govern the play of the game, mediation rules to resolve the inevitable impasse situations, and police rules to provide consequences for breaking any of the other rules. Individual players in some games have arbitrary constraints built into their roles; these constitute other kinds of rules.[14,15] It is assumed that individual players, in attempting to maximize their game winnings within both the freedom and the rules of the game, will develop transferable strategies.[16]

TYPES OF LEARNING GAMES

In a short, but very useful paper Paul Twelker and Ken Layden have differentiated four types of learning games:

Non-simulation games are competitive learning contexts in which participant success is determined by the degree of subject matter comprehension—of information, concepts, generalizations, and/or theories—demonstrated during game play.

Planning exercises are non-simulation games which focus on process rather than context by engaging the participant in the examination of selected social problems requiring solution. Committees cooperate in discussion and each proposes solutions which are in competition for adoption by the entire group after evaluation criteria have been established and applied.

Inter-personal simulation games are learning contexts in which the participant responds within the simulation game as if he were the actual system of interaction being simulated. Interaction is structured by rules and physical circumstances. Resultant interaction ranges from the highly restricted participant behavior of a computer simulation game through the less inhibited behavior of a so-called "board game" to the flexible, open-ended behavior of role-playing simulation games which allow participant behavior more closely proximate to that in the actual system of interaction being simulated. Whatever the format, inter-personal simulation games combine the competitive aspects of gaming with the reality replication of simulation to allow the participant a personal glimpse of how it "feels" to be in the dynamics of real system interpersonal interaction.

Large system simulation games are learning contexts for the examination of the dynamics of complex systems of interaction. Focus may range from looking at the variables affecting the urban community to a thorough-going analysis of the nation-state system of the international community. But, in all cases the participant engages himself in the simulated system—as a planner, decision-maker, or merely observer—in order to better comprehend the variables affecting the dynamics of aggregate human behavior within the context of the actual complex system being simulated.[17]

Since the objectives of each of these types of learning games are analogous to objectives of teaching library administration, it is easy to project game designs. Objectives with potential for gaming might include: comprehension of administrative theory; analytical examination of typical administrative problems; personal interaction in the daily administration of a library; institutional interaction in a cooperative network. Learner success in games depends to some degree on cognitive knowledge and skill, but an element of chance is also often present. Chance is usually incorporated in learning games to represent elements of the real world over which the individual has no control. It can also be included to add to the competitive aspect of the game and to augment the chosen means of scoring.

TWO LIBRARY SCIENCE GAMES

"LAG, A Library Administration Game"[18] is a board game designed to introduce neophytes to library functions, terminology, and values. The board is arbitrarily divided into areas representing typical library departments, such as administrative offices, circulation, reference, acquisition, cataloging, and staff lounge. The path of game play leads through these areas.

Each player is the library's administrator; all are in competition for "The Key to the Executive Washroom." Players roll a die, in turn, to determine how many steps to take along the game path. If a player stops in one of the functional areas, he takes a card from a pack representing that area. The card states something that has happened in the area and the "value" of the "activity" is reflected in rewards or losses to the player. For example, if the player stops in Reference, the card may say, "Copy machine breaks down—back up two spaces." In Acquisition, the card might say, "International flights grounded two weeks by strike. All European periodicals are late—lose one turn."

There are also chance rewards and losses unrelated to specific library functions—for example, on one space is printed, "The research paper you submitted to the *Journal of Library History* has been accepted for publication— move ahead five spaces." Spaces of a certain color represent the phone calls that interrupt the administrator's day. If a player stops on one of them, he picks up a card from the appropriate pack to learn the phone message, which, again, results in a reward or loss for him. LAG has three faces (board designs with related card packs): one each for academic, public and special libraries. It is useful in the introductory stages of an administration or type-of-library course. The LAG design is based on a content analysis of expressed values in relation to activities as described in library literature.

"Negotiation"[19] is a reference process game designed for beginners in librarianship. It illustrates first-hand to the players some of the problems encountered by the reference librarian in his effort to discover what the patron really wants to know when he asks a question at the reference desk. The game is played by three people: one player represents a reference librarian, one is a library patron, and the third is the referee. Roles are changed as the game progresses. The "patron" asks a question, and the "reference librarian" attempts to identify the "real question" by asking clarifying questions according to the game rules. The "patron" makes his answers incomplete, evasive, and off-target, but never dishonest. The "referee" decides what constitutes a dishonest response and disqualifies it. A scoring system identifies the winner in the triad.

The "Negotiation Game" was designed along the lines of the familiar parlor game "Twenty Questions" with the input of reference questions from an analysis of over five hundred "initial" and "real" questions collected in a medium-sized public library. It is useful with beginning reference students to convey the affective aspects of the reference interview.

USING GAMES IN LEARNING

Whether in classrooms or in continuing-education workshops, games must be integrated in the learning system rather than isolated from it. They should be chosen or designed on the basis of specific learning objectives. Briefing in advance of game play serves to input or review the cognitive base on which game play depends, as well as to present the operational information for play. The follow-up debriefing emphasizes the game learning and clarifies the game limitations through group discussion. Both cognitive and affective aspects of game learning should be considered during the debriefing.[20]

An important characteristic of games is that they both highlight and distort. In order to emphasize one aspect of reality and shoehorn it into a design for gaming, other aspects of reality are sacrificed. It is a trade-off deliberately chosen by a teacher, usually in order to gain the advantage of challenge and high interest generated among learners by games. The choice puts extra responsibility on the teacher for, as Shirts puts it, "Aside from the need to relate the simulation experience to the real world, some sort of mechanism is needed to correct the misimpressions that the simulations can create."[21] The caution applies equally to all forms of simulation instuction, and underscores the different role of the simulation learning director from that of the traditional didactic teacher.

Learning game experts have emphasized additional aspects of the teacher–director's role, illustrating the intellectual and managerial demands of the role. As planner, the director must weigh factors of learner readiness and potential dramatic impact against situational constraints before making scheduling decisions. As pacemaker, especially in the more complex interactional games, the director must be alert to slowdowns, which call for intervention if there is to be no loss of learning. As referee, he demonstrates interpersonal relationships and informed judgment as well as avoiding game-disruptive disputes. In many game designs, the distribution of feedback is also part of the referee's (or at least the director's) role. This feedback serves an evaluative, corrective function during game play, but it is also crucial in maintaining interest and competitive spirit.

Directors may reserve for themselves the scoring responsibility in game use, or they may share it with players or judges—indeed they may turn it over to them. They cannot, however, avoid it and still claim they have used a game effectively.

> Players should be able to determine the relative effectiveness of their playing, who won or lost (or played realistically or unrealistically), and what effective play means in the particular process being simulated in the game. Scoring also provides what psychologists call "closure" to the activity, completing it in a psychologically satisfactory way.[22]

Scoring, however, is one of the most difficult parts of game design. The more complex the game, the more significant the role of scoring as a part of understanding the process being simulated. For library science games, we may have to identify our elusive theory of librarianship in addition to compiling many facts and constructing more theories before we can design valid, sophisticated games.

REFERENCES

1. Sarane S. Boocock and E.O. Schild, eds., *Simulation Games in Learning* (Beverly Hills, Calif.: Sage Publications, 1968), pp. 15–18.

2. R. Garry Shirts, "Games Students Play," *Saturday Review*, May 16, 1970, pp. 81–82.

3. James S. Coleman, "Social Processes and Social Simulation Games," in *Simulation Games in Learning, op. cit.,* pp. 29–51.

4. Boocock and Schild, *op. cit.,* pp. 17–18.

5. Three games that might be useful are "The Neighborhood Game," "EDPLAN," and "SIMPOLIS," all available from Abt Associates, 55 Wheeler Street, Cambridge, Massachusetts 02138.

6. Coleman, *op. cit.,* pp. 30–31.

7. Boocock and Schild, *op. cit.,* p. 9.

8. *Ibid.,* p. 115.

9. Clark Abt, "Games for Learning," in *Simulation Games in Learning, op. cit.,* p. 72.

10. Clark Abt, *Serious Games* (New York: Viking Press, 1970), p. 11.

11. Duncan N. Hansen, "Game Theory," a mini-lecture distributed during the course EDR 567, Winter Quarter 1970, Florida State University. p. 5.

12. Abt, *Serious Games, op. cit.,* p. 20.

13. *Ibid.,* pp. 11–12.

14. Abt, "Games for Learning," *op. cit.,* pp. 73–74.

15. Coleman, *op. cit.,* pp. 32–35.

16. Hansen, *op. cit.,* p. 5.

17. Paul A. Twelker and Ken Layden, *Educational Simulation/Gaming* (Stanford University: ERIC Clearinghouse on Media and Technology, 1972), pp. 1–3. This paper was funded by the National Institute of Education and ERIC at Stanford.

18. Martha Jane K. Zachert and Veronica S. Pantelidis, "LAG, A Library Administration Game," c. 1970, rev. 1973. Unpublished.
19. Martha Jane K. Zachert and Veronica S. Pantelidis, "Negotiation," c. 1970, rev. 1972. Unpublished.
20. Abt, *Serious Games, op. cit.,* pp. 28–31.
21. Shirts, *op. cit.,* p. 82.
22. Abt, *Serious Games, op. cit.,* p. 33.

PART IV.
Research for
Simulation Teaching
of Library Administration

10.
The Design of
Simulation Teaching Materials
· ·

Studies of the uses and effectiveness of simulation in elementary, secondary and collegiate instruction have been going on steadily for some years. This body of research shows that "from simulations it is possible to learn winning strategies, principles and relationships, decision-making skills, identifications, procedural sequences, and skilled perceptual-motor acts."[1] A single simulation does not provide learning opportunities in all of these categories; nor do all apply equally to the teaching of library administration. On the other hand, the potential for simulation as a methodology for teaching library administration has not been fully explored. As they are now being used, library simulations appear to be limited to experiences with decision-making, personnel management and library/user relationships.[2,3] A great deal of research is needed before we will know with assurance what kinds of learning for administrative effectiveness are best accomplished with the aid of simulations.

In any use of simulation, however, other than experimental or developmental uses, the availability of valid, reliable materials is a prerequisite. This chapter will identify in an introductory way, therefore, three potentially fruitful kinds of research related to the provision of simulation materials: (1) background studies, (2) model design, and (3) learner response to instructional use of simulation. The discussion is limited to these particular needs because they appear to represent a prior condition to the significant incorporation of simulation into either initial or continuing instruction of library administrators. This is not to say that other kinds of research are not also needed; the limitation will simply keep the discussion within introductory bounds.

BACKGROUND STUDIES

The relationship of models to simulations has not been obvious in all of the developmental literature about this methodology. A recent study of taxonomic problems related to instructional simulations does, however, emphasize their central role.

> An instructional simulation is defined as a dynamic model representing the essential elements and phenomena of a real system, with provisions for students to manipulate the model, causing the model to exhibit to the students the various behavior of the real system.[4]

This definition postulates a concept within which a valid model is a prime requisite if a simulation is to be lifelike. The need for accurate information descriptive of the real system, as input into model design, is now obvious.

The Industrial Library Simulation was based on a case study; the Governmental Library Simulation, on a combination of survey and case research; the Lancaster Library Management Game, on a series of operations research studies. The models thus derived provide learners with descriptions of the settings for decision-making, as well as the limits within which alternative decisions can be projected and choices can be made. In all honesty it must be admitted that these specific simulations have not been experimentally validated. A large number of background studies into the nature and behavior of systems to be modeled is an essential research need, as is the validation of the models that incorporate the results of such descriptive studies.

To be more explicit about the kinds of studies needed: Broad general studies of administration in libraries are needed, with attention to comparative data on the fulfillment of each administrative function under differing normal and abnormal conditions. In-depth studies of the traditional types of libraries (academic, public, school, special) are needed, as well as studies of subtypes (e.g., governmental, industrial, special/academic, nonprofit research, as subtypes of "special"). These studies must regard their library subjects as systems. Studies of subsystems within each orbit are also needed, not forgetting that library administrators constitute one important subsystem. Furthermore, these studies should be coordinated in such a way that traditional assumptions will be challenged and that new insights, rather than restatements of currently accepted impressions, will result.

To return to the most recent definition of instructional simulations: Provision for manipulation of the model is as important an element in the definition as is the concept of centrality of a model. Model manipulation is essentially a stimulus/reaction sequence. There must be, therefore, a built-in capability for reaction whenever the learner provides a stimulus. In the Lancaster Library Management Game the model consists of quantifications required in the play of the game plus the logic to evoke each as needed. The learner provides a stimulus in the form of a decision, and the computer carries out the mathematical processes which constitute the reaction and informs the learner by printout of the results of his decision. In the simulations of special library administration designed to date, the reaction to the learner's decision-stimulus is usually one of interaction between library administration and management, between staff member and staff member, or between library and user(s). The teacher serves as referee. Designers of both computer and manual simulations need more information than is now available concerning (1) the range of behaviors in the universe they are modeling, (2) which behaviors can be considered typical and which are atypical, plus (3) insight into the more difficult problem of which behaviors are most appropriate in reaction to what kinds of stimuli. To be valid, this information should be based on research. Teachers also need research-based information (rather than subjective impressions) in order to evaluate learner behaviors exhibited during experiential learning.

Not only is all of this research needed, but in many instances methods of doing the research must also be studied and validated. It seems unlikely, given the prevailing patterns of library science research, that these kinds of background problems will be worked out systematically; rather, in all probability, a variety of kinds of studies will be carried out more or less simultaneously. As is often the case for those who wish to base actions on library science research, there is little solid ground. For some time to come the teacher who is motivated to use simulations in teaching library administration may feel he can forge ahead only in an experimental mode.

FACTORS IN MODEL DESIGN

There is little information in the literature of instructional systems about the design of models analogous to library models. One team of experienced researchers, however, has isolated five factors which, they claim, influence the design of models for the study of complex political entities. The first of these is the *purpose* of the simulation. Once that is decided, the *degree of abstraction*, the *time scale*, the *field situation* and the *field processes* to be simulated must be appropriate to that purpose.[5] These same factors appear to be relevant to the design of models for the study of processes in libraries, which are also complex entities.

Purpose

The underlying purpose of instructional simulations for teaching library administration is to provide a realistic base from which librarians (both potential and actual) can gain insight into the process of administration. My own first efforts have gone into the implementation of objectives that reflect planning and supervisory activities implemented in the spirit of participative management. Thus the simulation materials include specific explicit purposes related to the generally accepted functions of administration. (See Part VI, Industrial Library Simulation: Problems, Note to Instructors about Objectives.) In addition, the Industrial Library Simulation and the Governmental

Library Simulation include implicit purposes related to the management style which I feel is most important for special librarians. Explicit and implicit purposes are valid elements of a library model. Each designer must, of course, decide exactly what his own objectives will be within the underlying purpose of facilitating insight into the process of administration.

Degree of Abstraction

The designer has the choice of designing with either a low or a high level of abstraction. A design with a low level of abstraction would include a good deal of detail and would probably be very realistic in appearance; it runs the risk of being hard for learners to generalize from because of the minutia. A design with a high level of abstraction, on the other hand, would omit detail in favor of a more generic tone easy to generalize from, but possibly distorted in comparison to specific real situations. It must be remembered in designing that the amount of detail determines the degree of complexity of the model for the learner. Familiarization with the detail depicted, however, is an offsetting factor for an individual learner.[6] Thus the extent of library experience of the expected learners appears to be an important consideration in the decision whether to use a high or a low level of abstraction. Also to be considered is the often-expressed desire of learners—and some library employers—for emphasis on realism, rather than theory, in library education.

Time Scale

Choice of a time scale must be a conscious one because simulation, by its nature, can either slow down fast processes, or speed up slow ones. If the designer merely wishes to miniaturize an existing situation, the ratio of real time to simulation time might even be one to one. If, however, the designer wishes to simulate change in the real situation, he must decide whether he is concerned with short-term change, which can be expressed in a low ratio of real time to simulation time, or long-term change, which would require a high real time/simulation time ratio.[7] It is traditional to assume in teaching library administration that a series of processes must be included—the well-known planning, organizing, directing, staffing, coordinating, reporting, budgeting. We assume further that these processes recur over a period of time, one process dominating the administrator's attention more in one set of circumstances than another, but none ever completely dormant. The simulation must, therefore, interweave these administrative processes in some semblance of real time, or it must focus on one or two of the processes at a high level of abstraction with an accompanying low level of realism.

It seems almost axiomatic that any realistic portrayal of the administration of libraries must acknowledge the probability of change in the life of the library modeled. Descriptions and problems of the old, the new, their interrelationships, and their effects on library processes and personnel could well form a central core for the study of all administrative process and behavior. Short-term change appears easiest to predict, and the low real time/simulation time ratio may be easiest to design. The question does arise, however, of whether it is fair to provide learners primarily with concepts of short-term change in their basic education for career service. In the span of a library career the long-term social and technological changes may well be of greater importance. Predicting such changes for inclusion in a model, however, calls for a precision of futurism that may be beyond the present capability of library model designers.

A more practical problem for the designer may be that of the compressibility of various administrative processes. Compressibility refers to the foreshortening or time collapse made possible by isolating a single administrative process, or a few related processes, from others with which, in real life, it is intermingled. For example: Given the proper background documents, a job interview can be conducted in a 30-minute roleplay with little difficulty. The time of the roleplay is very close to real time for such an interview and the time compression in the roleplay is slight. The task of planning new library services, on the other hand, may encompass phases, among others, of surveying user needs, ascertaining the attitudes of library fiscal managers, collecting data related to the nature and the cost of the desired services, and involving staff in the planning. It is very important for learners to have the experience of all of these tasks, but how realistically can the learning experience be compressed into roleplay, in-basket exercises, action mazes or games? Over-compression may violate the validity of the chosen time scale; less compression may be impossible within the constraints of real course time. All of the designer's knowledge of administrative processes and behaviors and his ingenuity in design are called into play in devising a time scale. This is an aspect of design in which a great deal of research is needed, not the least of which is that leading to the development of tests to determine the validity of a chosen time scale.

Field Situation

The "field situation" might be defined as a description of the real world of librarianship, as possibly different from the portrayal of that world in library literature and in the library science classroom. The designer will be influenced in his decisions about the features of the field situation to be incorporated in the model by his prior decisions made during the design process. Many aspects of the real situation will have to be omitted from the model in order to focus attention on those of central importance for the purposes of a specific simulation. There are as yet no guidelines to help the designer; choices depend on his detailed understanding of the field situation to be simulated.[8] In an ideal situation the designer's understanding is a composite of his personal and necessarily limited experience enhanced by the results of research studies

available to him. In simulating the administration of industrial and governmental libraries, the designer had little significant, generalizable research to
use; other types of libraries may be easier to simulate because of the greater
availability of research studies. Even so, additional design methods should be
developed to offset the limitations of both personal experience and the unsys-
tematic research characteristic of library science.

Field Processes

Finally, field processes both at the level of administrative strategies and at
the level of daily transactions must be included in the simulation. The major
problem is to devise ways in which ongoing processes can be miniaturized, or
to devise "substitute mechanisms that will have approximately the same
consequences for the miniature system that the corresponding mechanism has
for the full-scale system."[9] Again, knowledge of these processes must come
either from the designer's experience or from research that is sufficiently
broad-based for its results to be generalizable.

Criteria for Evaluation

Some criteria for judging an instructional simulation are implicit in the
foregoing, though not at a level of precision that a designer might wish. Braby
has stated his criteria as "(1) The subject is perceived as a dynamic system;
(2) the essential features and behavior of the system are represented by a dynamic model with internal logic; and (3) the model can be manipulated by
students and provide them with feedback in the form of changing model behavior."[10]

LEARNER FEEDBACK

Not only must a model be a valid representation of a segment of real life,
but it must also convey its information in such a way that learners can inter-
nalize this information and use it in problem-solving, first in the classroom
and later on the job. The validity of a model as a representation of "real life"
in libraries is essential; the reliability of that model in the sense of its capability to communicate information successfully to learners is equally important. Until the twin criteria of validity and reliability are met, a model must
be in a constant state of revision. Field research is one significant source of input for revision; learner feedback expressive of affective reaction and cognitive achievement is another.

Instructional simulations designed for teaching school administrators are
perhaps the nearest analogy to the kinds of library simulations under discussion. Four methods of evaluation used in combination have become virtually standard: (1) observation and critique by instructional staff and/or outside evaluators, (2) learner/instructional staff critical discussion at intervals

during the simulation and/or post-simulation, (3) affective "reactionnaires" during and after the simulation, (4) cognitive pre- and post-tests. Several tests of school administration instructional simulations have included, in addition, a follow-up evaluation some time after the simulation study to determine whether or not changes had taken place in the behavior of the learners.[11,12]

Observers, simulation designers and others have pointed out that learner reactionnaires and critiques lack perspective for a variety of reasons: unidentifiable intervening forces; halo effects; the absence of control group; learner/instructor relationships that develop during experiential learning; and, where academic credit is at stake, learners' efforts to push the grade as high as possible through psychological, as well as other, strategies. Few instructors would debate the possibility that such contaminating factors are at work. Still, if we accept the proposition that learners are most highly motivated in relation to cognitive content when they feel the information is relevant to their self-perceived needs, especially in career preparation and in-service education, then it is important to know how the learners feel. We must use the best means available, though we acknowledge the imperfections of those means.

CONCLUSION

Does simulation hold promise for the teaching of library administration? Yes, in the opinion of a growing number of teachers, administrators and learners who have tried it. It has been demonstrated that teachers who did not participate in the design of a simulation can, and will, use it enthusiastically,[13] and that learners attest to the learning values of the simulation experience both in master's-level study and in continuing education.[14,15] If additional models were to be developed by researchers, there would be advantages for both teachers and learners.

The research needs center on obtaining valid descriptions of field situations and field processes for input into model design. This research should emphasize obtaining information that is generalizable within carefully stated limits about both libraries and library administrators. Studies of administrative behavior, of decision-making responsibilities and of patterns of administrative communication are especially needed. Results of such studies would permit simulation designers to challenge traditional assumptions of instruction for library administration and of the behavior of library administrators.[16]

Given a series of valid models and problems that involve manipulation of the models, every teacher of library administration would have available a choice of tested materials to use singly or in combination, for initial or continuing education purposes. Learning materials could then be used for pedagogical reasons rather than because they were the only ones the teacher had the time and personal experience to prepare himself.

REFERENCES

1. Paul A. Twelker, *Simulation: An Overview*, 1968. (Available as ED 025 459) Abstracted in *Research in Education* 4 (May 1969): 89.

2. P. Brophy et al., *A Library Management Game* (Lancaster, England: University of Lancaster Library, 1972).

3. Martha Jane K. Zachert, "The Library Administration Course: Simulation as a Technique," *Journal of Education for Librarianship* 11 (Winter 1971): 243–250.

4. Thomas R. Braby, "Guidelines for Describing Instructional Materials Incorporating Simulation Techniques" (Ed. D. dissertation, Teachers College, Columbia University, 1969). Abstracted in *Dissertation Abstracts* 31 (1971): 4030-A.

5. Andrew M. Scott, William A. Lucas and Trudi M. Lucas, *Simulation and National Development* (New York: Wiley, 1966), pp. 160–161, 165.

6. *Ibid.,* p. 160.

7. *Ibid.*

8. *Ibid.,* p. 161.

9. *Ibid.*

10. Braby, *op. cit.*

11. Hollis A. Moore, Jr. and Francis M. Trusty, "The Use of Simulated Situations at Stanford University," in *Simulation in Administrative Training* (Columbus, Ohio: The University Council for Educational Administration, 1960), p. 26.

12. Harold J. McNally and D. Richard Wynn, "The Use of Simulated Situations at Teachers College, Columbia University," *Simulation in Administrative Training*, p. 34.

13. Thomas Slavens, "Teaching Special Librarianship: Some Current Approaches," *Special Libraries* 63 (1972): 477–481.

14. Unpublished reaction reports in the author's files, primarily from the Catholic University of America, Florida State University, and workshops conducted by the author.

15. Barbara Conroy, *A Descriptive and Evaluative Report of the Washington Seminar: Library Career Development Institute* (Washington: The Catholic University of America, Department of Library Science, 1971), pp. 61, 64, 76.

16. Since this chapter was written, an excellent manual for simulation designers has been published: Robert Maidment and Russell H. Bronstein, *Simulation Games: Design and Implementation* (Columbus, Ohio: Charles E. Merrill Publishing Company, 1973).

PART V.
Bibliography

This bibliography of selected references includes monographs, research reports, state-of-the-art reviews, and examples of simulations and experiential methodologies, as well as some articles of comment and exhortation which appeared from approximately 1965 to mid-1973. It is, in fact, a culled version of my working bibliography which is intended to be of practical use to other library science teachers. As such, rather than a systematic bibliography of teaching simulation information, it excludes the purely theoretical, most of the research related to materials designed for disciplines other than library science, much of the repetitive literature, and all foreign language literature. All of the initial statements of ideas that were seminal for me are included, plus the best of the statements that I discovered belatedly, as well as evaluative and update materials.

This is not to say that there has been no systematic searching, for certain sources were thoroughly searched in 1967–1968, and the search was updated in 1970 and again in the fall of 1973. These sources were *Education Index*, *Dissertation Abstracts*, *Research in Education* and, partially, *Business Periodicals Index*. To the citations thus gleaned have been added those that have appeared in library literature. Several nonlibrary publications found to be especially valuable have been monitored on a continuing basis, especially *American Behavioral Scientist*, *Educational Technology*, *Journal of Applied Behavioral Science*, and *Training and Development Journal*. Most of the systematic searching was done by Veronica Pantelidis, then my graduate assistant at Florida State University, Vivian Templin, my research assistant at Catholic University of America, and Karola Rac, my graduate assistant at the University of South Carolina. Bibliographic assistants neither die nor fade away; they go right on searching and continuously update their former teachers. My appreciation to these bibliographers is considerable.

It should be noted for those who wish to cover the field thoroughly that there is a great deal of simulation teaching going on in the field of medical and health science education. As it has been reported, however, it seems less analogous to the teaching of library *administration* than does simulation development in business and educational administration. For this reason, it has been omitted from this bibliography. It does appear to me to have some potential for possible future development of simulation teaching of other aspects of librarianship, for example reference service, and it should be winnowed for ideas and applications. It should also be noted that many of the research reports omitted from this bibliography because of their specific relationship to materials for other disciplines include ideas for research designs of possible usefulness in library science. Furthermore, the use of simulations in research, as separate from teaching, has been excluded. As stated above, this is a working bibliography of items most useful in the design and classroom utilization of simulation and experiential techniques for teaching library administration.

The bibliography arrangement is virtually self-explanatory. The "Background" section includes a variety of items about learning psychology, communication, instructional design, and innovative classroom techniques. It is intended for brief orientation for those unfamiliar with current ideas in these areas. The sections "Simulation," "Roleplay," "In-Basket Techniques," and "Games" include the items that relate specifically to those topics. Because of some fumbling for terminology during the period of initial development of these techniques, there is some overlap and occasional semantic incongruity. I have tried to place items according to current definitions and terminology. A very few items that cross arbitrary boundaries and include important material related to more than one technique have been listed more than once. Those who wish a comprehensive bibliography should consult *The Literature of Gaming, Simulation, and Model-Building: Index and Critical Abstracts*, by Martin Shubik, G. Brewer and E. Savage (Santa Monica, Calif.: Rand, 1972), and *Reviews of Selected Books and Articles on Gaming and Simulation*, by Martin Shubik and Garry D. Brewer (Santa Monica, Calif.: Rand, 1972).

BACKGROUND

Alderfer, Clayton P., and Lodahl, Thomas M. "A Quasi Experiment on the Use of Experiential Methods in the Classroom," *Journal of Applied Behavioral Science* 7 (January/February 1971): 43–69.

Bormann, Ernest G., and Bormann, Nancy C. *Effective Small Group Communication.* Minneapolis: Burgess Publishing Company, 1972.

Broadwell, Martin M. *The Supervisor as an Instructor.* Reading, Mass.: Addison-Wesley Publishing Company, 1968.

Cherryholmes, Cleo H. "Some Current Research on Effectiveness of Educational Simulations: Implications for Alternative Strategies," *American Behavioral Scientist* 10 (October 1966): 4–7.

Dubin, Robert, and Taveggia, Thomas C. *The Teaching-Learning Paradox: A Comparative Analysis of College Teaching Methods.* Eugene, Oreg.: Center for the Advanced Study of Educational Administration, 1968.

Evans, Richard I., and Leppmann, Peter K. *Resistance to Innovation in Higher Education.* San Francisco: Josey-Bass, 1968.

Friedlander, Frank. "The Primacy of Trust as a Facilitator of Further Group Accomplishment," *Journal of Applied Behavioral Science* 6 (1970): 387–400.

Kapfer, Miriam B., ed. *Behavioral Objectives in Curriculum Development.* New York: Educational Technology Publications, 1971.

Knowles, Malcolm S. *The Modern Practice of Adult Education.* New York: Association Press, 1970.

Kohl, Herbert R. *The Open Classroom.* New York: New York Review, 1969.

Krumboltz, John D., and Potter, Beverly. "Behavior Techniques for Developing Trust, Cohesiveness, and Goal Accomplishment," *Educational Technology* 13 (January 1973): 27–30.

Mager, Robert F. *Preparing Instructional Objectives.* Palo Alto, Calif.: Fearon Publishers, 1962.

Matlin, Norman. *The Educational Enclave.* New York: Funk and Wagnalls, 1969.

Popham, James, and Baker, Eva. *Establishing Instructional Goals.* Englewood Cliffs, N.J.: Prentice-Hall, 1970.

Popham, James, and Baker, Eva. *Planning an Instructional Sequence.* Englewood Cliffs, N.J.: Prentice-Hall, 1970.

Schmuck, Richard, Chesler, Mark, and Lippitt, Ronald. *Problem Solving to Improve Classroom Learning.* Palo Alto, Calif.: Science Research Associates, 1966.

Thompson, James J. *Instructional Communication.* New York: American Book Company, 1969.

Ullmer, Eldon J. "Instructional Development in Higher Education: Basic Premises of a Learner-Centered Approach," *Educational Technology* 9 (April 1969): 10–16.

Zoll, Allen A., III. *Dynamic Management Education.* Reading, Mass.: Addison-Wesley, 1969.

SIMULATION

Amstutz, Arnold E. *Computer Simulation of Competitive Market Response.* Cambridge: Massachusetts Institute of Technology Press, 1967. Chapter 14, "Educational Applications of Behavioral Simulation," pp. 413–430.

Bartlett, Alton C. "Changing Behavior Through Simulation—An Alternate Design to T-Group Training," *Training and Development Journal* 21 (August 1967): 38–52.

Basil, Douglas C., Cone, Paul R., and Fleming, John. *Executive Decision-Making Through Simulation.* Columbus, Ohio: Charles E. Merrill Books, 1965.

Bessent, Wailand. "A Feedback Procedure for Simulation of Administrative In-Basket Problems." Paper presented at the American Educational Research Association Symposium on Feedback in Simulation Techniques, New York, February 1967.

Boardman, Robert. "The Theory and Practice of Educational Simulation," *Educational Research* 11 (June 1969): 179–184.

Boocock, Sarane, and Schild, E.O. *Simulation and Gaming.* New York: American Management Association, 1961. Report No. 55.

Braby, Thomas R. "Guidelines for Describing Instructional Materials Incorporating Simulation Techniques." Ed. D. dissertation, Teachers College, Columbia University, 1969.

Brophy, Peter, and Buckland, Michael K. "Simulation in Education for Library and Information Service Administration," *Information Scientist* (September 1972): 93–100.

Cruickshank, Donald R. "The Notions of Simulations and Games: A Preliminary Inquiry," *Educational Technology* 12 (July 1972): 17–19.

Cruickshank, Donald R. "Simulation," *Theory Into Practice* 7 (December 1968): 190–202.

Culbertson, Jack, et al. "The Design and Development of Prototype Instructional Materials for Preparing Educational Administrators." Available as ED 019 723/ EA 001 229. Abstracted in *Research in Education* 3 (November 1968): 40.

Culbertson, Jack A., and Coffield, W.H. *Simulation in Administrative Training.* Columbus, Ohio: University Council for Educational Administration, 1960. See especially Chapter IV, "Simulated Situations and Instruction: A Critique," pp. 39–46.

Fattu, Nicholas, and Elam, Stanley. *Simulation Models for Education.* Bloomington, Ind.: Phi Delta Kappa, 1965. Fourth Annual Phi Delta Kappa Symposium on Educational Research.

Garvey, Dale M. "A Preliminary Evaluation of Simulation." Paper presented at the 46th Annual Meeting of the National Council for the Social Studies, Cleveland, Ohio, November 23–26, 1966.

Guetzkow, Harold, ed. *Simulation in Social Science: Readings.* Englewood Cliffs, N.J.: Prentice-Hall, 1962.

Guy, Leonard C. "Simulated Management," *Library Journal* 94 (January 15, 1969): 37–41.

Guy, Leonard C. "Teaching the Management of Libraries," *Library Association Record* 70 (April 1968): 91–95.

Heinkel, Otto A. "Evaluation of Simulation as a Teaching Device," *Journal of Experimental Education* 38 (Spring 1970): 32–36.

Hinrichs, J.R. "Comparison of 'Real Life' Assessments of Management Potential with Situational Exercises, Paper-and-Pencil Ability Tests, and Personality Inventories," *Journal of Applied Psychology* 53 (October 1969): 425–432.

Lavin, Richard. "Simulation, Standards and the Seventies," *Library Journal* 94 (November 15, 1969): 4216–4217.

Maidment, Robert, and Bronstein, Russell H. *Simulation Games: Design and Implementation.* Columbus, Ohio: Merrill, 1973.

Ochoa, Anna. "Simulation and Gaming: Simile or Synonym?" *Peabody Journal of Education* 47 (September 1969): 104–107.

Raia, Anthony P. "A Study of the Educational Value of Management Games," *Journal of Business* 39 (1966): 339–352.

Ramey, James W. "Simulation in Library Administration," *Journal of Education for Librarianship* 8 (1967): 85–93.

Reed, Luton R. "A Study of the Feasibility of Using Operational Simulation Techniques for Evaluating Administrative Skills Possessed by Instructional Communications Specialists." Ph. D. dissertation, Syracuse University, 1966.

Rowell, Glennon. "The Model in Use (Simulation)," *Theory Into Practice* 7 (December 1968): 194–196.

Schild, E.O. "The Shaping of Strategies," *American Behavioral Scientist* 10 (November 1966): 1–4.

Scott, Andrew M., Lucas, William A., and Lucas, Trudi M. *Simulation and National Development.* New York: Wiley, 1966. Chapter 9, "The Procedures and Uses of Simulation," pp. 159–177.

Twelker, Paul A. "Designing Simulation Systems." Available as ED 028 964/SP 002 237. Abstracted in *Research in Education* 4 (September 1969): 97–98.

Twelker, Paul A. "Simulation: An Overview." Available as ED 025 459/SP 001 930. Abstracted in *Research in Education* 4 (May 1969): 89.

Twelker, Paul A. "Simulation Applications in Teacher Education." Available as ED 025 460/SP 001 931. Abstracted in *Research in Education* 4 (May 1969): 89.

Twelker, Paul A. "Simulation: Status of the Field," Paper presented at the Conference on Simulation for Learning, Boston, Massachusetts, 1968. Available as ED 028 974/SP 002 384. Abstracted in *Research in Education* 4 (September 1969): 99.

Weinberger, Morris J. "The Use of Simulation in the Teaching of School Administration." Ed. D. dissertation, Columbia University, 1965.

Widgerson, Harry I. "The Name of the Game—Simulation." Visalia, Calif. ADAPT, A PACE Supplementary Education Center, 1968. Research Brief No. 1. Available as ED 028 647. Abstracted in *Research in Education* 4 (September 1969): 53.

Zachert, Martha Jane K. "The Design of Special Library Teaching Models," *Special Libraries* 64 (September 1973): 362–369.

Zachert, Martha Jane K. *The Governmental Library Simulation for the Study of Administration of a Special Library.* Part I. The Federal Library Model. Part II. Participant's Resource-Log. Part III. Director's Guide. Washington, D.C.: The Catholic University of America, Department of Library Science, 1971.

Zachert, Martha Jane K. "The Library Administration Course: Simulation as a Technique," *Journal of Education for Librarianship* 11 (Winter 1971): 243–250.

Zachert, Martha Jane K., and Pantelidis, Veronica S. "Experiential Methods of Teaching Special Librarianship," *Special Libraries* 63 (December 1972): 545–548.

ROLEPLAY

Chesler, Mark, and Fox, Robert. *Role-Playing Methods in the Classroom.* Chicago: Science Research Associates, 1966.

Corsini, Raymond J., Shaw, Malcolm E., and Blake, Robert R. *Roleplaying in Business and Industry.* New York: Free Press of Glencoe, 1961.

Cruickshank, Donald R. *Inner-City Simulation Laboratory.* Chicago: Science Research Associates, 1969.

Cruickshank, Donald R., Broadbent, Frank W., and Bubb, Roy L. *Teaching Problems Laboratory.* Chicago: Science Research Associates, 1967.

Elbing, Alvar O., Jr. "The Influence of Prior Attitudes on Role Playing Results," *Personnel Psychology* 20 (Autumn 1967): 309–321.

John, Martha A. "The Relationship of Role-playing to Futuristic Thinking," *Journal of Education* 152 (April 1970): 4–10.

Klein, Alan F. *Role Playing in Leadership Training and Group Problem Solving.* New York: Association Press, 1956.

Levit, Grace, and Jennings, Helen H. "Learning Through Role Playing," *Adult Leadership* 2 (October 1953), 9–16.

Maier, Norman R.F., Solem, Allen R., and Maier, Ayesha A. *Supervisory and Executive Development: A Manual for Role Playing.* New York: Wiley, 1957.

Paniagua, Lita, and Jackson, Vivian C. "Role Playing in New Careers Training." New York: New York University, School of Education, 1968. Available as ED 025 820/CG 003 541.

Shaftel, Fannie R., and Shaftel, George. *Role-playing for Social Values: Decision-making in the Social Studies.* Englewood Cliffs, N.J.: Prentice-Hall, 1967.

"Six Practical Ideas for Role Playing," *SM/Sales Meetings Magazine*, 19 (May 1970): 55–67, 70–72, 75–76, 79–81, 83–84, 86–87.

Van Dersal, William R. *The Successful Supervisor in Government and Business*. New York: Harper and Row, 1968.

Zoll, Allen A., III. *Dynamic Management Education*. 2d ed. Reading, Mass.: Addison-Wesley Publishing Co., 1969.

IN-BASKET TECHNIQUES

Daly, Andrew. "In-Basket Business Game," *American Society of Training Directors Journal* 14 (August 1960): 8–15.

Davis, Joan A.M., and Taylor, William. "Teaching the Head: Simulated Management," *The Times Educational Supplement* (London), June 12, 1964, 1624.

Frederiksen, Norman. "Factors in In-Basket Performance," *Psychological Monographs* 76 (1962): Whole No. 541.

Frederiksen, Norman. "In-Basket Tests and Factors in Administrative Performance," in *Simulation in Social Science: Readings*, ed. Harold S. Guetzkow. Englewood Cliffs, N.J.: Prentice-Hall, 1962.

Frederiksen, Norman, Saunders, D.R., and Wand, Barbara. "The In-Basket Test," *Psychological Monographs* 71 (1957): Whole No. 438.

Gibson, George. "A New Dimension for 'In-Basket' Training," *Personnel* 38 (July–August 1961): 76–79.

Greenlaw, Paul S. "The In-Basket as a Training Instrument," in *Marketing Keys to Profits in the 1960's*, ed. Wenzil K. Dolva. Chicago: American Marketing Association, 1960.

Herron, Lowell. *Executive Action Simulation*. Englewood Cliffs, N.J.: Prentice-Hall, 1961.

Iannizzi, Elizabeth. ". . . Through Experience in Making Decisions," *Business Education Forum* 21 (February 1967): 9–13.

Immegart, Glenn L., and Brent, Daniel. "Sister Monica's In-Basket," *Catholic School Journal* 68 (May 1968), 34–38.

Jaffee, Cabot L. *Problems in Supervision: An In-Basket Training Exercise*. Reading, Mass.: Addison-Wesley, 1968.

Joyce, Robert D. "In-Basket Training for Engineering Managers," *Educational Technology* 10 (January 1970): S20–S26.

Knudson, H.R., Jr. *Human Elements of Administration*. New York: Holt, Rinehart and Winston, 1963.

Lopez, Felix M., Jr. *Evaluating Executive Decision Making: The In-Basket Technique*. New York: American Management Association, 1966. Research Study No. 75.

Meckley, Richard F. "Simulation in Leadership Training," *American Vocational Journal* 45 (September 1970): 26–27, 40, 57.

Roberts, R.S. "Training Managers to Make Decisions: The In-Basket Method," *Personnel* 42 (September–October 1965): 58–66.

Zachert, Martha Jane K., and Pantelidis, Veronica S. *SIBE: A Sequential In-Basket Technique, The Pilot Study*. Tallahassee, Fla.: CAI Center, Florida State University, 1971.

Zoll, Allen A., III. *Dynamic Management Education*. Reading, Mass.: Addison-Wesley, 1969.

GAMES

Abt, Clark C. "Games Can Have Bonuses and Obstacles," *Nation's Schools* 80 (October 1967): 92.

Abt, Clark C. *Serious Games.* New York: Viking, 1970.

Babb, E.M., and Eisgruber, L.M. *Management Games for Teaching and Research.* Chicago: Educational Methods, 1966.

Boocock, Sarane S. "An Experimental Study of the Learning Effects of Two Games with Simulated Environments," *American Behavioral Scientist* 10 (October 1966): 8–17.

Boocock, Sarane S. "Games Change What Goes on in Classrooms," *Nation's Schools* 80 (October 1967): 94–95, 122.

Boocock, Sarane S., and Schild, E.O., eds. *Simulation Games in Learning.* Beverly Hills, Calif.: Sage Publications, 1968.

Brophy, Peter, and Buckland, Michael K. *A Library Management Game: A Report on a Research Project.* Lancaster, England: Library Research Unit, University of Lancaster, 1972.

Buckland, Michael K., and Hindle, A. "The Case for Library Management Games," *Journal of Education for Librarianship* 12 (Fall 1971): 92–103.

Calvert, Donald E. "Management Games as Teaching Devices," *Training and Development Journal* 24 (February 1970): 16–18.

Carlson, Elliot. *Learning Through Games.* Washington, D.C.: Public Affairs Press, 1969.

Cohen, K.J., and Rhenman, E. "The Role of Management Games in Education and Research," *Management Science* 7 (1961): 131–166.

Coleman, James. "Academic Games and Learning," *National Association of Secondary School Principals Bulletin* 52 (February 1968): 62–68.

Coleman, James. "Introduction: In Defense of Games," *American Behavioral Scientist* 10 (October 1966): 3–4.

Coleman, James, Boocock, Sarane S., and Schild, E.O. "Simulation Games and Learning Behavior," *American Behavioral Scientist* 10 (1966): Entire issues October and November.

Colley, D.I., and Russell, J. "The Manchester Public Libraries Library Management Game," *Library World* 69 (July 1967): 10–11.

"Games Can Teach the Boss His Business," *Changing Times* 24 (November 1970): 45–47.

Giammatteo, Michael C. "Sample of a Gaming Exercise." 1969. Available as ED 030 169/CG 004 212. Abstracted in *Research in Education* 4 (November 1969): 28.

Glazier, Ray. *How to Design Educational Games: A Game Design Manual for Teachers and Curriculum Developers,* 2nd ed. Cambridge, Mass.: Abt Associates, 1970.

Graham, Robert G., and Gray, Clifford F. *Business Games Handbook.* New York: American Management Association, 1969.

Greene, Jay R., and Sisson, Roger. *Dynamic Management Decision Games.* New York: Wiley, 1959.

Kasperson, Roger E. "Games as Educational Media," *Journal of Geography* 67 (October 1968): 409–422.

McKenney, James L. *Simulation Gaming for Management Development.* Cambridge, Mass.: Division of Research, Graduate School of Business Administration, Harvard University, 1967.

McKenney, James L., and Dill, William R. "Influences on Learning in Simulation Games," *American Behavioral Scientist* 10 (October 1966): 28-32.

Moore, Larry F. "Business Games vs. Cases as Tools of Learning, Results of Research at the University of Colorado," *Training and Development Journal* 21 (October 1967): 13-23.

Rapoport, Anatol, and Chammah, Albert M. "The Game of Chicken," *American Behavioral Scientist* 10 (November 1966): 10-27.

Rogers, Virginia M., and Kysilka, Marcella L. "Simulation Games: What and Why," *Instructor* 79 (March 1970): 94-95.

Stoll, Clarice S., and Boocock, Sarane S. "Simulation Games for Social Studies," *Audiovisual Instruction* 13 (1968): 840-842.

PART VI.
Simulation Examples

Industrial Library Simulation

. . . .

DOCUMENT A. ORGANIZATION CHART OF THE DOUBLE XYZ OIL
COMPANY PARENT ORGANIZATION

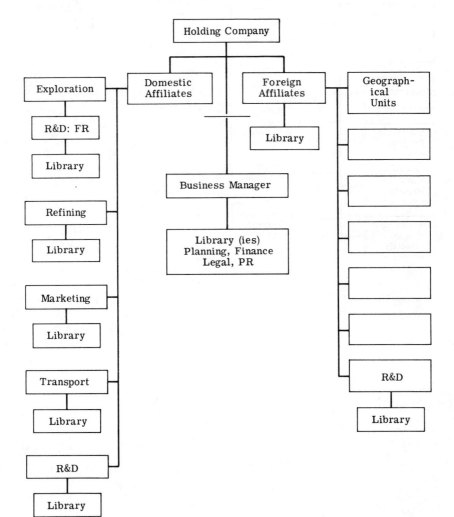

DOCUMENT B. ORGANIZATION CHART OF THE DOUBLE XYZ OIL
              COMPANY FIELD RESEARCH LABORATORY

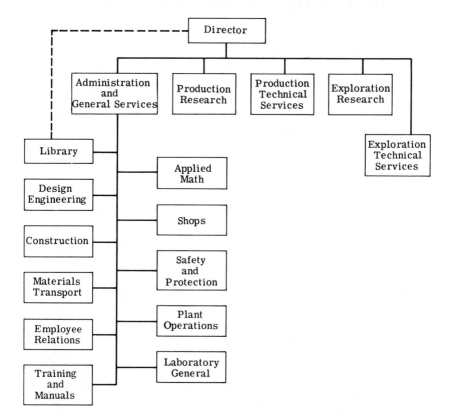

DOCUMENT C. ORGANIZATION CHART OF THE FIELD
RESEARCH LABORATORY LIBRARY

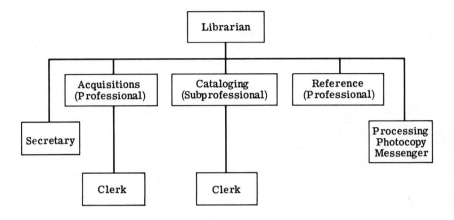

DOCUMENT D. FLOOR PLAN OF THE FIELD RESEARCH LABORATORY LIBRARY

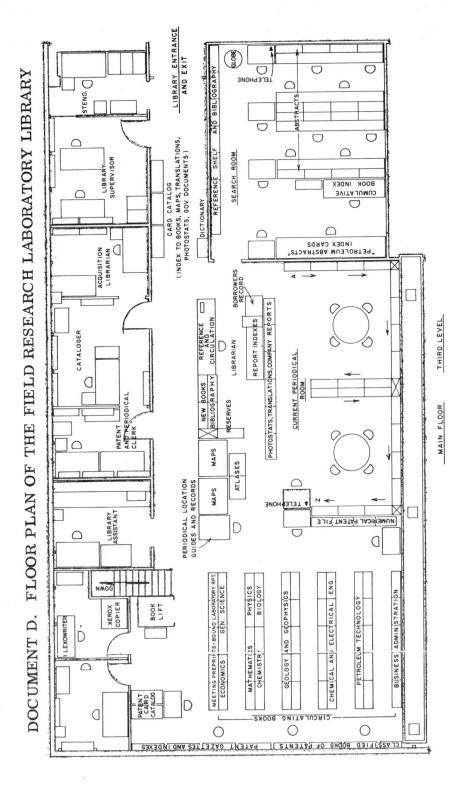

DOCUMENT D (Continued)

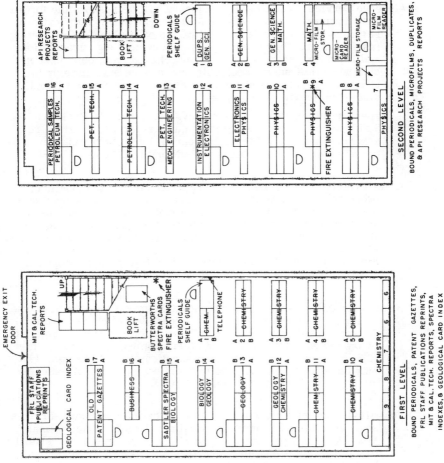

FIRST LEVEL

BOUND PERIODICALS, PATENT GAZETTES,
FRL STAFF PUBLICATIONS REPRINTS,
MIT & CAL. TECH. REPORTS, SPECTRA
INDEXES, & GEOLOGICAL CARD INDEX

SECOND LEVEL

BOUND PERIODICALS, MICROFILMS, DUPLICATES,
& API RESEARCH PROJECTS REPORTS

DOCUMENT E. FRL LIBRARY POLICY MANUAL (SELECTIONS)

Reference Service: The Research Library will be responsible for all
informational needs of the Field Research Staff. Informational
services will be available to libraries of Double XYZ affiliates
insofar as possible. Some types of services, e.g., translations
and literature searches, may be purchased from outside agencies when this seems desirable to conserve staff time or to
utilize additional resources, and when it can be done without
disclosing privileged company information.

Specific informational services available to Field Research
Staff include current awareness, quick reference, search, research, translation, literature search, interlibrary loan, internal reports management, and editorial services.

Special Projects: The Library will engage in special informational
projects to the limit of its resources. Such projects may be
internal efforts to meet specific company informational needs,
or external cooperative efforts to increase or improve the industry's informational resources. In cases where the project
will be an ongoing one, where it will command appreciable staff
time, or where additional personnel will be needed, proposed
projects should be cleared with the Director of Research.

Circulation: All materials may be checked out by Company personnel.
Materials in constant demand are loaned on a 24-hour basis.
All other materials are loaned on an indefinite basis, subject to
two-week recall on request of other Company personnel. Interlibrary loans are made at the discretion of the librarian. (These
may be filled by photocopies to avoid having material inacces-
sible to Company if librarian desires.)

Acquisition: Any materials needed to provide informational services
shall be obtained. There are no limitations on forms of materials. Decisions on form (i.e., original, photocopy, etc.) shall be
based on factors of time, permanence, availability, and cost.
Duplicates may be obtained at the librarian's discretion.

Organization Policy: Books, maps, translations, photostats and government documents are organized by the Dewey Decimal Classification. Patents are organized by their numbers. Company
reports and other special files are organized as need dictates.

Budget Policy: A budget request is prepared annually by the librarian
in consultation with the Director of the Field Research Laboratory. It is submitted to the Head of Administration and General
Services. The budget (exclusive of salaries) is prepared on the
principle of internal allocation of funds; major allotments only
need show in the budget request. Departments ordering specific
items will have these charged to their respective budgets.

DOCUMENT F. FRL LIBRARY ANNUAL REPORT: STAFF

Appreciable effort in 19x8 was spent in training and upgrading the Library Staff.
A library school student from the University of Texas was employed during the
summer for the prime purpose of potential staff development. In addition, each
member of the Library staff has been encouraged and given the opportunity to
participate in special training programs related to library science, documentation techniques, and research seminars.

— from 19x8 Annual Report

TABLE I. STATISTICAL SUMMARY OF SELECTED FUNCTIONS
IN THE STAFF WORKLOAD, 19x2-19x8

Function	19x2	19x3	19x4	19x5	19x6	19x7	19x8
Acquisition							
Journal issues	3,000[a]	3,718	4,237	5,446	7,450	12,174	12,761
Patents[b]				3,565	4,557	5,001	4,611
Other items	2,128	2,226	2,340	2,396	2,063	3,167	3,312
TOTAL	5,128	5,944	6,577	11,407	14,070	20,342	20,684
Cataloging							
Total cards typed	7,775	14,893	12,763	10,383	6,707	39,729	30,515
Total cards ordered							
Total cards filed							
Circulation							
Items checked out	3,012	3,366	2,526	4,148	4,001	5,583	6,788
Items checked in	2,831	3,727	2,897	3,799	3,313	5,215	7,024
TOTAL	5,843	7,093	5,423	7,947	7,314	10,798	13,812
Readers Services							
Questions							
answered	2,492	2,056	1,920	4,245	3,906	4,364	4,617
Literature search							
Translations	52	149	134	205	148	155	128
ILL requests	633	668	844	793	603	752	615

a. Estimate (19x2 only).
b. Patent Library was operated separately until November 19x8.

DOCUMENT G. FRL LIBRARY ANNUAL REPORT: SERVICES

Reference

The services offered are the usual ones offered by special libraries.
Because the staff is small and the demand for depth reference service
is not constant (or because the specialized resources needed are not
available in the parent library), service is sometimes supplied through
contract with outside agencies, e.g., in the case of translations, literature searches and patent searches.

During the year, more research staff members requested Library reference service than in any prior year. The 194 technical men aver-
aged 78 visits each to the Library in 19x8, 30 phone calls, 35 loans of
materials from the parent library and 3 interlibrary loans. Their reference questions took many forms. Some of the questions were for
information on people, such as names, addresses, positions, training,
and included both U.S. and foreign scientists. In addition to supplying
biographical information, the Library also provided a bibliography of
articles or patents produced by the individual. Other questions pertained to information on companies, such as the names of directors,
products, government contracts, and patents assigned. Information
on specific oil fields was requested many times by both FRL staff people and the field offices. Information needed varied from the location
of a field to a detailed search on the geology, and exploratory and production history. The Library is presently compiling a list of reference aids which contain this type of information. Another category of
questions received frequently during 19x8 pertained to government research contracts. Information needed ranged from a detailed procedure of how to procure a government contract and included such items
as the policy of a particular agency in granting contracts, of companies recently receiving contracts for certain types of work, and what
areas are now open to contracting. This type of question involved
rather extensive searching in U.S. Government Research Report literature. Another type of question frequently received during the year
pertained to information on foreign countries. Information needed
varied from climatic conditions or geographical-political information
to a detailed and extensive compilation of a bibliography of the geology
of certain countries. Another type of question frequently received
concerned FRL's own internal reports and publications. An increasing need for suitable indexes to FRL's Reports and Lab Memos is obvious. There is an increasingly strong interest in FRL's patent position in certain subject areas. Samples of questions received are
available in a separate memo.

In addition to giving increased reference service, the Library also
increased its efforts to train research staff members in the use of
literature and Library facilities. Our objective is to make each researcher as literature competent as possible. Approximately twenty
research individuals were given instructions on how to search for
specific information they required. In order to simplify the searching problem, the Search Room was set up during the year. Most of
the main searching tools are concentrated in this room. Subsequently,
it is believed that during 19x8 the Library began to show maturity in
reference service.

During the year, the Patent Library was merged with the Main Library. An increase in the emphasis and the use of the patent literature is evident from the number of orders received for patents and from the number of reference questions pertaining to patents. It is also evident that there is an increasing need for foreign patent information. During 19x8, a total of 4,611 U.S. patents were ordered at the request of the Patent Engineers and the research staff. The Patent Section of the Library is now well organized and is "ready for action."

Appreciable progress was made during 19x8 in documenting the published literature and the Company's literature. Due to the diligent efforts of the Library staff, a current and up-to-date file of 180,000 abstract cards of the published literature and patents in petroleum exploration and production is now a vital part of the literature resources of many of the research staff. A breakdown by geographical areas or countries of cards pertaining to foreign and domestic locations permits, for the first time in the history of this Library, a researcher to pinpoint the geology of a specific area. The usefulness of this file cannot be described in words. More and more of the research staff people are taking advantage of this file. However, as the file increases in size (and therefore in usefulness), more time is required to maintain and interfile the approximately 1,600 cards per week.

Appreciable effort was expended during the year in assisting in the development of exploration and production indexing tools. We worked with the Society of Petroleum Engineers Information Retrieval Committee as well as with the University of Tulsa and the American Petroleum Institute groups. We have continued in our diligent efforts to evaluate "Petroleum Abstracts" and to see that these maintain a high level of quality.

With regard to the documentation of Company internal material, the year 19x8 marked the beginning of preparation of abstracts of FRL Reports, Laboratory Memoranda, and Newsletters. These abstracts are now being sent to many Division and District offices. The year 19x8 also marked the first full year in which the FRL Library received and cataloged reports from operating departments of subsidiary and related companies. This program has been, in general, highly successful and has provided to our research staff more internal Company material than under the earlier system. Additional effort needs to be expended on this program in order to insure its maximum success.

Circulation

At the time of the 19x8 annual report, 6,289 items, 41% of the total, were checked out of the Library. Thirteen borrowers, 9% of the technical staff, have checked out 34% of the current checkouts. We have done appreciable study of the distribution of checked-out items among the research staff. We have also calculated a "retention coefficient" for each borrower. A plot of the individual retention coefficient versus all items currently checked out indicates that some borrowers exhibit an excessively long retention of an excessively large number of items. Our study of retention time of checked-out items shows that 63% of all items currently checked out have been checked out to the same person for more than two years. In like manner, 24% of all items currently checked out have been checked out to the same person for more than five years. These data confirm and justify the numerous complaints we have recently been receiving; that is, that new employees, or those employees not retaining checked-out items, are finding it increasingly difficult to locate books needed during the course of their research. There are several plans of action which could be implemented in order to result in greater accessibility of more books to more people. We intend to implement some of these in the immediate future.

We are continuing with our study of ways of streamlining our circulation system. We are now using the Xerox Copier to prepare call-in and "come-and-get-it" notices. Due to the large number of items of current check-out, we are being asked more frequently to call in more items. At present, persons have requested to see approximately 8%, that is, 400 books, which are presently checked out to other people. During 19x8, we have attempted to follow a rigorous two-weeks call-in schedule for these reserves. This has helped disperse needed items, but is not completely successful.

TABLE II. SUMMARY OF SERVICES RENDERED TO RESEARCH STAFF, 19x2-19x8[a]

Service	19x2	19x3	19x4	19x5	19x6	19x7	19x8
Visits to Library by FRL Staff Members	7,436	9,775	8,359	15,978	11,821	14,347	15,193
Phone calls for service	3,948	4,229	3,613	2,765	2,706	5,084	5,891
Reference Service							
Questions answered	2,492	2,056	1,920	4,245	3,906	4,364	4,617
ILL requested	633	668	844	793	603	752	615
Translations	52	149	134	205	148	155	128
Circulation							
Items checked out	3,012	3,366	2,526	4,148	4,001	5,583	6,788
Items checked in	2,831	3,727	2,897	3,799	3,313	5,215	7,024

a. Includes yearly data for Parent Library which was operated separately until November, 19x8.

DOCUMENT H. FRL LIBRARY ANNUAL REPORT: ACQUISITIONS

The parent library serves 194 technical personnel who in 19x8 produced 226 reports and 42 journal articles relating to their fields of
research. The total overall expenditure per technical man in 19x8
was $275.52. Analysis of the Library purchasing habits of these tech-
nical men during 19x8 showed that 68% of the technical staff participated in ordering material for the library. However, 48% of the purchased items were requested by 6% of the staff. This is typical of
experience in many special libraries, i.e., a relatively small number
of research staff members are the most avid requesters of the literature.

Analysis of recent acquisition figures (Table III) shows that the Library growth rate is approximately 4.5% per year. Of the various
types of materials added to the library (books, photostats, maps,
translations, reports, etc.) the only type to show a steady annual increase over the last five years is the reports. In 19x8 this increase
jumped from its former level of 12-15% in 19x6 and 19x7 to 60%.

TABLE III. ANALYSIS OF LIBRARY ACCESSIONS, 19x4, 19x6, 19x8,
            BY TYPE OF MATERIALS

Type of Material	19x4	19x6	19x8
Books			
New	1,000	855	1,444
Recataloged	364	113	44
Total Books	1,364	968	1,488
Lab Reports			
FRL	137	140	226
Eastern Lab	185	268	265
Operating Dept.[a]			161
Outside Reports	308	371	534
Total Reports	630	779	1,186
Translations			
Oral	53	40	0
Written	81	108	128
Total Translations	134	148	128
Photostats	117	143	208
Microfilm	33	25	5
Maps[a]			255
Journals	4,237	7,450	12,761
TOTAL ACCESSIONS	6,515	9,513	16,031

a. First started accessioning in 19x8.

TABLE IV. ANALYSIS OF LIBRARY ACCESSIONS, 19x4, 19x6, 19x8,
           BY SUBJECT

Classification	19x4		19x6		19x8	
	#	%T	#	%T	#	%T
000-019 Bibliographies	23	3.79	34	3.86	42	3.12
020-029 Library Science	7	1.10	8	.91	12	.89
030-099 General Works	2	.32	8	.91	21	1.56
100-199 Philosophy	0		0		1	.07
300-399 Economics & Law	1	.16	16	1.82	49	3.65
400-499 Linguistics	14	2.21	9	1.02	5	.37
500-509 Pure Science, General	5	.79	7	.79	8	.60
510-519 Mathematics	48	7.57	42	4.77	83	6.18
520-529 Astronomy	6	.95	7	.79	6	.45
530-539 Physics	108	17.03	121	13.72	173	12.87
540-549 Chemistry	61	9.62	67	7.60	94	6.99
550-559 Earth Science	151	23.82	118	13.38	214	15.92
560-569 Paleontology	10	1.58	4	.44	3	.22
570-579 Biological Science	14	2.21	5	.57	21	1.56
580-589 Botany	10	1.57	11	1.25	2	.14
590-599 Zoology	19	3.00	3	.34	0	
600-609 Applied Science, General	1	.16	1	.11	5	.37
620-621 Mechanical Engineering	42	6.62	110	12.48	87	6.47
622 Mining Engineering	27	4.26	35	3.97	83	6.18
623-629 Other Engineering	0		10	1.13	12	.89
630-639 Agriculture	1	.16	0		4	.30
650-659 Business	2	.32	13	1.47	26	1.93
660-669 Chemical Technology	17	2.68	30	3.40	39	2.90
700-799 Arts & Recreation	3	.47	1	.11	2	.15
800-899 Literature	6	.95	0		2	.15
900-999 History (Maps)	0		0		87	6.47

TABLE V. SUMMARY OF LITERATURE EXPENDITURES PER TECHNICAL
          MAN BY VARIOUS SECTIONS, 19x6, 19x7, 19x8

Section	19x8 Average Technical Personnel	19x8 $/Man	19x7 $/Man	19x6 $/Man
Applied Math	9	127.26	61.80	29.72
Production Research Division	68	84.12	119.88	55.18
Production Technical Services	37	36.35	14.05	9.83
Exploration Research Division	51	121.43	128.62	46.00
Exploration Technical Services Division	5	110.58	116.72	42.59
Exploratory Research	2	122.87	66.71	0.00
Administration and General Services	18	31.51	35.67	46.30
Training and Manuals	3	140.18	73.06	0.00
Library	1			
TOTALS	194			

DOCUMENT J. FRL LIBRARY ANNUAL REPORT: BUDGET

TABLE VIA. Operating Expense Budget, 19x4, 19x6, 19x8, 19x9

Expense	19x4	19x6	19x8	19x9
A. Wages and Salaries	68,000	72,000	79,000	86,000
Labor Burden		17,000	18,500	20,000
B. Services and Supplies				
Employee Expense	1,000	2,000	2,500	2,500
Equipment	15,000	5,000	2,000	1,000
Labor	7,000			
Materials and Supplies				
Library Supplies	2,000	2,000	3,500	3,500
Office Supplies		1,500	1,500	2,000
Professional Fees and Services		500	1,000	2,000
Miscellaneous Operating Expense		4,000	4,500	6,000
Publications	18,000	22,000	45,000	48,000
Miscellaneous Direct Expense				500
Rent			2,000	7,000
TOTAL OPERATING EXPENSE	111,000	126,000	159,000	178,500

TABLE VIB. Detail of Expenses

Code	Description of Expense		Amount
1	Wages and Salaries: Professional Librarian (3) Technician (1) Secretary (1) Clerk (3)		85,150
		Salary increases	375
		Overtime	583
	Total		86,000
7	Labor Burden: 23.2% of Gross Wages		20,000
9	Employee Expenses Travel on Company Business and to Professional Training Courses and Library Meetings		2,500
15-1	Materials and Supplies Library Supplies		
	Catalog Cards	500	
	Book Cards	75	
	Book Pockets	125	
	Misc. Binding and Mending Supplies	1,225	
	Card Tabs and Dividers	200	
	Patent Binders	350	
	Interlibrary Loan Forms	250	

TABLE VIB (Cont.)

Code	Description of Expenses	Amount	
	Interlibrary Loan Shipping Boxes	85	
	Princeton Pamphlet Files	300	
	Microfilm Reels and Boxes	200	
	Misc. Circ. Desk Supplies	90	
	Flexowriter Supplies	340	
15-2	Stationery and Office Supplies		
	Misc. Supplies	610	
	Xerox Supplies	1,150	
	Total Supplies		5,500
16	Facilities and Equipment		
	Miscellaneous Equipment		1,000
20	Professional Fees and Services		
	Translators		2,000
29	Miscellaneous Operating Services		
	Binding	4,000	
	Microfilming	500	
	Printing	500	
	Delivery Service	1,000	
	Total Miscellaneous Operating Services		6,000
37	Publications		
	Books	9,450	
	Photostats	2,200	
	Microfilm	500	
	Translations	5,300	
	Periodical Subscriptions	8,075	
	Reprints	3,300	
	Maps	525	
	LC Cards	225	
	Spectra Indexes	1,300	
	Patents	1,600	
	U. of Tulsa Abstracts	15,000	
	Literature Searches	525	
	Total Publications		48,000
39	Miscellaneous Direct Expense		
	Postage and Freight	150	
	Tuition Fees	350	
	Total Miscellaneous Direct Expense		500
50	Rent Expense		
	Xerox 914		7,000
	TOTAL OTHER OPERATING EXPENSE		178,500

TABLE VII. Operating Expense Budget, 19x9, Summary

General Services: Library

Code	Expense Items	Amount
1	Wages and Salaries	86,000
7	Labor Burden	20,000
	Other Operating Expense	
9	Employee Expenses	2,500
15	Materials and Supplies	5,500
16	Facilities and Equipment	1,000
20	Professional Fees and Services	2,000
29	Miscellaneous Operating Services	6,000
	Other Direct Expenses	
37	Publications	48,000
39	Miscellaneous Direct Expense	500
50	Rent Expense	7,000
	Total Other Operating Expense	
	Total Expense Items	178,500

DOCUMENT K. FRL LIBRARY PROFESSIONAL BOOKSHELF

Ashworth, Wilfred., ed. Handbook of Special Librarianship and Information Work. 3rd ed. London: Aslib, 1967.

Burkett, Jack., ed. Trends in Special Librarianship. London:
Archon, 1969.

Cowgill, Logan O., and Robert J. Havlik. "Standards for Special
Libraries," Library Trends 21 (1972), 249-260.

Dougherty, Richard M. Scientific Management of Library Operations.
Metuchen, N.J.: Scarecrow, 1966.

Fisher, Eva L. A Checklist for the Organization, Operation and Evaluation of a Company Library. 2nd ed. N.Y.: SLA, 1966.

SLA. Illinois Chapter. Special Libraries: A Guide for Management.
N.Y.: SLA, 1966.

SLA. Objectives and Standards for Special Libraries. N.Y.: SLA,
1964.

SLA. Profiles of Special Libraries. N.Y.: SLA, 1966.

Strauss, Lucille, Irene M. Shreve, and Alberta L. Brown. Scientific
and Technical Libraries: Their Organization and Administration.
N.Y.: Wiley, 1972.

Woods, Bill M. "The Special Library Concept of Service," American
Libraries 3 (1972), 759-768.

Library Resources and Technical Services, v.4-   , 1960-   .
Special Libraries, v.5-   , 1960-   .

NOTE TO INSTRUCTORS

In each of the six problem units that follow, the objectives are stated in terms of the Industrial Library Model, the Double XYZ Oil Company. Underlying these objectives, of course, are more generalized ones. It is the instructor's responsibility to provide the general cognitive input for learners during the briefing, and to help learners generalize from the specifics of the simulation during the debriefing.

The underlying objectives of each unit might be stated as a series of experiences for learners in the administrative areas of planning services, staffing services, providing materials, providing physical facilities, planning financial support, and record-keeping/communicating. It is understood that appropriate cognitive content accompanies each unit.

Unit I.   Planning Special Library Service

    1. To participate in interactive planning between library staff and users;

    2. To formulate policies inclusive of the results of the planning.

Unit II.   Providing Personnel to Perform Service

    1. To correlate staffing with service policies in terms of job descriptions, number and level of staff;

    2. To carry through all steps in staff procurement (job advertisement, interviewing, hiring, orientation of new staff);

    3. To plan an in-service training program;

    4. To experience selected problems of supervision.

Unit III.   Providing Materials to Implement Plans for Service

    1. To participate in interactive planning for collection development;

    2. To design procedures for implementation of plans.

Unit IV.   Providing Physical Facilities for Service

    1. To participate in interactive planning for space and equipment for service (staff and staff; staff and management);

    2. To plan utilization of new space;

    3. To plan growth adjustments in an existing facility.

Unit V.   Financial Planning for Service

    1. To plan for "start-up," "operating," and "adjustment" financial needs;

    2. To justify requests for financial support.

Unit VI. Recording and Communicating Library Service

    1. To prepare anticipatory and follow-up communications and records related to planning, meetings and policy-making. (Unit I)

    2. To prepare records and communications related to personnel management. (Unit II)

    3. To prepare records and communications related to acquisition and cataloging procedures. (Unit III)

    4. To prepare floor plans for the utilization of new space and for growth adjustment of existing space. (Unit IV)

    5. To prepare documents for "start-up" budgets, "operating" budgets, statements of "adjustment" needs complete with justification. (Unit V)

    6. To design one or more library forms.

    7. To prepare one or more public relations communications.

UNIT I.* PLANNING SPECIAL LIBRARY SERVICE

Unit Objectives:
1. To plan appropriate service to researchers at a location distant from the company's home office library;
2. To incorporate the plan in the policy manual of the Field Research Laboratory Library (FRLL) of the Double XYZ Oil
   Company;
3. To make the agreed-on plans known to the staff of the Field
   Research Laboratory.

Roleplay Activities:
1. Participating (through an assigned role) in a library/user
   planning meeting;
2. Reaching a consensus among library staff members about
   the nature of the service and the policies for providing the
   service.

Communication Activities:
1. Preparation of a call to a meeting;
2. Preparation of minutes of a meeting;
3. Stating the agreed-on policy for remote site service in a
   form suitable for inclusion in the library's staff manual;
4. Preparation of a publicity release to FRL personnel about
   the new plans.

———————

Roleplay 1. A committee composed of Double XYZ Oil Company's
             Field Research Laboratory Library staff members,
             FRL management and researchers is convened to plan
             the information services to be offered Company person-
             nel at the remote location.

Roles:
   FRLL Librarian, who calls the meeting and presides
   FRLL Reference Librarian
   FRL Director
   ECEP Director
   FRL Head, Administration and General Services Division
   FRL researchers, some of whom will be assigned to ECEP
   FRLL Secretary, who will prepare the minutes of the meeting

Roleplay Time:
   45 minutes maximum

Communication:
   Call to the meeting
   Minutes of the meeting

———————

*Note: All unit materials which follow are printed here in compressed
       form to save space. For use with a class, supplementary doc-
       uments and in-basket items would be distributed on separate,
       individual pieces of paper.

<u>Roleplay 2</u>. The FRLL Librarian and Department Heads meet to in-
corporate plans for the remote site information service
in the existing library policy.

Roles:
FRLL Librarian
FRLL Reference Librarian
FRLL Acquisitions Librarian

Roleplay Time:
30 minutes

Communication:
Revised policy statement(s)

<u>In-basket Exercise</u>:

ABC for XYZ
Office of the Editor
Memo

To: FRLL Librarian

From: Editor, <u>ABC for XYZ</u>

Re: Story on plans for information service to ECEP

An upcoming issue of <u>ABC for XYZ</u> will be devoted to informing company personnel about the new project "ECEP." Will you or one of
your staff write an article on the information services that will be
given to project personnel? If you anticipate that the article will exceed 1000 words, please call me for a redefinition of this assignment.
I would appreciate having your article in a week or ten days. If you
need any help, don't hesitate to call me. Many thanks.

<u>Suggested Preparation</u>:

1. Review how to preside at meetings.

2. Review how to take minutes.

3. Review how to write public relations releases.

<u>Suggested Reading</u>:

1. Industrial Library Model

2. <u>Objectives for Special Libraries</u>, ed. Ruth Leonard. (N.Y.:
Special Libraries Association, 1964) 21 p.

3. (As many up-to-date articles about planning special library
service as the leader feels are necessary.)

Supplementary Document

MEMORANDUM

Double XYZ Oil Company
Field Research Laboratory
Administration and General
Services Division

To: Librarian, Field Research Laboratory

From: Head, Administration and General Services

The attached memo tells the story. Although we knew this was in the offing, we didn't realize how soon we'd be expected to implement the operation. And—since this will be the Company's first venture outside of Texas—we're feeling our way.

The Director tells me library services at the site are essential. Let me know as soon as you can what plan you will suggest for providing such services. If I can help, holler.

Attachment
cc: Director, Field Research Laboratory
    Head, Everglades City Exploration Project

. . . .

Attachment

MEMORANDUM

Double XYZ Oil Company
Field Research Laboratory
Director's Office

To: All Divisions and Departments

The Company has decided to lease off-shore exploration rights to a parcel of land in the Gulf of Mexico near Everglades City, Florida. Exploration activities at this site will begin six months from this date. Maximum exploration time is two years. The operation will be known as ECEP (Everglades City Exploration Project).

The exploration task force will consist of a maximum of thirty researchers plus necessary technical support personnel, approximately three to one. Some personnel will be transferred from FRL, Houston, to this project; others will be hired specifically for the project. The Director's Office will have overall responsibility for the selection and assignment of personnel, with implementation and assistance from AGS Division. Transportation and local housing arrangements will be made through AGS.

This memo will authorize division and department heads normally concerned with support of exploration activities to initiate planning. Extra-normal support deemed necessary should be requested directly from the Director's Office. Preliminary budget requests will be due in sixty days. The newly appointed ECEP Project Head and other key personnel are identified in a separate ECEP Personnel Memo.

. . . .

UNIT II. PROVIDING PERSONNEL TO PERFORM SERVICE

Unit Objectives:

1. To determine the nature of the work at the remote site and/ or at the home library generated by the agreed-on service and policy;
2. To determine how many staff members will be needed at the remote site and/or at the home library to perform the added service;
3. To determine the level (i.e., professional, subject specialist, technician, clerical) of the added position(s);
4. To select and hire new staff members;
5. To plan an in-service training program for beginning FRLL clerks;
6. To plan selected details of staff supervision.

Roleplay Activities:

1. Writing new job description(s);
2. Interviewing job applicant(s);
3. Selecting new staff member(s);
4. Conducting in-service training session(s).

Communication Activities:

1. Preparation of application form(s);
2. Preparation of interview form(s);
3. Writing a job advertisement;
4. Preparation of staff evaluation form(s);
5. Amending organization chart to show new staff and/or new library responsibilities and relationships;
6. Preparation of a typical personnel schedule.

———————

Roleplay 1. The FRLL Librarian and Department Heads meet to determine the nature of the added work, number and level of positions needed.

Roles:
FRLL Librarian
FRLL Reference Librarian
FRLL Acquisition Librarian

Roleplay Time:
30 minutes maximum

Communication:
Job description(s), including job qualification(s)

Roleplay 2. In two time segments one or more applicants for the same position are interviewed by the FRLL Librarian and/or by two Department Heads, and these three individuals meet to make their selection.

Roles:
> FRLL Librarian
> FRLL Reference Librarian
> FRLL Acquisition Librarian
> Applicant(s)

Roleplay Time:
> Segment 1. 20-30 minutes per interview
> Segment 2. 20 minutes

Communication:
> Letter of commitment to selected applicant

Roleplay 3. A staff member from technical services initiates a new clerk into the mysteries of one simple clerical routine (e.g., distributing the mail, typing a catalog card, checking in an issue of a periodical, completing a bindery instruction form).

Roles:
> Technical services staff member
> Library clerk

Roleplay Time:
> 30 minutes maximum

Communication:
> Statement of procedure to be followed (as if from FRLL Staff Procedure Manual)
> Any other instructional material needed for the particular training

Note: The student playing the role of the instructor must prepare whatever materials are needed for the roleplay, but some of this material need be in one copy only, not for distribution to the class. Samples of value to the class in debriefing or for personal files should be distributed to all.

In-basket Exercise 1:

> PHONE MESSAGE

> From: Head, Employee Relations, Division of Administration and General Services

> To: FRLL Librarian

> Message: Please select 3-5 important publications for placing an ad for professional librarians. Write appropriate ad(s) and forward to me along with an estimate of cost.

In-basket Exercise 2:

MEMO   Double XYZ Oil Company
                                             Division of Administration
                                                  and General Services

To: FRLL Librarian

From: Head, DAGS

Re: New library responsibility; new position

Your plan for providing information service to ECEP and your
new library position have been authorized as requested. Please
send me an amended organization chart to reflect the changes at
your earliest convenience.

In-basket Exercise 3:

MEMO   Double XYZ Oil Company
                                             Division of Administration
                                                  and General Services
                                             Employee Relations Office

To: All Unit Supervisors

From: Head, Employee Relations

In line with company policy of sampling all supervisory activities, please send me, by next Monday, a copy of your schedule of
assigned personnel duties for the second week of this month.

————————————

Suggested Preparation:

1. Look up how to determine the number and level of staff needed.

2. Review interviewing and staff selection procedures.

3. Study in-service training methods.

4. Review supervisor's responsibility in staff evaluation.

Suggested Reading:

(As many up-to-date articles about personnel management and
form design as the leader feels are necessary.)

————————————

Supplementary Document(s)

Completed application forms should be distributed in advance of
Roleplay 2. If students have been assigned the design of an application form (Communication Activity 1), the leader should add
information about one or more hypothetical applicants and distribute the documents in time for everyone to study them in advance. If the leader does not wish to make the assignment for
the design of such a form, then he should choose or design a
form himself and present the necessary information about the
applicants so that it will be in hand during Roleplay 2.

UNIT III. PROVIDING MATERIALS TO IMPLEMENT PLANS
           FOR SERVICE

Unit Objectives:
1. To develop a plan for collection development to implement
   agreed-on services (both "opening-day collection" and continuing selection);
2. To design procedures for acquisition and cataloging of
   "opening-day collection";
3. To plan a process for the revision of acquisition and catalog
   records, if necessary, to incorporate information about
   materials for added services.

Roleplay Activities:
1. Participating in technical services planning meetings;
2. Reaching a consensus about technical services procedures
   and policies.

Communication Activities:
1. Stating the agreed-on policy for collection development in
   support of services to remote site personnel, as part of the
   FRLL staff manual;
2. Preparation of a PERT chart for assemblying an "opening-
   day collection";
3. Preparation of procedure manual statements for implementation of agreed-on policies.

———————

Roleplay 1. The FRLL Librarian and Department Heads meet to plan
             policies for acquisition of materials for service to
             remote site personnel.

Roles:
  FRLL Librarian
  FRLL Reference Librarian
  FRLL Acquisition Librarian

Roleplay Time:
  20-30 minutes

Communication:
  Revised policy statement(s)

Roleplay 2. The FRLL Acquisition Librarian presents a PERT chart
             for preparation of the ECEP "opening-day collection" to
             the FRLL Librarian and Technical Services Staff. (Rep-
             resentatives of the Division of Administration and Gen-
             eral Services may be invited to this meeting to represent
             the purchasing agent and the personnel officer.)

Roles:
  FRLL Acquisition Librarian
  FRLL Librarian
  FRLL Cataloging Librarian

Roleplay Time:
  15-20 minutes

Communication:
  PERT Chart
  Personnel time involvement chart (optional)

In-basket Exercise 1:

MEMO   FRLL
                                           Office of the Librarian

To: Acquisition Librarian
    Cataloging Librarian

Please submit to me by two weeks from today a statement defining the
changes in acquisition and catalog records, if any, necessitated by developing plans for service to ECEP personnel. If new forms are
needed, please submit drafts.

In-basket Exercise 2:

MEMO   FRLL
                                           Office of the Librarian

To: Reference Librarian

Please critique for me the accompanying material relating to the implementation of service to ECEP personnel. I would appreciate having
your reaction in a week or ten days.

Attachement(s): Suggested changes in acquisition and catalog records

In-basket Exercise 3:

MEMO   FRLL
                                           Office of the Librarian

To: Acquisition Librarian
    Cataloging Librarian

Now that the plans and policies for collection development for service
to ECEP have been completed, please prepare procedure manual
statements for the staff. The new statements should be completed
within three weeks.

Suggested Preparation:

1. Review acquisition procedures, including record-keeping.

2. Learn to prepare a PERT chart.

3. Review formats for procedure manuals.

Suggested Reading:

(As many up-to-date articles about collection building, acquisition procedures, and work-flow in technical services as the leader feels are necessary.)

UNIT IV. PROVIDING PHYSICAL FACILITIES FOR SERVICE

Unit Objectives:

1. To plan to meet the physical needs of the projected service
   at the remote site;
2. Given the external form and dimensions of the space allocated for the expansion of service, to prepare a floor plan;
3. To plan a revision of stack space for the FRL Library which
   will extend the library's capacity by five years;
4. To prepare a specification list for new furniture/equipment
   needed for the expanded service.

Roleplay Activities:

1. Participating in a physical facilities planning meeting;
2. Justifying physical facilities requests to management.

Communication Activities:

1. Writing a program presenting the physical facilities needs of
   the projected service to personnel at the remote ECEP location;
2. Preparation of a floor plan for the space allocated for expansion of service, given the external form and dimension of the
   space;
3. Preparation of a floor plan for the revision of stack space for
   the FRL Library which will extend the library's capacity by
   five years;
4. Preparation of a specification list for new furniture/equip-
   ment needed for the expanded service.

Roleplay 1. The FRLL Director and Department Heads (including
             professional staff allocated to ECEP if such a staffing
             pattern has been decided on) meet to plan the physical
             facilities of the service expansion to personnel at the re-
             mote site.

Roles:
    FRLL Director, who calls the meeting and presides
    FRLL Reference Librarian
    FRLL Acquisition Librarian
    (ECEP Professional Staff, if separate or additional staff have
    been hired)

Roleplay Time:
    45 minutes maximum

Communication:
    Call to meeting, with statement of responsibilities
    Program for revision or addition of space

Roleplay 2. The Director of Administration and General Services Di-
             vision, FRL, asks the Library Director to justify space
             requests. (Option: Justify space requested for ECEP ser-
             vice, or justify space modification for five year growth.)

Roles:
> FRL, Administration and General Services Division Director
> FRLL Director

Roleplay Time:
> 30 minutes maximum

Communication:
> Memo to accompany oral presentation

In-basket Exercises 1-4:

> Note to instructor: The in-basket exercises comprise Communications Activities 1-4. The items presented to students must be "written to order" for each class to preserve the logic of the earlier decisions of each class. The most common decision is to have a full-fledged branch library in Everglades City; the alternate decision sometimes arrived at by a class is to give service from the home library in Houston invoking one or more forms of rapid communication. Occasionally, with the alternate decision, a class will elect to have a service desk and staff member in Everglades City.

> In-basket Exercise 1. This calls for the writing of a facility program for the use of an architect. If the class has chosen to request a branch in Everglades City, they should receive a memo from the FRL Director asking that a program be submitted. Be careful not to promise or imply that a building will be built specifically for the library; merely request the program. If the class has chosen to give service from Houston, have the FRL Director inquire about possible additional space needs and invite a program for a new home office library.

> In-basket Exercise 2. This exercise follows Exercise 1 logically. If the class has decided on a branch library and has written a program for it, choose one of the following options and inform the Library Director in a memo from the Head, Division of Administration and General Services:

> Option 1: "The Company has decided to house all land-based units of ECEP in a trailer complex, ground for which has already been leased. Trailer shells will be 65' x 12' with multiple units used where needed. External specifications have been prepared and submitted to contractors for bids. Prepare a floor plan to fit your internal needs and submit by (date)."

> Option 2: "The Company has decided to house all land-based units of ECEP in a complex of abandoned stores in Everglades City which have already been leased. External renovation is being planned by DAGS. Individual store units are 62' deep and 15', 30' or 45' wide. Choose the size you need and prepare a floor plan to accommodate your equipment. Submit by (date)."

Option 3: If the class has decided to give service from the home
office library, additional space will be needed. The
FRL Director should write a memo to the Library Director, allocating space on a third level of the building,
equivalent to the present second-level space, and request floor plans.

In-basket Exercise 3. If Option 3 in In-basket Exercise 1, has been
assigned, the instructor may wish to omit In-basket Exercise 3
as its objective will have been met. Otherwise, the assignment
to prepare a floor plan for revision of present space can be used
in several ways at the instructor's option.

Option 1: If the class plans for a branch library are unrealistically opulant in terms of space and staff, ''management'' can refuse, but grant an additional amount of
space for the home office library. Realistically, this
has to be a third level, equivalent in size to the existing second level. The in-basket memo should inform
the Library Director of the decision and request a
floor plan showing the changes required in existing
levels as well as requests for the third level. (Caution:
This option requires a lot of rethinking and longer time
should be allotted to complete the assignment than for
Option 2.)

Option 2: Plans for a branch library can be accepted with the
acknowledgment that additional space will be needed
for branch back-up plus normal expansion at the home
office library. Space on the third level of the building,
equivalent to the present second level space, is available. The instructor can allocate as much of this
space as he wishes to the library.

Option 3: Plans for a branch library can be accepted, and the
FRL Director can inform the Library Director that he
is reviewing the laboratory's growth rate and future
space needs and request a proposal to cover anticipated library growth for a given period of time (usually five or ten years). Any conditions or limitations
the instructor wishes to invoke should be included in
the memo.

In-basket Exercise 4. This assignment is to familiarize learners
with the preparation of specification lists. It can be a very
lengthy one if limits are not imposed. The instructor should
weigh the value of the experience against the required investment of time and decide whether to require specifications for (1)
the entire branch library, (2) a portion of the branch library, (3)
the new level of the home office library, or (4) renovation of
some portion of the home office library. If experience with
some special type of library furnishing is desired, the assignment could be limited to (1) microforms collection and service
area, (2) map collection and service area, (3) expansion of stack
area, (3) browsing or periodicals reading area, etc. (Caution: A
collection of catalogs of library and special equipment available

from various sources must be available for consultation by the
learners in order to obtain furniture and equipment specifications.)

Suggested Preparation:

  1. Study how to write a building program.
  2. Study a variety of floor plans with emphasis on "special areas"
     and on adjusting to limited space.

Suggested Reading:

  (As many up-to-date articles about space allocation and planning
  as the leader feels are necessary.)

UNIT V. FINANCIAL PLANNING FOR SERVICE

Unit Objectives:

1. To plan financing of the remote site service, both "start-up" and "first period of operation" budgets;
2. To plan modification of the FRL Library budget to accommodate the projected change in operation;
3. Given the form of the budget documents, to prepare appropriate documents with justifications.

Roleplay Activities:

1. Participating in a financial planning meeting;
2. Justifying financial planning to top management.

Communication Activities:

1. Preparation of a "start-up" budget for the service to the remote site;
2. Preparation of a "first year of operation" budget for the new service;
3. Preparation of a supplementary or a modified budget to accommodate change in the operation of FRLL.

Roleplay 1. The FRLL Director and Department Heads (including professional staff allocated to ECEP if such a staffing pattern has been decided on) meet to plan the start-up budget for the expansion of service to the remote location.

Roles:
FRLL Director, who calls the meeting and presides
FRLL Reference Librarian
FRLL Acquisition Librarian
(ECEP Professional Staff, if separate or additional staff have been hired)

Roleplay Time:
45 minutes maximum

Communication:
Call to meeting, with statement of responsibilities
"Start-up" budget

Roleplay 2. The FRLL Director and Department Heads (including professional staff allocated to ECEP if such a staffing pattern has been decided on) meet to plan the budget for the first year of operation of the service to the remote location.

Roles:
FRLL Director, who calls the meeting and presides
FRLL Reference Librarian
FRLL Acquisition Librarian
(ECEP Professional Staff, if separate or additional staff have been hired)

Roleplay Time:
45 minutes maximum

Communication:
    Call to meeting, with statement of responsibilities
    "First year of operation" budget

Roleplay 3. The FRLL Director and Department Heads (including pro-
            fessional staff allocated to ECEP if such a staffing pattern
            has been decided on) meet to plan the request for addi-
            tional funds for FRLL to accommodate added work neces-
            sitated by ECEP service.

Roles:
    FRLL Director, who calls the meeting and presides
    FRLL Reference Librarian
    FRLL Acquisition Librarian
    (ECEP Professional Staff, if separate or additional staff have
        been hired)

Roleplay Time:
    45 minutes maximum

Communication:
    Call to meeting, with statement of responsibilities
    Request for addition to budget

Note: If the class is large enough, it works well to roleplay 1, 2 and
      3 simultaneously. After the three budgets have been pre-
      pared, they can be critiqued by the entire class. Roleplay 4
      would then be the justification of one of the budgets.

Roleplay 4. The Director of Administration and General Services Di-
            vision, FRL, asks the Library Director to justify a budget
            (any one of the three prepared in Roleplays 1, 2, 3).

Roles:
    FRL, Administration and General Services Division Director
    FRLL Director

Roleplay Time:
    30 minutes maximum

Communication:
    Memo to accompany oral presentation

Supplementary Document for Roleplay 1:

                                    Double XYZ Oil Company
                                    Field Research Laboratory
                                    Office of the Director
MEMO

To: All ECEP planning units

From: Director, ECEP

Re: Start-up Budgets

This is a reminder that your start-up budgets are due (date). These
budgets should include all expense outlay anticipated in advance of the

beginning date of the Project. Capital expenses related to physical facilities should <u>not</u> be included. If you have any questions, please call my office.

. . . .

Supplementary Document for Roleplay 2:

Division of Administration
and General Services

MEMO

To: ECEP Library Services Director

From: Head, DAGS

Re: ECEP first year operating budget

Please submit an operating budget for ECEP library services for one year, in the usual form. The following codes have been assigned:

201 Wages and Salaries
207 Labor Burden
209 Employee Expenses
215 Materials and Supplies
216 Facilities and Equipment
220 Professional Fees and Services
237 Publications
239 Miscellaneous Direct Expense

N.B. The budget you submit should cover expected expenditures during the one-year period following the beginning of the service. It should take into account the fact that the start-up budget is separate and has already been taken care of.

In-basket Exercise 1:

MEMO

Double XYZ Oil Company
Field Research Laboratory
Office of the Director

To: Heads, All Units

From: FRL Director

Re: PPBS budgeting

The Company is considering the use of PPBS, and we need to find out just how realistic it would be to convert from our present system.

Please plan a tentative PPBS budget on a five-year base and submit to me with your comments on how adoption of this system would affect your unit. Is it realistic to ask for this by (date)?

Note to instructor: This can be either a very long, or more reasonable
    assignment depending on the amount of input provided the learners,
    and on whether or not a model of a PPBS budget is available to
    them.

———————

Suggested Preparation:

1. Review library budgeting.

2. Learn about, or review, PPBS.

Suggested Reading:

(Specific articles on PPBS, plus as many up-to-date articles
about budgeting as the leader feels are necessary.)

UNIT VI. RECORDING AND COMMUNICATING LIBRARY SERVICE

Unit Objectives:

1. To prepare a variety of written records and/or communications typically used in special libraries.

Communication Activities:

1. Preparation of anticipatory and follow-up communications and records related to planning, meetings and policy-making (see Unit I);

2. Preparation of records and communications related to personnel management (see Unit II);

3. Preparation of records and communications related to acquisition and cataloging procedures (see Unit III);

4. Preparation of floor plans for the utilization of new space and for growth adjustment of existing space (see Unit IV);

5. Preparation of budget documents (see Unit V);

6. Design of one or more library forms (see Units II, III);

7. Preparation of one or more public relations communications (see Units I, II).

Note to Instructors: The content of this unit can be scheduled separately or as part of the units shown above. In a one quarter course, it seems to be time-saving to schedule the first five units and to integrate the objectives and activities related to records and communication into those units. Related readings or examples of types of forms and communications must be made available to learners at the same time that assignments are made.

A group of additional communications in the form of in-basket items follows. These, along with those presented as potential test items in Chapter 7, Exhibit 9, may be used at the instructor's option as in-class exercise items, assignments, or test items.

Communication 1

DOUBLE XYZ OIL COMPANY
FIELD RESEARCH LABORATORY

Interoffice Memo

Administration and
        General Services
Division Office

To: FRLL Director

From: Head, DAGS

Re: Consultant for Systems Analysis

Your "Proposal for a Systems Analysis of the Library's Acquisition Procedures" made interesting reading and has been the subject of

several conferences between myself and the FRL Director. We agree
that such a study could have important implications for library service
for FRL. Both of us feel, however, that you are already overloaded
with normal work plus the initiation of the ECEP project and that, although you are quite capable, you should not take on the analysis yourself. We prefer that you recommend a consultant to do the job and reserve yourself for liaison with the consultant and general supervision
of the study. Such a recommendation from you will have a high priority in next quarter's planning budget (on which we are now working).

Communication 2

DOUBLE XYZ OIL COMPANY
FIELD RESEARCH LABORATORY LIBRARY

Interoffice Memo

To: Director, FRLL

From: Acquisitions Assistant

Re: Request for a conference

When the position of reference librarian became vacant recently, I
thought you would consider me for the position. Now I hear you have
hired a new person and given her the reference job. After all, I have
worked in this library for five years and I know it well. If I cannot
advance here, I feel I should look for another job. May I have a conference with you about my chances for advancement?

Note to Instructor: It is anticipated that the first response to the
    above would be a look at the employee's file or a mental review of
    her capabilities and work record. The following may be used in
    anticipation of such a request, or you may wait until the request is
    made and then distribute the following:

PERSONNEL SUMMARY OF SUBPROFESSIONAL
ASSISTANT IN ACQUISITIONS, FRLL

Miss_____ joined the company in 19x3 after completing an Associate of Arts degree in secretarial science at a nearby junior college. She had no library science courses, but was taught on the job
certain routine procedures in acquisition work. At the present time
she searches all English-language trade publications, places and
controls routine orders for monographs and serials. She performs
other assigned acquisition duties under the supervision of the Acquisition Librarian. Her work record is good, absenteeism low,
and she has had four annual merit increases and is due a fifth at the
beginning of the fiscal year. She has never requested Company assistance in furthering her education although the Company has a
liberal policy in this regard.

Communication 3

DOUBLE XYZ OIL COMPANY
FIELD RESEARCH LABORATORY

Interoffice Memo	Administration and
	General Services
	Division Office

To: FRLL Director

From: Head, DAGS

Re: Dress for Employees

It has come to my attention that some employees in the library are
dressing in a manner which is detrimental to the Company image. I
request that you take such steps as are necessary to see that employees under your supervision are appropriately dressed for work. Ex-
treme fashions such as see-through blouses and blue jeans are not to
be worn. The Company feels within its rights in establishing limits
and requiring employees to stay within these limits inasmuch as the
appearance of our employees reflects directly on the Company.

P.S. Specifically, I refer to the person who was filing at the card catalog Friday morning at 10:30.

———————————

Communication 4

MEMO

Production Technical
Services
Division Office

To: FRLL Director

From: Head, DPTS

Re: Annual Report

Your latest annual report has just reached my desk. May I point out
to you that by publishing a table such as your "Summary of Literature
Expenditures per Technical Man by Various Sections," you make
DPTS look very bad. It appears that we are uninterested in the library
since we do not spend as much money per man as any other technical
division. I certainly would not want management to draw this conclusion, since it does not happen to be true. Therefore, I am requesting
that you stop including this kind of information in your reports to management. Otherwise—well, we can always improve the look of DPTS's
library use by spending more money, can't we?

———————————

Communication 5

DOUBLE XYZ OIL COMPANY
FIELD RESEARCH LABORATORY

> ECEP Project
> Office of the Director

To: Director, FRLL

From: Director, ECEP

Re: Library Newsletter to ECEP

Your suggestion that the FRLL provide a newsletter service to Project members is an excellent one. In addition to library news, lists of new materials here that could be requested by Project personnel, etc., as outlined in your memo, I would like to have you include general Double XYZ news that comes into FRL in various forms and updates on the research going on here in Houston.

Please submit format specifications, sample newsletter and cost projections for a three-month trial period.

Communication 6

DOUBLE XYZ OIL COMPANY
FIELD RESEARCH LABORATORY

> ECEP Project
> Office of the Director

To: Director, FRLL

From: Director, ECEP

Re: Florida Newspaper Subscriptions

One of the Project members has just suggested to me that the Library might begin to subscribe to Everglades City and Collier County newspapers now so that personnel and wives could begin to "get the feel" of where we will be living and working. I believe you said during your briefing on the area that you could do this if we wanted it.

Please subscribe to five or six papers and send the invoice to me for payment from Project funds.

B.
Governmental Library Simulation
· ·

DOCUMENT A. EXCERPT FROM THE GOVERNMENTAL
ORGANIZATIONAL MANUAL

THE DEPARTMENT OF ECOLOGY

Creation and Authority: The Department of Ecology was established
by the Ecology Act of December 3, 19x0 (14 Stat. 667; U.S.C. 627). The
act, which became effective February 3, 19x1, transferred to and in-
vested in the Secretary of Ecology all the functions, powers and duties
of the Commission on Environment Utilization, the Office of Conserva-
tion of Natural Resources, and the Bureau of Power Resources of the
Department of Interior; the Offices of Biological Interface and Statistical Interpretation of the Department of Agriculture; the Bureau of
Pollution Management, the Board of Minority Enterprises and the
Office of Legal Sanctions of the Department of Health, Education,
and Welfare.

Purpose: The Department was established for the purpose of unify-
ing the administration of activities pertaining to the relationship of
living things to their environment with the intent of raising the standard of living and preserving the resources of the nation.

Organization: The organization plan reflects the concept of an executive team comprised of the Secretary and the Heads of the eight operating agencies. The structure of the Department is shown in the organization chart.

Excerpted from The Government
Organization Manual,
19x1.*

---

*The dating scheme for the simulation communications is a system
that avoids real dates which quickly appear out-of-date. Relative
dates are, however, necessary for internal logic. Therefore, 19x0
was chosen as the year of founding the Department of Ecology and
its Library; 19x1 was the first year of existence. At the time of the
action DOE is in 19x5, the fifth year of existence. March 20 is a
Wednesday.

DOCUMENT B. MEMORANDUM TO THE DIRECTOR

DEPARTMENT OF ECOLOGY

Memorandum
April 5, 19x5

To: Assistant Secretary for Administration

From: Director, DOE Library

Re: Transfer of the OAES Library to the DOE Library

In accordance with your memo of March 28, 19x5, I have visited the
OAES Library to acquaint myself with the situation and to prepare for
the transfer. My report to you follows.

When the Department of Ecology was established in 19x0 there was a
unit in the Department of Space which logically should have been
placed in DOE along with the units from Agriculture, Interior and
HEW. DOS did not want to lose the unit and was able to prevent its
transfer. Now, in 19x5, the transfer is finally to take place, though
reluctantly from the standpoint of the personnel of the unit and its
library.

The Office of Aerial Environmental Surveys is the office in question;
its library must now be merged with the DOE Library. The OAES Library consists primarily of aerial photographs and aerial maps—
50,000 of them—plus about 3,000 books and 25 journal subscriptions.
The OAES Library is growing at the rate of 20-22,000 photographs and
maps per year, and approximately 300 books per year. Space must be
found for these materials in the DOE Library.

The OAES Library is under the direction of a geographer (MS level)
who "picked up" a little library science as a student assistant during
his graduate school days. The second in command has had BS training in geography, cartography and biology, but no library science. Between them they have devised a classification scheme for arranging
the maps and photographs. This scheme serves also as an index for
purposes of information retrieval. Three clerks round out the personnel complement of the Library. Two of these clerks spend their entire time retrieving specific maps and photos on request and refiling
them after use. The third clerk is responsible for circulation and reprography. These workers must be incorporated into the DOE Library staff.

The major services of the OAES Library are the archival management
of the primary materials, information retrieval in cooperation with
the Office's researchers, and a small amount of ready reference work.
Typically, a researcher in OAES will ask whether the files contain a
certain area map. If not, he will want the available photographs from
which to construct a map. A copy of the map is then added to the
OAES Library files. If no photographs are available, they are ordered
from other staff members. OAES staff are busy continuously with
aerial mapping. All photographs and maps related to this activity are
fed into the Library files. Fast entry of materials into the system is
imperative, as is fast retrieval. No automation of the system has been
attempted. The classification scheme is partially satisfactory for retrieval purposes; for the rest, everyone depends on the personal

knowledge of the head librarian and his assistant, both of whom have been with the OAES Library since its beginning.

The OAES Library issues a daily list of maps and photographs added to the files. This list is distributed to all personnel of the Office by 2 p.m. each day, and serves as the major current awareness service of the Office. There is no current awareness service for other library materials.

There is no real organization for the books and journals. Books are listed in a catalog by author and title short forms, the citation form being an in-house one. Books are arranged on the shelves in broad subject categories; journals are arranged by titles. Journal subscriptions are controlled by a Cardex system. Head librarian and assistant do this work as it comes to hand; there is no specific break-down of tasks or responsibilities. Both spend most of their time working with the maps and photographs, assisting researchers, and preparing the daily CA bulletin. All of these materials must be integrated into the DOE Library (note especially the instant cataloging backlog we inherit).

All of the services to researchers must be continued when the OAES Library is merged with the DOE Library. Experience shows that when a unit such as OAES is merged with a larger agency with a more sophisticated library, the new group of researchers learn of additional services which would benefit them. It should be anticipated, therefore, that the OAES personnel will create an additional workload in relation to DOE Library services as well as a continuance of the workload the OAES Library has experienced. This additional service workload will have to be evaluated in terms of both personnel and materials needed.

Attachment: OAES Library Equipment List

AERIAL ENVIRONMENTAL SURVEY LIBRARY

Equipment List

Item	Description	Amount
Map Cases	Steel; 5-drawer; stackable 48'' x 75'' x 16''	4
	Wood; 5-drawer; stackable 24'' x 37'' x 16''	16
Book Stacks	Steel; 36'' x 72'' x 12'': 7 shelves In use New	24 2
Magazine Rack	Wood; 42'' x 37'' x 17''	1
Card Catalog	Wood; 60'' x 41'' x 18''	1
Desks	Steel; 60'' x 30''	5
Chairs	Steel; upholstered; Stenographic type Wood; for reader's use	5 8

Item	Description	Amount
Tables	Wood; 36'' x 72''	2
Typewriters	Underwood Standard: to be discarded	1
	Underwood Standard: good condition	1
	Remington Standard: good condition	1

DOCUMENT C-1. DEPARTMENT OF ECOLOGY ORGANIZATION CHART: STAFF

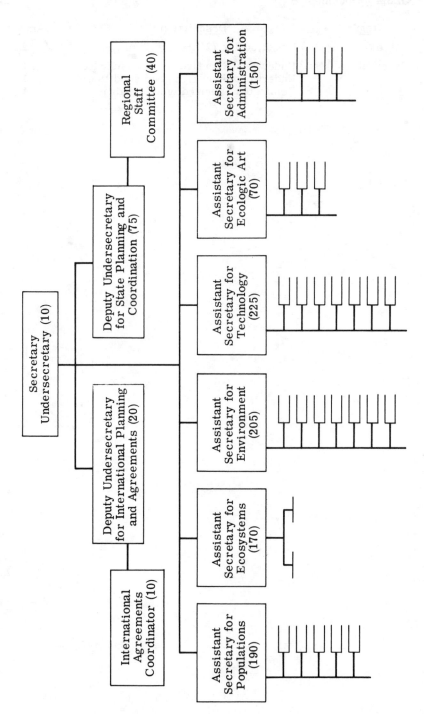

DOCUMENT C-2. DEPARTMENT OF ECOLOGY ORGANIZATION
CHART: BUREAU OF ADMINISTRATION

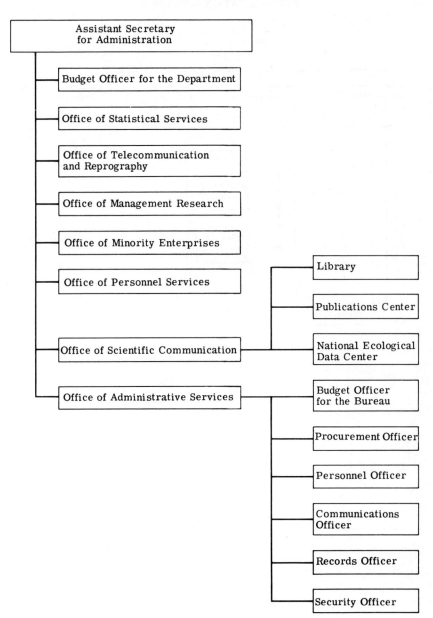

DOCUMENT C-3. DEPARTMENT OF ECOLOGY ORGANIZATION
CHART: OFFICE OF SCIENTIFIC
COMMUNICATION LIBRARY

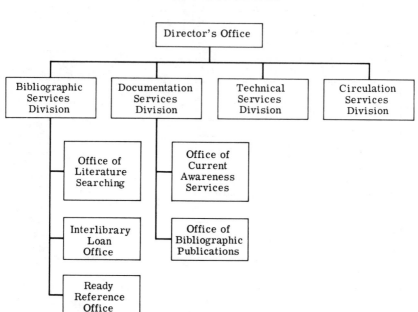

DOCUMENT C-4. DEPARTMENT OF ECOLOGY STAFFING
PATTERN: LIBRARY

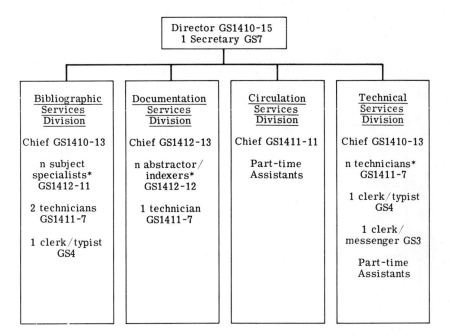

Director GS1410-15
1 Secretary GS7

Bibliographic Services Division	Documentation Services Division	Circulation Services Division	Technical Services Division
Chief GS1410-13	Chief GS1412-13	Chief GS1411-11	Chief GS1410-13
n subject specialists* GS1412-11	n abstractor/ indexers* GS1412-12	Part-time Assistants	n technicians* GS1411-7
2 technicians GS1411-7	1 technician GS1411-7		1 clerk/typist GS4
1 clerk/typist GS4			1 clerk/ messenger GS3
			Part-time Assistants

Note: Several positions in the DOE Library are represented in the
Governmental Library Simulation by one incumbent, whereas in
a real library of this size there would be several individuals at
the same level. This modification is made to reduce the number
of individuals needed for role-playing. The positions are
marked with an asterisk; the number is indicated by n.

DOCUMENT D. DEPARTMENT OF ECOLOGY LIBRARY FLOOR PLAN

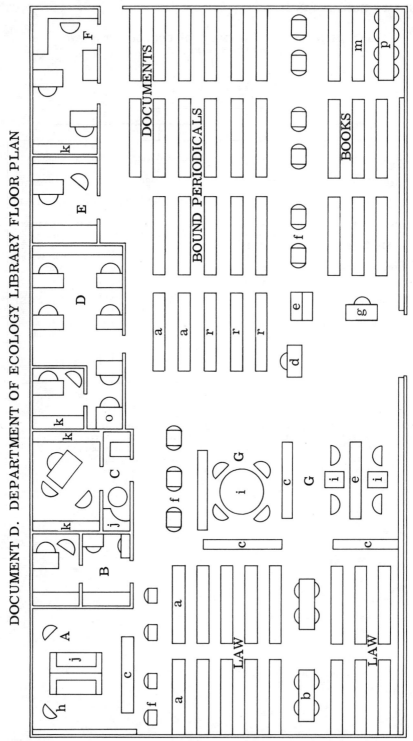

KEY TO THE FLOOR PLAN

A   Law Reading Room
B   Office of Documentation Services
C   Office of the Director of the Library
D   Office of Bibliographic Services
E   Office of Acquisitions
F   Mail Room
G   Reading Area

a   Ranges of Bound Periodicals and Books
b   Study Tables
c   Current Periodicals—Counter High

d   Ready Reference Librarian
e   Card Catalog
f   Study Carrels
g   Circulation Desk
h   Chair
i   Table
j   Sofa
k   Storage
m   Microform Storage
o   Teletypewriters
p   Reader–Printers
r   Reference Books

DOCUMENT E. DEPARTMENT OF ECOLOGY LIBRARY BUDGET
(Excerpt)

	Current Fiscal Year	Projections	
	19x5	19x6	19x7
STAFF:			
Personnel (See Attachment)	181,540	201,509	225,690
Personnel Benefits[a]	19,970	22,167	24,827
Travel[b]	1,800	1,888	1,995
Training Expenses[c]	2,000	2,220	2,486
CAPITAL EXPENSES:			
Electric Typewriter	450	550	560
Micro Reader-Printer	400	440	493
Vertical File	200	222	249
MATERIALS:			
Books (app. 4000)	52,000	57,720	64,646
Periodicals (app. 3600)	64,500	71,595	80,186
Serials (app. 2000)	170,683	189,458	212,193
Microforms (app. 5000)	20,000	22,200	24,864
Miscellaneous	3,000	3,330	3,730
SUPPLIES:[d]	2,250	2,498	2,798
COMMUNICATIONS:[e]	2,760	3,064	3,432

Note: There is no pretense that this is a realistic budget for a departmental library; it is, in fact, closer to the budget for a library
somewhat lower in the organizational structure.

a. Personnel Benefits are calculated as 11 percent of salaries.
b. Allowance is made for one-third of the professional staff to attend one national
meeting of their professional association yearly, with an extra amount to be shared
among the remaining professional staff to attend local meetings. The allowance includes $200 travel plus $25 per day for a maximum of four days per national meeting. $1/3 \times 6 [\$200 + 4(25)] = 2(300) = \$600$, plus $200 for the local meetings. Since
only actual expenses are paid, in some years more staff will be able to attend national meetings, in other years, fewer, depending on distance and length of meeting.
Required field trips require approximately $1000 per year.
c. Allowance is made for one-half of the staff to take one three-semester hour course
(or equivalent) per year, at the rate of $75 per semester hour course (or equiva-
lent) per year, at the rate of $75 per semester hour plus $25 for books. $1/2 \times 15$
$[(75 \times 3) + 25] = 8 (225 + 25) = \$2000$.
d. Allowance is made at the rate of $150 per staff member. $15 \times 150 = \$2250$.
e. Allowance is made for: (a) one phone for each staff member ($15 \times 6 = 90$) per month
($90 \times 12 = \$1080$) plus long distance ($3 \times 10$ per day$= 30 \times 225 = \$6750$); (b) 1500 letters
per quarter ($1500 \times 4 = 6000 \times .08$ per letter$= \$480$); (c) ILL mailing, $500; (d) 2 teletype terminals, $65 per terminal per month rental, plus $50 per machine per
month for messages. $2 [(65 \times 12) + (50 \times 12)] = 2(780 + 600) = 2(1380) = \$2760$.

DOCUMENT E ATTACHMENT

DOE LIBRARY BUDGET: PERSONNEL DETAIL
(Excluding Part-time Assistants)

Positions	Series	GS Level	Range, Steps 1-10a			Present Salary
Chief Librarian	1410	15	22,885-29,752			23,000
Secretary		7	8,098-10,525			8,341
Chief, Bib. Ser. Div.	1410	13	16,760-21,791			16,760
Subject Specialists	1412	11	11,905-15,478	Position A		11,905
				Position B		12,362
Technicians	1411	7	8,098-10,528	Position A		8,098
				Position B		8,584
Clerk-typist		4	5,853- 7,608			5,853
Chief, Doc. Ser. Div.	1412	12	14,192-18,449			15,892
Technician	1412	7	8,098-10,528			9,313
Subject Specialist	1412	12	14,192-18,449			14,192
Chief, Cir. Ser. Div.	1411	11	11,905-15,478			13,276
Chief, Acq. Ser. Div.	1410	12	14,192-18,449			14,617
Technician	1411	7	8,098-10,528			8,098
Clerk		4	5,853- 7,608			6,038
Messenger		3	5,212- 6,778			5,212
						181,540

a. As of Summer 1970.

DOCUMENT F. DEPARTMENT OF ECOLOGY AGENCY MANUAL

Section R. Library Facilities and Services

A. Scope and Objectives

The mission of the DOE Library is to support agency programs
through a variety of information services; to fulfill the bibliographically related information requirements of Department of Ecology
personnel; to develop and maintain a comprehensive ecology management library and to disseminate ecology management information to
the agency staff members, to Federal officers, to the academic community and to scholars and researchers engaged in serious inquiry.
The Library also serves as information advisor to the state and international agencies with which DOE maintains liaison.

B. Organization and Responsibility for Library Services

1. It is the policy of the Department of Ecology to have one central
library which shall provide all library needs and services required by Agency personnel in Washington. Field services are
supplied by transmission of documents and by telecommunica-
tion to field libraries and personnel.

2. The DOE librarian is responsible to the Assistant Secretary for
Administration for:

a. Identifying the bibliographically related information requirements of the Agency on a continuing basis; analyzing
and organizing these requirements into a rational system;
and developing and implementing policies and procedures
for the selection, organization and utilization of the resources necessary to fulfill these requirements.

b. Organizing and directing the library for efficient workload
management, staffing it with highly qualified personnel and
providing necessary training, planning, and budgeting for
the most effective utilization of available resources, and
for promoting the full utilization of library services and
collections, and providing informative reports on library
operations to management.

c. Developing a comprehensive collection of materials in
ecology management, supplemented by utilitarian collections in law and other fields related to Agency programs.

d. Purchasing or otherwise acquiring all books, periodicals
and other materials added to the library collections or
needed for reference use within the guidelines specified
in Section E (below).

e. Providing library services such as answering reference
and management questions, supplying current awareness
services, preparing bibliographies, abstracts, state-of-
the-art and other special literature reviews, lending materials, providing interlibrary loan services and routing
periodicals.

    f. Conducting legal and legislative research, including prep-
aration of digests of the <u>Congressional Record,</u> analytics
of appropriation hearings and Congressional Hearings.

    g. Publishing literature reviews, digests, abstracts, and bib-
liographies in areas relating to ecology, including <u>Ecology
Literature</u> (monthly); <u>Ecology Literature Index</u> (annually);
<u>Ecology Bibliography Series</u> (periodically).

    h. Maintaining a collection of all Department of Ecology pub-
lications, both current and historical, for permanent reference purposes.

    i. Systematically providing information about the Library's
resources, services and programs to encourage maximum
utilization of the Library by its various publics through
such media as a library handbook, flyers, library tours
and oral presentations, reports and articles; maintaining
contacts with professional organizations, library schools,
and other librarians on matters pertaining to ecology.

    j. Coordinating field library services.

3. Bureau directors, staff officials and regional directors are responsible for:

    a. Informing the librarian of their library needs. When a
project is expected to involve extensive bibliographic or
documentary services on the part of the Library, the
earliest possible advance notice should be given to the
librarian.

    b. Certifying to their need for periodicals necessary to their
work.

    c. Cooperating with the librarian to insure that all Library
materials are fully utilized in ecology programs.

    d. Reviewing the availability and use of bureau publications
when requested to do so by the librarian, and supplying an
appropriate number of copies for the Library collection.

C. <u>Library Services and Facilities</u>

1. <u>Library Facilities</u>. The Library is located on the eighth floor
of the Department of Ecology Building. Hours are from 8:15
a.m. to 4:45 p.m. Monday through Friday. All stacks are open;
a few carrels are available for long-term use. Typewriters
may be used in the library; microfilm readers and reader-
printers are available. Copying equipment is available on the
eighth floor for the convenience of authorized personnel.

2. <u>Availability of Services</u>.

    a. All Library services are available to Agency personnel.
Requests may be made by telephone, teletype, or memorandum, or on Form 768.

    b. Researchers working in the field of ecology may use the
Library facilities and secure reference assistance. Borrowing privileges are not available except through interlibrary loan.

3. <u>Reader Assistance and Referral Service.</u> Staff members will
   explain the arrangement and resources of the Library generally, assist readers in selecting and locating publications to
   meet a particular need, and explain the use of the card catalog,
   <u>Ecology Literature Index</u>, and other specialized reference tools.
   They may also refer the patron to related resources within the
   Agency or in the Washington area, specialized subject matter
   experts in the field, or other researchers known to be working
   in the same subject area.

4. <u>Reference and Research Assistance.</u> The Library staff will
   answer reference questions requiring factual information in
   response to specific inquiries; conduct literature searches in
   required areas. Staff members do not provide interpretations
   of laws, regulations or involved research; instead, they refer
   the question to an appropriate specialist.

5. <u>Current Awareness Services.</u> The Library staff identifies, to
   the fullest extent possible, the specialized interests of the
   Agency personnel, analyzes them in relation to Library resources and services, and systematically tries to keep staff
   members abreast of newer materials in their fields through its
   publications. The Library cooperates with a commercial current awareness service in ecology by providing and interpret-
   ing Agency publications in advance of publication. In return,
   the Library receives copies of the service for distribution and
   for retention.

6. <u>Bibliographic Services.</u> Upon request of Agency personnel, the
   Library will compile a bibliography on any subject of interest
   to the Agency, using its own resources and those of other libraries, as necessary.

7. <u>Loan Services.</u> All materials in the Library, except reference,
   archival and microform, may be borrowed by Agency employees.
   Requests and renewals may be made either in person or by telephone. The loan period varies with the type of materials and is
   indicated on the attached circulation slip. Publications should
   not be transferred to another borrower without notifying the Library. All materials should be returned to the Library prior
   to extended leave or separation. If Library materials are still
   charged to an employee when his property clearance is received
   in the Library, appropriate measures will be taken through the
   Budget and Finance Division to secure reimbursement.

8. <u>Interlibrary Loan Services.</u> Upon request, the Library will borrow, <u>for official use</u>, items, including films, from other government libraries or other local sources. Since government libraries limit their interlibrary loan privileges exclusively to materials needed in the conduct of official business, the Library
   staff cannot accept other types of requests. Publications borrowed from other libraries may be retained only for the loan
   period designated by the lending library. A uniform agreement
   exists among Federal libraries whereby all interlibrary materials shall be kept available for immediate return if the need
   should arise. In order to retain our borrowing privileges, the
   Library is obligated to insist that this agreement be honored by
   borrowers.

9. Periodical Routing. The Library routes major periodicals to Agency personnel. Employees who wish this service make their selections from the Subject List of Periodicals, Form 257, and forward the request to the Library Circulation Division.

10. Legislative Service. The staff will prepare digests, on request, of information in subject areas of interest to Agency personnel that are recorded in the Congressional Record, including both floor and committee action on bills, statements on the floor, public laws signed, hearings scheduled, etc. The Library compiles legislative histories on all new ecology legislation on a current basis.

The Library is responsible for distributing to Agency personnel all bills, reports, documents, hearings and public laws needed in their work. Requests may be made for individual items as the need arises. Copies for extensive distribution should be ordered directly by the appropriate bureau.

D. The Collections

1. Ecological Management. The Library secures and retains permanently all books, pamphlets, brochures, serials, documents, unpublished papers, periodicals, and microforms which relate to ecological management. Selected commercial publications are also maintained currently. Major materials on ecology generally, and state, local and foreign publications are also secured and retained on a selective basis according to prescribed acquisitions policy.

2. Social and Physical Sciences. The Library selects major materials in the social and physical sciences, including political science, economics, statistics, biology, oceanography, meteorology, sociology and demographic studies. Only latest editions are kept, and generally the collection is weeded more stringently than the ecology management materials. Retention is determined by use.

3. Ready Reference Collection. Major bibliographic, biographical, statistical and other reference materials are selected for the Library and retained primarily for current use only. Bibliographic and other tools which have cumulative value may be retained permanently.

4. Law Collection. This collection consists of the National Reporter System, the Code of Federal Regulations, citators such as American Digest, Federal Digest, Shepard's, encyclopedic books and other legal research tools. This collection is retrospective for twenty years or less, as current demand indicates.

5. Legislative Reference Collection. This collection contains selected copies of bills, reports, hearings, documents, and public laws from the 70th to the current Congress. In addition, the Library has compiled legislative histories on all major ecology laws. Basic research tools are also included.

6. Periodical Collection. The Library subscribes to or receives free approximately 2000 periodicals in fields of interest to the Department. A Subject List of Periodicals is maintained currently, and a master list of all titles held, both current and non-

current, is available for reference use. The most recent issues
of periodicals are shelved near the entrance to the Library so
that users may see them before they are circulated. Periodicals
received by the Library are retained for five years. Those
which are to be retained permanently are kept in microform.

7. Archives Collection. This collection consists of one copy of
every Department of Ecology publication, both historical and
current, including all editions. All major releases of the
Agency are also available.

E. Development and Maintenance of Collections

1. Acquisition and Retention Policy. The Library develops and
revises as necessary a written acquisitions policy which provides general guidelines for the addition and retention of materials in the collections. The Library solicits recommendations
and suggestions from Department personnel for appropriate
items to be added to the collection, and for changes in policy.

2. Procurement Policy for Library Collections. The Library pur-
chases or secures free all materials to be added to the Library
collections; evaluates all gifts, and determines whether they
should be permanently retained; arranges all exchanges, including the management of all materials deposited with it for exchange; places Agency memberships in professional organizations approved by the Assistant Secretary for Administration;
places subscriptions to journals requested by Department personnel for routing.

3. Procurement Policy for Bureaus and Staff Officers. Authorized
personnel, through their administrative officers, may request
the librarian to secure publications for reference use in their
offices. Requisition form 719 should be used.

a. The librarion will review the request, determine whether
loan copies are already available, and if not, whether
this is an item which the Library would normally add to
its collection according to approved acquisition policy,
or whether other Department members might also need it.

b. Items to be added to the collection will be ordered and
paid for from Library funds, cataloged, and sent to the
requesting office through the administrative officer on a
long-term loan not to exceed one year.

c. All offices having long-term loans will be inventoried once
a year by the librarian with the assistance of the administrative officer. All items will be verified according to
location, responsible borrower, and continuing need.

d. Requested items which the librarian determines do not
meet library acquisition criteria will be ordered by the
Library out of bureau funds as a service. They will not
be cataloged, but a record card will be made for each.
Items will be stamped "For Permanent Retention" and
sent to the requesting office through the administrative
officer of the bureau, who will be solely responsible for
them.

e. The Library does <u>not</u> order the following classes of materials: (1) multiple copies of publications intended as handouts for informational or training purposes; (2) Government publications, such as <u>The Congressional Directory</u> or the <u>U.S. Government Organization Manual</u> (desk copies); (3) dictionaries, atlases and similar tools needed by various offices and purchased in quantities by the Office of Administrative Services; (4) office copies of newspapers.

4. <u>Organization of the Collection.</u> All books and near-books are classified and cataloged according to the Library of Congress classification scheme by a contracting agency under the supervision of the Library. Other materials are organized in a manner suitable to their format and expected usage and in such a way as to be conducive of their maximum utilization.

F. Ecology Publications Program

1. <u>Ecology Literature.</u> The Library compiles monthly a selected list of new books, pamphlets, periodical articles, microfilms, government documents and other materials received in the Library. These are classified by subject and annotated as necessary. Internal distribution is made through the Publications Center on the basis of individual requests. Other Federal agencies may receive up to ten copies free on request to the Library. Others desiring to receive the publication may purchase it on annual subscription from the Superintendent of Documents. DOE personnel who wish to borrow items listed may request them by telephone, teletype, or memo, citing the item number only.

2. <u>Ecology Literature Index.</u> A topical index to all materials listed in <u>Ecology Literature</u> is published quarterly, with an annual cumulation, and distributed in the same manner as the monthly list. The index is available in the Library on a current basis in printout form. A thesaurus of descriptors used in indexing is available in the Library.

3. <u>Ecology Bibliography Series.</u> The Library compiles and updates on a regular schedule a series of annotated bibliographies on special aspects of ecology and ecology management. All bibliographies are reviewed by subject specialists before publication. A current list of bibliographies available will be supplied on request. Copies of individual bibliographies are available to Department staff on request; others may purchase copies from the Superintendent of Documents.

4. <u>Bibliography of Department of Ecology Publications.</u> The Library publishes annually, for internal use, a complete list of publications issued by the various bureaus and staff offices during the year. A subject index is included. The index for the current year may be used, pre-publication, in the Library. Information compiled for this bibliography is supplied to both government and commercial indexing agencies, and is therefore not distributed to the general public by the Library.

5. Selected Ecology Publications of Federal Agencies. The Library issues quarterly for distribution to DOE personnel a selected list of ecology publications received on exchange from various Federal agencies, with a single index. Individuals may secure retention copies of publications listed by applying to the issuing agency; loan copies are available from the Library. DOE personnel who wish to borrow items from the list may request them by telephone, teletype or memo, citing item number only.

DOCUMENT G. DEPARTMENT OF ECOLOGY LIBRARY ANNUAL
REPORT 19x4

Summary of Personnel

POSITIONS AUTHORIZED

ADMINISTRATION:

Director (GS15): Performs over-all administration of library;
coordinates liaison with field units of DOE.

Secretary (GS7): Performs routine secretarial duties for Director.

BIBLIOGRAPHIC SERVICES DIVISION:

Chief (GS13): Directs the provision of personal reference and
bibliographic services; administers the Division.

Subject Specialists (GS11): Two positions; conduct literature
searches and prepare bibliographies on demand.

Technicians (GS7): Position 1, Reference Technician, answers
non-complex questions, aids users in locating materials in library and in using bibliographic tools.
Position 2, Interlibrary Loan Technician, locates materials in
other libraries and performs routines of borrowing.

Clerk/Typist (GS4): Performs general clerical and typing duties for the Division.

DOCUMENTATION SERVICES DIVISION:

Chief (GS12): Directs the computer managed dissemination and
bibliographic services; administers the Division.

Abstractor/Indexers (GS12): Two positions; abstract periodical
articles, code bibliographic information for computer.

Technician (GS7): Performs routine coding and computer liaison.

CIRCULATION SERVICES DIVISION:

Chief (GS11): Administers the Division; trains part-time assistants; directs lending and dissemination activities.

Part-time Assistants: Perform Division routines under direction.

ACQUISITION SERVICES DIVISION:

Chief (GS12): Administers the Division; directs the acquisition
of materials; supervises the contracts for cataloging and preparation of materials.

Technician (GS7): Performs routine duties under direction.

Clerk/Typist (GS4): Performs clerical duties for the Division.

Clerk/Messenger (GS3): Performs routine duties of mail clerk,
stock clerk, and messenger, under direction.

PROBLEMS

1. Several positions have higher requirements than their ratings indicate. These positions are hard to fill, and to keep filled, because of the technical level of the work performed in relation to

salaries paid. Employees quickly become dissatisfied when they
compare their responsibilities with those of others who have similar or even higher ratings.

The following positions fall within this category:
Chief, Circulation Services Division
Chief, Documentation Services Division
Reference Technician, Bibliographic Services Division
Technician, Documentation Services Division

2. In some cases advancement to a higher grade has been denied, and,
as a result, valuable employees have left to take positions where
they could receive promotions more rapidly. Not only does the Department lose the benefits of their experience, but the long training period necessary with each new employee causes an undue burden on the entire library staff. At times, this situation causes inconvenience to library users.

3. In addition to the established positions described above, several
new positions are needed. DOE field offices have multiplied in the
last two years more rapidly than was anticipated, and the resulting
branch library work has therefore increased exponentially. Demands on the DOE Library, as the responsible back-up library for
all field agencies, have thus increased proportionately, frequently
causing severe limitations in the library's ability to carry out
planned services. Two new positions are needed to meet this
added work load in the immediate future, and realistic long-range
planning should begin.

Liaison Librarian (GS12): Full-time, duties to include coordination of interlibrary work between DOE Library and branch
libraries, and the training of semiprofessional personnel in
the branch libraries in order to relieve DOE Library of some
of the overload.

Clerk/Typist (GS4): Full-time, duties to include many clerical
tasks now performed by Chief, Circulation Services Division,
and by part-time assistants. A full-time trained person in this
position would free the Chief, CSD, to plan updating of the circulation system to meet more efficiently the increased requests
from the branches.

DOCUMENT H. DEPARTMENT OF ECOLOGY LIBRARY ANNUAL
              REPORT 19x4

Statistical Abstract

TABLE I. BIBLIOGRAPHIC SERVICES

A. Reader Service Transactions

Type of Transaction	19x4				19x3			
	In-House	Other Federal Agencies	Liaison Agencies	TOTAL	In-House	Other Federal Agencies	Liaison Agencies	TOTAL
1. Ready Reference Question	7,750	1,275	1,275	10,300	6,970	1,150	1,147	9,267
2. Reader Assistance	2,550	125	125	2,800	2,240	112	115	2,467
3. Reader Referral	2,550	125	125	2,800	2,240	110	112	2,462
4. Literature Search	425	10	25	460	385	8	22	415
5. Bibliography Compiled	65	10	15	90	60	7	13	80
6. State-of-the-Art Review Compiled	115	0	10	125	103	1	8	112
7. Legislative Digest	80	0	0	80	72	0	0	72
8. Legislative History	15	0	0	15	13	0	0	13
Total Transactions	13,550	1,545	1,575	16,670	12,083	1,388	1,417	14,888

A. Reader Service Transactions (Continued)

Type of Transaction	19x2				19x1			
	In-House	Other Federal Agencies	Liaison Agencies	TOTAL	In-House	Other Federal Agencies	Liaison Agencies	TOTAL
1. Ready Reference Question	5,995	1,079	1,034	8,108	5,636	1,014	998	7,647
2. Reader Assistance	1,945	96	95	2,136	1,820	87	82	1,989
3. Reader Referral	1,926	96	90	2,112	1,804	85	98	1,987
4. Literature Search	343	7	10	360	322	4	8	334
5. Bibliography Compiled	51	7	6	64	20	5	4	29
6. State-of-the-Art Review Compiled	88	0	7	95	35	0	0	35
7. Legislative Digest	62	0	0	62	25	0	0	25
8. Legislative History	11	0	0	11	5	0	0	5
Total Transactions	10,421	1,285	1,242	12,948	9,666	1,195	1,190	12,051

TABLE I (Cont.)

B. Housekeeping Transactions

Type of Transaction	19x4	19x3	19x2	19x1
1. Items selected for purchase[a]	5,550	6,500	4,940	6,655
2. Items searched, but not acquired[b]	2,015	1,780	1,450	725
3. Items weeded[c]	4,000	1,425	1,250	100
TOTAL	11,565	9,705	7,640	7,480

a. Represents bibliographic work incidental to the internal selection of library materials. Bibliographic verification required for purchase requests made by library users is included under Acquisition Services, Table IV.
b. Represents bibliographic work incidental to searching, but not included under Item 1, above, or Table IV, because no purchase resulted.
c. Represents bibliographic work incidental to maintenance of internal records for material withdrawn from the collection.

TABLE II. DOCUMENTATION SERVICES

A. Reader Service Transactions

Type of Transaction	19x4	19x3	19x2	19x1
1. Current awareness profiles negotiated	360	310	285	235
2. Current awareness printed-out	5,400	4,650	3,410	1,410
3. Demand bibliography printed-out	75	40	0	0
TOTAL	5,835	5,000	3,695	1,645

B. Publication Services

Publication	Number of Issues Prepared			
	19x4	19x3	19x2	19x1
1. Ecology Literature	12	12	12	6
2. Ecology Literature Index	4	4	4	2
3. Selected Ecology Publications of Federal Agencies	4	4	4	0
4. Bibliography of DOE Publications	1	1	1	1
5. Ecology Literature Thesaurus	1	1	1	1
6. Subject List of Periodicals	1	1	1	1
7. Ecology Bibliography Series	12	6	8	2
TOTAL	35	29	31	13

TABLE III. CIRCULATION SERVICES

A. Loan Transactions

Type of Transaction	Books and Pamphlets	Journal Issues	Docu- ments
1. DOE Loans			
In-House	19,125	3,825	2,550
Teletype	1,000	125	380
2. Interlibrary Loans			
Outgoing	1,275	0	275
Incoming	1,280	50	130
TOTAL	22,680	4,000	3,335

B. Reprography Transactions

Type of Transaction	Books and Pamphlets	Journal Issues	Docu- ments
1. Microform print-out	1,000	300	1,050
2. Hard copy photocopy[a]	2,000	500	700
TOTAL	3,000	800	1,750

C. Library Publications Circulated[b]

Type of Transaction	19x4	19x3	19x2	19x1
1. Library Periodicals Routed	1,275	1,055	900	850
2. Ecology Bibliographic Services Distributed	1,550	1,275	1,125	60
TOTAL	2,825	2,330	2,025	910

a. For Field Agency and Liaison Agency personnel only. Personnel in the Ecology Building photocopy their own in the Reprography Center on the third floor.
b. Other Library publications are distributed by the Office of Personnel Services.

TABLE IV. ACQUISITION SERVICES

A. Materials Acquired

Type of Material	19x4	19x3	19x2	19x1
1. Books	4,000	4,000	3,500	3,500
2. Journals (Titles)	2,000	1,750	1,250	1,000
3. Serials (Titles)	4,000	2,500	1,000	1,000
4. Documents	14,000	12,500	11,000	12,500
5. Pamphlets	1,850	1,700	1,000	1,000
6. Microforms	1,000	900	500	300
7. Archival Items	775	650	550	520
8. Other[c]	450	400	300	450
TOTAL	28,075	24,400	19,100	20,270

B. Materials Discarded

Type of Material	19x4	19x3	19x2	19x1
All Materials (i.e., Items)[a]	4,000	1,425	1,250	100

a. Includes reprints, unpublished papers, in-house bibliographies, legislative digests, literature reviews, etc.

DOCUMENT J: DEPARTMENT OF ECOLOGY LIBRARY
PROFESSIONAL BOOK SHELF

No bibliography is included here because this document should be
the instructor's bibliography for the course or workshop. As such,
it should be completely up-to-date and should consist of the specific
items to be referred to during the instruction. The topics covered
in the original GLS Professional Book Shelf were:

Administration

Government: The Federal Government
              Libraries in the Federal Government

Skills: Locating Information
              Communication
              Interpersonal Relations

DOCUMENT K. AERIAL ENVIRONMENTAL SURVEY LIBRARY
ORGANIZATION CHART

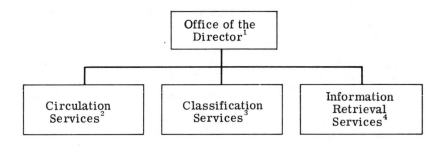

---

1. Director (GS12): Administers Aerial Environmental Survey Library; assists users.
2. Library Technician (GS4): Performs circulation and reprography duties under supervision.
3. Library Technician (GS5): Performs classification and other clerical duties under supervision.
4. Subject Specialist (GS9): Performs information services for users.

NOTE TO INSTRUCTORS

The twelve problems that follow were designed for course study by
trained librarians experienced in special librarianship in the federal
government of the United States. The aspects of administration which
they represent were identified by a group of federal librarians. The
problems emphasize planning, directing, staff management and communication. For use with other groups of learners additional problems would have to be designed or these problems would have to be
refocused in order to meet specific objectives of those groups.

In the original format of the Governmental Library Simulation a separate Director's Guide was provided. Since it was not feasible to reproduce the entire guide here, each of the problems reproduced is
followed by suggestions to assist an instructor in the use of the material.

PROBLEM 1. PLANNING LIBRARY CONSOLIDATION

Incorporation of the library of hold-out agency into the department
library has been ordered and must be accomplished in a given period
of time. Resistance is evident at the planning meeting. It is the intention of the department administrative officer that two initial goals
will be accomplished at this meeting: (1) the department library mission statement will be revised to include the mission of the incoming
library; (2) at least the policy, if not the details, of assignment of
personnel from the incoming library to the merged library staff will
be agreed on.

Roles: DOE Assistant Secretary   DOE Personnel Officer
           for Administration   DOE Librarian
       OAES Administrative   OAES Librarian
           Officer   DOE Library Secretary

Roleplay Time: 30 minutes

Suggestions for Preparation: Review:
    1. How to conduct a meeting.
    2. How to take minutes.
    3. Dynamics of participation in a group.
    4. Statements relating to DOE Library.
    5. Management of personnel reassignment.
    6. Special library services.

Sources:

    Federal Library Model

    Cantor, D.D. "Communications, the Personnel Approach,"
        Personnel Journal 48 (May 1969), 337-339.

    "How to Get the Most Out of Meetings" (Condensed from Direc-
        tion, the CNA Magazine), Management Review 59 (February
        1970), 39-43

    Lawrence, Paul R. "How to Deal with Resistance to Change,"
        Harvard Business Review 47 (January-February 1969), 4-12,
        166-76.

    Levinson, Harry. "A Psychologist Diagnoses Merger Fail-
        ures," Harvard Business Review 48 (March-April 1970),
        139-147.

    Morse, John J. and Lorsche, Jay W. "Beyond Theory Y," Har-
        vard Business Review 48 (May-June 1970), 61-8.

    Swope, George S. "Interpreting Executive Behavior," Manage-
        ment Review, 59 (April 1970), 2-14.

    Tannenbaum, Robert and Schmidt, Warren H. "How to Choose a
        Leadership Pattern," Harvard Business Review 36 (March-
        April 1958), 95-101.

Communication 1

Department of Ecology   memorandum   March 20, 19x5

to: Assistant Secretary of Environment

from: Secretary of Ecology
         Office of the Secretary

subject: Transfer of the Office of Aerial
         Environmental Surveys to the
         Department of Ecology

The enclosed memo from the Secretary of Space explains the reason
for the transfer of OAES. Will you please manage this transfer and
keep me informed?

. . . .

Communication 1: attachment

                                         Office of the Secretary
Department of Space   memorandum   March 15, 19x5

to: Secretary of Ecology

from: Secretary of Space

subject: Transfer of the Office of Aerial Environmental Surveys to
         the Department of Ecology

The President's Commission on Efficiency in Government has recommended that the Office of Aerial Environmental Surveys be incorporated into the Department of Ecology. The President is anxious to accomplish the Commission's recommendations and has urged all agencies to begin implementation immediately. Since most activities will
be under the direction of your Assistant Secretary for Environment,
according to the Recommendations, we will be ready to cooperate in
the transfer of OAES at any time and suggest that it be done by September 15, 19x5. If you can complete the transfer of all activities in
a shorter time, it will be to our mutual advantage.

Communication 2

Department of Ecology   memorandum   April 27, 19x5

to: Director, DOE Library

from: Assistant Secretary for Administration

subject: Transfer of the Office of Aerial Environmental Surveys to
         the Department of Ecology

The enclosed copy of a letter from the Assistant Secretary for Environment explains the transfer of OAES. Will you please manage the
transfer of the Library and keep me informed?

To get things started, I will call a meeting in the near future with
DOE and OAES administrative officers affected. I would like to discuss, at that meeting, revision of the DOE Library mission and DOE
Library personnel assignments to incorporate the needs of this new
unit.

. . . .

Communication 2: attachment

Department of Ecology   memorandum   March 26, 19x5

to: Assistant Secretary for Administration

from: Assistant Secretary for Environment

subject: Transfer of the Library of the Office of Aerial Environ-
         mental Surveys from the Department of Space to DOE

I have been directed to incorporate the entire Office of Aerial Environmental Surveys into the Department of Ecology, primarily into
the Office of Environment, as soon as possible. As you know, it is
the policy of our Department to keep all libraries in the Washington
area consolidated. Therefore, would you begin immediately to plan
the incorporation of OAES Library into DOE Library?

The move should be completed by September 15, 19x5, sooner if possible. Keep me informed of any major difficulties—a brainstorming
session will probably bring forth fruitful solutions.

_____

SELF-ANALYSIS AND EVALUATION*

Directions: Answer A, and B or C.

A. Before roleplay:
   1. What do you understand the immediate goals of the meeting to
      be?

   2. If you were chairman, how would you attempt to accomplish
      these goals?

B. After roleplay: Roleplayers:
   1. Were the goals of the meeting accomplished? Yes___ No___
      If no, why not?

   2. Were you able to act as you think you would act in a similar
      situation? Yes___ No___
      If no, why not?

   3. Thinking back over the roleplay, was there anything you feel
      you should have done differently? Yes___ No___
      If yes, what? Explain.
_____
*Self-analysis and evaluation should follow each roleplay as ex-
plained in Chapter 4. Forms are not included in Problems 2-12
in order to save space.

C. After roleplay: Observers:
   1. Where the goals of the meeting accomplished? Yes___ No___
      If no, why not?

   2. Which roleplayers took a leadership role in accomplishing
      the business of the meeting?

   3. Which roleplayers did little to accomplish the business of the
      meeting?
      What could these roleplayers have done to improve their
      performances? Explain.

Note to Instructors: The following role cards should be typed in advance of the class meeting and given privately to the students who are
assigned these roles. The class will expect resistance during the
roleplay on the basis of the statement of the problem. The detailed
directions are for the roleplayers only.

Problem 1: Library Consolidation
Role: OAES Administrative Officer

You don't care one way or the other what happens to the OAES
Library, but your boss in the Department of Space is very un-
happy over the transfer and has instructed you not to waste
time over it. "They are getting our library as a gift; let them
do the work." Therefore, though not openly hostile, you aren't
going out of your way to help. Furthermore, you want to get the
meeting over in a hurry. Try to postpone, delegate or otherwise dispose of everything the chairman suggests. If the meeting
isn't over in fifteen or twenty minutes, excuse yourself on a
flimsy excuse and leave.

Problem 1: Library Consolidation
Role: OAES Librarian

You have a soft berth in the library, with no real accountability
to anybody for the way you do things. You and your assistant
librarian have worked together for years, are spare-time bud-
dies as well, and don't want to break it up. You resent having to
move, having a professional librarian over you (you have no library training), and having to change your working habits in any
way. You don't like whatever is suggested for your assistant librarian either. Do everything you can to impede the change
through words, gestures and actions except downright refusal
to move. You must give lip service to the idea or lose your job.
You may be agressively hostile, however.

The student assigned to roleplay the DOE Assistant Secretary for Administration should prepare a call for the meeting, which will be
distributed to all students. The DOE Library secretary should take
the minutes of the meeting and these should be distributed. Both
documents should be critiqued later by the class.

The debriefing after this roleplay should center around the conduct of the meeting, the feasibility of actual plans suggested and the
identification of alternatives, as well as the attitudes displayed and
expected in a situation in which a library staff includes hostile individuals.

PROBLEM 2. PRESENTATION AND JUSTIFICATION OF RECOM-
MENDATIONS FOR REVISION OF LIBRARY SPACE

The Committee on Space Revision must present its recommendations
for the physical accommodation of the OAES Library (services, materials, personnel) to the Head of the DOE Office of Administrative Services. With his approval the recommendations can then be sent
through channels for final approval.

Roles: Head, DOE Office of Administrative Services
        Director, DOE Library
        Chief, Office of Documentation Services

Roleplay time: 20-30 minutes

Suggestions for Preparation: Review:

    1. Physical facilities for special libraries
    2. Federal Library Model, Document D

Sources:

American Library Association. Problems in Planning Library Fa-
    cilities. Chicago: American Library Association, 1964.

Anthony, L.J. "Library Planning," Handbook of Special Librarian-
    ship and Information Work. 3d ed. edited by W. Ashworth.
    London: Aslib, 1967, 309-364.

"If Your Office is Typical, It's a Bad Place to Work," Management
    Review 59 (June 1970), 47-51.

Laub, Kenneth D. "Tips on Leasing Office Space," Management
    Review 58 (November 1969), 36-41.

McDonald, J. "How the Man at the Top Avoids Crises," Fortune
    81 (January 1970), 120-122.

Special Libraries, 1961-1965. [Series of articles on planning
    physical facilities.]

Note to Instructors: As a preliminary to this problem three individ-
    uals should be assigned the roles of DOE Administrative Ser-
    vices Officer, DOE Librarian and DOE Chief of Documentation
    Services. These three, meeting outside of class, should con-
    sider the space problems of integrating the two libraries and pre-
    pare recommendations to meet the situation. The recommenda-
    tions should be distributed and the class given time to study them
    before the Problem 2 roleplay begins. It is helpful during both
    the roleplay and the debriefing to have transparencies of the DOE
    Library floor plan and an overhead projector.

The debriefing should focus on the special services of the OAES
Library and the ways in which they create space problems. Alternatives should be brought out and considered. There will
probably be different problems of communication in the Problem
2 roleplay (in which there was no built-in discord) than in the
Problem 1 roleplay. All aspects of the group communication
should be discussed.

PROBLEM 3. COORDINATION AND DIRECTION OF AN
            INTERN PROGRAM

A proposal for an intern program to develop professional personnel
for the DOE Library, submitted over a year ago, is funded rather
suddenly. Three interns have been selected and have arrived for
work. Their first two weeks on the job they spend in a training institute for new Federal library employees. This institute is held at
the department library of the Department of Space. During this time,
the DOE Library staff must make specific plans for the utilization of
the interns. The Library Director calls his four chiefs into a planning session for this purpose.

Roles: Director, DOE Library   Chief, Bibliographic Services
       Chief, Documentation   Chief, Circulation Services
       Services   Chief, Technical Services

Roleplay time: 30-40 minutes

Suggestions for Preparation: Review: Principles of Internships

Sources:

Berkner, D.S. "Two Library Work-Study Programs in the Boston
    Area," College and Research Libraries 28 (March 1967), 120-128.

Connor, J.M. "Medical Librarian Trainee Program in a Medical
    Society Library," Special Libraries 58 (July-August 1967), 428-429.

Denova, Charles. "Is This any Way to Evaluate a Training Activity?
    You Bet It Is!" Personnel Journal 47 (July 1968), 488-493.

Graham, R.G. and Valentine, M.A. "Dealing with On-the-Job Identity
    Problems," Management Review 58 (September 1969), 41-48.

Hekimian, J.S. and Jones, C.H. "Put People on Your Balance Sheet,"
    Harvard Business Review 45 (January-February 1967), 105-113.

Herzberg, Frederick. "One More Time: How Do You Motivate Em-
    ployees?" Harvard Business Review 46 (January-February
    1968), 53-62.

Imberman, A.A. "The Missing Element in Supervisory Training,"
    Management Review 59 (March 1970), 15-19.

Immelman, R.F.M. "The Continuing Education of Library Person-
    nel," South African Libraries 37 (December 1969), 128-143.

Jones, F. "Practical Training Schemes for Library School Stu-
    dents," Library Association Record 68 (August 1966), 281-283.

Livingston, J.S. "Pygmalion in Management," Harvard Business Re-
    view 47 (July-August 1969), 81-89.

Maier, N.R.F. and Thurber, J.A. "Problems in Delegation," Per-
    sonnel Psychology 22 (Summer 1969), 131-139.

Netz, D.J. and Wood, D.E. "The Human Element: A Retrospective
    Evaluation of the Ohio State University Libraries Internship Pro-
    gram," American Libraries 1 (March 1970), 253-254.

North, D. "The Misfit: A Corporate Need," Vital Speeches 34 (August 1968), 630-632.

Paul, William J., Robertson, Keith B., and Herzberg, Frederick. "Job Enrichment Pays Off," Harvard Business Review 47 (March-April 1969), 61-78.

Peele, D. "Performance Ratings and Librarians Rights," American Libraries 1 (June 1970), 595-600.

Communication 3

Department of Ecology   memorandum   March 1, 19x4

to: Assistant Secretary for Administration, DOE

from: Library Director

subject: Proposal for a Library Internship Program

Following our conversation yesterday about the Library's continuing personnel problems, I drafted a statement incorporating some of the ideas we talked about. This is a first effort, and the details are open to negotiation.

. . . .

Communication 3: attachment

Department of Ecology   Library
                                                              March 1, 19x4

Subject: Proposal for a Library Internship Program

Purpose of Program: To develop top quality professional personnel for the DOE Library from among graduates of accredited library schools through a planned six month internship.

Justification: Since the establishment of the DOE Library we have experienced difficulty in attracting and keeping top quality librarians. As the Library's responsibilities expand to include service to more agencies, liaison with state and international agencies, and expanded involvement in government-wide information networks, the personnel crisis will accelerate. The problem is compounded by the length of time required for any employee to become thoroughly familiar with the special services and problems of the DOE Library and by the slowness of the normal pathways to promotion. Good young people are discouraged and seek jobs elsewhere before they reach peak productivity and eligibility for promotion here.

Characteristics of Proposed Program:
  1. Rigorous selection of interns.
  2. Planned rotation through all library activities.
  3. Increased responsibilities as internship progresses.
  4. Close observation and direction of each intern.
  5. Continuous evaluation and rigorous weeding of interns.
  6. An approved rapid promotion plan for successful interns.

Schedule for Program: Six months of each of three successive years: either July through December (for June graduates), or September through May (for August graduates).

Number of Interns Requested: First year, four interns; succeeding years, negotiable on basis of first year experience.

Responsible Official: Director, DOE Library

Communication 4

Department of Ecology   memorandum

to: Director, DOE Library

from: Assistant Secretary for Administration

subject: Library Internship Program

date: March 2, 19x5

Executive Order D4201, Improved Career Opportunities in Federal Service, January 10, 19x5, opened the way to fund your Proposed Internship Program of March 1, 19x4.

This memo will authorize you to publicize the Program and to select three interns to begin the program on April 15, 19x5 at the GS grade 9. Please work with the Training Officer in the Personnel Office in the detailed planning of the internship program.

Please keep me informed of the progress of the program; it is of particular interest to the Secretary.

cc: Personnel Officer

Communication 5

Department of Ecology   memorandum

to: Division Chiefs, DOE Library

from: Director, DOE Library

subject: Planning Conference for Internship Program

date: April 10, 19x5

We will meet on April 23 at 10 a.m. in my office to finalize plans for rotating the interns to all departments.

Please bring to the meeting your plans for the training of the interns in your respective divisions, making these plans as specific as possible in relation to objectives, in-service training required, tasks to be assigned, and time required for each intern in your department. The schedule will have to account for each intern from May 1 to

September 15, 19x5. We will also have to plan for the in-depth evaluation of each intern, though these plans do not have to be finalized
at the present time.

I am enclosing copies of the applications of the three interns selected for your program. In preparing plans for the work of these
interns in your department, you should consider the prior training
and special capabilities of these individuals.

Attachments: 3

. . . .

Communication 5: attachment 1*

DEPARTMENT OF ECOLOGY
LIBRARY MANAGEMENT DEVELOPMENT INTERNSHIP PROGRAM
APPLICATION

Name: John Blalock   Male: x   Female:_
Address: 1042 Ewer Dr., Tarpa, Va.   Citizenship: U.S.
Permanent address, if different: Military status:
                                         Veteran—Korea

Education: State in chronological order, degrees earned, where, sub-
          ject major:

B.S.   Princemont College   Physics
M.L.S.   Dacron University   Special Libraries

Significant non-degree programs completed: What, where, when:

   Law   John Adams Law University 19x5 (-7 yrs.) (for 2 yrs.)
   Seminary St. Jehosephat   19x5 (-4 yrs.) (for 1 yr.)

Experience: State library positions held, where, when:

   Student aide—circulation—Princemont College for 2 years
   Shelved books while in law school.

Significant non-library positions, especially managerial positions:
   (Do not include student, summer, or other temporary jobs.)

Personal Data:

Date of birth:_____   Place of birth: Tarpa, Virginia
Marital status (check)   Health status (check)
   Single   x   Excellent x (glasses)
   Married ___   Good   ___
   Divorced ___   Fair   ___
   Widowed ___   Poor   ___

If married, name of spouse: Any handicaps: If so, explain:

If unmarried, name of nearest   Serious illness in last 12
   kin: months: If so, explain:
Mrs. Paul Blalock

---

* The underlined material in Communication 5 attachments represents the students handwritten information.

Honors and awards: Hobbies: <u>Classical music, puz-
                                               zles, mountain climbing</u>

Summarize your reasons for interest in the internship program:

     Even though I have traveled extensively, I believe it is time I
settled down and established a home for my mother and myself. This trainee program offers a challenge that makes
staying put sound exciting. Furthermore, my travel experiences
coupled with my ability to read German, Russian, Latin and
French should enhance my usefulness. Because I love the out of
doors, I am especially interested in working for the Department
of Ecology.

List the names and addresses of three individuals who have taught you
or supervised you to whom we may write for a statement about your
professional and personal capabilities in relation to this internship
program.

    1. Gordon Rogers
       Head Librarian
       Princemont College
       Alaska, Virginia

    2. Roland Thomas
       Prof. of Law
       Dacron University
       Dupont, Delaware

    3. William K. Moore
       Prof. of Special Libraries
       Dacron University
       Dupont, Delaware

. . . .

<u>Communication 5</u>: attachment 2

DEPARTMENT OF ECOLOGY
LIBRARY MANAGEMENT DEVELOPMENT INTERNSHIP PROGRAM
APPLICATION

Name: <u>Sara Goodman (Mrs. Edward)</u>   Male:__ Female:<u> x</u>
Address: <u>3024 Quennell Ave., Wash., D.C.</u> Citizenship: <u>U.S.</u>
Permanent address, if different: _____   Military status:

Education: State in chronological order, degrees earned, where,
          subject major:

<u>Alabama Teachers College</u> <u>B.A.</u>   <u>Elementary Education</u>
<u>University of Guam</u>   <u>M.L.S.</u> <u>Special Librarianship</u>

Significant non-degree programs completed: What, where, when:
    <u>None</u>

Experience: State library positions held, where, when:
    <u>None</u>

Significant non-library positions, especially managerial positions:
(Do not include student, summer, or other temporary jobs.)
   None

Personal Data:
   Date of birth:___   Place of birth:_____
   Marital status (check)   Health status (check)
      Single   ___   Excellent _x_
      Married _x_   Good   ___
      Divorced ___   Fair   ___
      Widowed ___   Poor   ___

If married, name of spouse: Any handicaps: If so. explain:

Edward Washington Goodman   None

If unmarried, name of nearest Serious illness in last 12
   kin: months: If so, explain.

                               None

Honors and awards: Hobbies:
   None   Dancing, civil rights

Summarize your reasons for interest in the internship program:

I'll be living in the area because my husband, who is in the military, has been assigned to Andrews Air Force Base, and therefore we will be making our home in Washington, D.C. for the next three years.

There are government libraries everywhere so that experience in a civil service library will be particularly valuable when we are re-assigned.

This internship provides supervised experience, and promises faster promotions for internees. We Blacks need to take advantage of every opportunity in order to compete with whites in the labor market.

List the names and addresses of three individuals who have taught you or supervised you to whom we may write for a statement about your professional and personal capabilities in relation to this internship program.

1. James Peterson
   Assoc. Prof. of Library Science
   Graduate School of Library Studies
   University of Guam

2. Donald Brooks
   Assoc. Prof. of Library Science
   Graduate School of Library Studies
   University of Guam

3. Constance Williams
   Instructor, Library Science
   Graduate School of Library Studies
   University of Guam

. . . .

Communication 5: attachment 3

DEPARTMENT OF ECOLOGY
LIBRARY MANAGEMENT DEVELOPMENT INTERNSHIP PROGRAM
APPLICATION

Name: Helen Moore   Male:____ Female: x
Address: 10911 New Mexico Ave,   Citizenship: U.S.
         Silver Spring, Illinois   Military status:

Education: State in chronological order, degrees earned, where,
          subject major:

B.A.   Torrence College, Arta, Indiana—Political Science
M.L.S.   Univ. of Sylta, Chicago, Illinois—Special Libraries

Significant non-degree programs completed: What, where, when:
    Dale Carnegie, Chicago, Illinois   19x5 (-10 years)
    Group Dynamics, YWCA   19x5 (-3 years)

Experience: State library positions held, where, when:

Significant non-library positions, especially managerial positions:
    (Do not include student, summer, or other temporary jobs.)

    Precinct Chairman 5 years—Silver Spring, Ill.
    State Committee—(Republican Party) 3 years

Personal Data:
    Date of birth: 19x2 (-40 years)   Place of birth: Chicago, Ill.
    Marital status (check)   Health status (check)
       Single   ___   Excellent x
       Married   x   Good   ___
       Divorced ___   Fair   ___
       Widowed ___   Poor   ___

If married, name of spouse: Any handicaps; If so, explain:
    John Henry Moore

If unmarried, name of nearest   Serious illness in last 12 months:
kin: If so, explain:
                              Hysterectomy

Honors and awards: Hobbies:

    Republican Woman of the   Politics, Bonsai
       Year for Illinois, 19x2

Summarize your reasons for interest in the internship program:

    My experience as a volunteer in politics convinces me that
women have the same capabilities as men and the world needs
those capabilities desperately. I want to get back into the labor
market and be a contributing member of society as well as set
an example to my three children, who are now self-sufficient,
of how women can be wife, mother and careerist.

    I believe a government library is the place a librarian can have
the most impact on the world today, and since ecology is so

important to every life, the Department of Ecology Library is the optimum combination for greatest impact.

List the names and addresses of three individuals who have taught you or supervised you to whom we may write for a statement about your professional and personal capabilities in relation to this internship program.

1. Dr. Gilda Jensen
    Professor of Library Science
    University of Sylta
    Chicago, Illinois

2. Dr. Abe Broome
    Professor of Library Science
    University of Sylta
    Chicago, Illinois

3. Peter Barbarollis
    State Central Committee
    915 Park Place
    Chicago, Illinois

Note to Instructors: The roles for Problem 3 should be assigned far enough in advance that each roleplayer will have time to prepare a plan. Copies of these plans should be distributed to all students so they will be prepared both for observation and discussion.

The debriefing should focus on how each roleplayer prepared his plan as well as on its substance. Hopefully there will be sufficient differences in the plans that compromise will be necessary in preparing a final plan. The group process of the roleplayers should be observed very carefully and compromise behavior should be discussed fully in the debriefing. Another question, in relation to the plan finally accepted, is "Does it allow for teamwork between each intern and each Division staff, or does it allow only for observation and independent work by the intern?" Discuss the implications of these different ways of teaching subordinates.

When a plan has been accepted, some members of the group can be assigned to write a public relations release to the professional press about the internship program. Others can be assigned to write an in-house release for distribution throughout DOE. These communications can be critiqued later by the entire group.

PROBLEM 4. PRESENTATION AND JUSTIFICATION OF
             REVISED BUDGET

The Library Director must present his recommendations for acco-
modating the OAES Library (services, materials, personnel) in the
DOE Library budget for the following fiscal year to the Assistant
Secretary for Administration and the DOE Budget Officer. With their
approval the recommendations can then be sent through channels for
final approval.

Roles: Assistant Secretary for Administration   DOE Budget Officer
        Director, DOE Library   OAES Librarian

Roleplay time: 20-30 minutes

Suggestions for Preparation: Review:
    1. Federal Library Model
    2. Budget practices and procedures.

Sources:

    Anthony, Robert N. "What Should 'Cost' Mean?" Harvard Busi-
        ness Review 48 (May-June 1970), 121-131.

    Flarsheim, H. "How 15 Executives Handle Their Annual Battle of
        the Budget, "Business Management 37 (November 1969), 22-26.

    Hughes, C.L. "Why Budgets Go Wrong," Personnel 42 (May 1965),
        19-26.

    Ott, D.J. and Ott, A.F. Federal Budget Policy. Rev. ed. Wash-
        ington, D.C.; Brookings Institution, 1969.

    Pondy, L.R. and Birnberg, J.G. "An Experimental Study of the
        Allocation of Financial Resources within Small Hierarchical
        Task Groups," Administrative Science Quarterly 14 (June 1969),
        192-201.

Communication 6

                    DOE LIBRARY PHONE MESSAGE

To: Director   May 8, 19x5
From: Assistant Secretary for Administration   9:30 am

The Assistant Secretary wishes to set up review of your revised
budget for 19x7 (incorporating OAES Library costs) for May 22 at
10:30 a.m.
If o.k., please inform OAES Librarian, who is to be present.

                              Your calendar is clear at that time,
                              so I agreed tentatively. O.K.?

                                        Marge

Note to Instructors: As a preliminary to this problem, and with as
    long a lead time as possible, two students should be assigned the
    preparation of the documents to be used during roleplay and copies
    should have been distributed to the class before the class meeting.

If there is no member of the class with the nature and critical
judgment necessary to play the role of a senior executive officer
of the federal government, the following role card may be given
out or the instructor might choose to combine both positions into
one role and himself fill that role.

    Problem 4: Budget Justification
    Roles: DOE Assistant Secretary for Administration
          DOE Budget Officer

    The positions of these two officers require that they under-
    stand library costs, yet neither is trained as a librarian. Years
    of experience have taught them many things, so "stupid" ques-
    tions are out of order. Questions should be critical and de-
    tailed, however. And, neither officer should be satisfied with
    superficial answers or generalizations. If the librarian is un-
    able to answer certain questions, the logical follow-up is,
    "What are you doing to get this information?" and/or to sug-
    gest ways and means. After all, you are thinking in the best
    interests of the Department.

Since the budgets are made two years in advance and approved one
year in advance in the Executive Branch, it would be safe to assume that the Department of Space budgets for 19x6 and 19x7 include OAES Library needs. Was the possibility of a transfer of
funds considered? This alternative should be brought out during
the debriefing if it did not come up during the roleplay. Another
point is that appropriations have been made on the basis of two
separate services to two separate audiences (OAES and DOE). Has
the budget, or the discussion, allowed for the possibility that as a
merged operation there will be a synergistic effect requiring, in
effect, more services and more funds? How can this idea be gotten across to management?

Usually, the budget document has to be revised on the basis of decisions made during the roleplay. This should be assigned to different students than those who originally prepared the budget so
that as many as possible get experience in budget preparation.
Finally, a student should be assigned to write a letter of transmittal to accompany the budget and this letter should be critiqued
by the group.

PROBLEM 5. QUALITY CONTROL OF LIBRARY OPERATIONS

The Secretary of Ecology has called for a Department-wide performance review at the conclusion of the Department's first five years
of existence, six months hence. The Library Director has instructed his Division Chiefs to work with their respective staffs to develop
procedures that will relate productivity to library programs and
budgets.

The problem calls for simultaneous roleplay, with each class member assigned to one of the four Division staffs. In the roleplay, each
student is to act as a professional librarian, even though this is not
the staffing configuration of the DOE Library.

Roles: Chief, Bibliographic Services
       Chief, Documentation Services
       Chief, Circulation Services
       Chief, Acquisition Services

       Every other class member is assigned to one of these four
       staffs.

Roleplay time: 45 minutes

Suggestions for Preparation: Review:
    1. Federal Library Model, Document F, Agency Manual; Docu-
       ment H, Statistical Abstract of Annual Report 19x4; Docu-
       ment E, Library Budget.
    2. Scientific management of libraries.
    3. Performance budgeting.
    4. Library statistics.

Sources:

    Baker, Samuel W. "Writing an Annual Report Worth Reading,"
       Management Review 59 (January 1970), 28-30.

    Brutcher, Constance, Gessford, Glen, and Rixford, Emmet.
       "Cost Accounting for the Library," Library Resources and
       Technical Services 8 (Fall 1964), 413-431.

    Coover, R.W. "User Needs and Their Effect on Information
       Center Administration: A Review 1953-1966," Special Li-
       braries 60 (September 1969), 446-456.

    DeWitt, Frank. "A Technique for Measuring Management Pro-
       ductivity," Management Review 59 (June 1970), 2-11.

    Drage, J.F. "User Preferences in Technical Indexes," Indexer 6
       (Autumn 1969), 151-155.

    Fazar, Willard. "Program Planning and Budgeting Theory: Im-
       proved Library Effectiveness by Use of the Planning-Pro-
       gramming-Budgeting System," Special Libraries 60 (Septem-
       ber 1969), 423-433.

    Ferguson, John. "Getting Better Results from Brainstorming,"
       Management Review 59 (August 1970), 18-23.

Geller, W.S. "Gauging Progress," Library Journal 90 (September 1965), 3559-3562.

Hamill, Harold L. "The Numbers Game: Performance Budgeting," Library Journal 90 (September 1965), 3563-3567.

Kuhn, James P. "Setting Up an Effective Quality Assurance Program," Management Review 59 (February 1970), 10-14.

Offenbacher, E. "The Economics of Reprography for Technical Communication, "UNESCO Bulletin for Libraries 24 (January-February 1970), 23-26.

Peterson, Stephen L. "Patterns of Use of Periodical Literature," College and Research Libraries 30 (September 1969), 422-430.

Randall, Gordon E. "Budgeting for a Company Library," Special Libraries 58 (June 1970), 2-11.

Tuttle, Helen W. "TSCOR: The Technical Services Cost Ratio," Southeastern Librarian 19 (Spring 1969), 15-25.

Communication 7

Department of Ecology   memorandum

to: All Professional Staff

from: Director, DOE Library

date: June 7, 19x5

As I mentioned at the last staff meeting, the time has come to begin planning for the five-year performance review requested by the DOE Secretary. The development of methods for review of each division will be under the general direction of the chief of the division, and all professional personnel will participate. To provide planning time I am assigning the initial division meetings for the following times, with the personnel of divisions not meeting to be deployed to carry on essential services (chiefs please coordinate):

> June 19 9-11 a.m. Bibliographic Services
> Acquisition Services
>
> June 21 9-11 a.m. Documentation Services
> Circulation Services

From this point on, it is up to each division. I will plan a meeting in about a month for representatives of each division to work with me to coordinate the division plans. Meanwhile, I will appreciate being kept informed of your progress.

Note to Instructors: For Problem 5 each student is assigned the role of a professional librarian in one of the DOE Library's four divisions, even though this distorts the organization chart staffing pattern. The different pattern is used so that every student will

have the responsibility to immerse himself in the literature relating to measuring and evaluating performance in library tasks.
Each student should study the documents of the Federal Library
Model that relate to the division to which he is assigned. After
he learns the work of the division in detail he should then look for
methods to relate cost, productivity and benefit to his division's
operations.

During class there will be four roleplays going on simultaneously
and the instructor will have to move from group to group to observe and help. If additional information about the divisions and
their work is requested before or during the roleplay, the teacher
will have to supply it from his experience or tell the inquirer that,
since that information has not been collected in the past, he will
have to get along without it. Since it will be obvious that the reporting (as represented in the documents) is not perfect, part of
the problem is to revise the statistical reporting procedures of
the DOE Library.

The debriefing should include an analysis of the faults of the
present statistical reports and agreement as to what is needed. In
critiquing the plans the chief criterion is that each plan be feasible.
Students should have considered the objectives, the procedures and
the problems of implementation of the plans. If they have not,
questions should be raised and carefully discussed. The problems
of coordinating four different plans into a final plan for the library as a whole should be left for Problem 7.

It should be noted that Problem 7, Coordination of Division Plans,
is the follow-up of Problem 5. Some extra cognitive instruction
may be needed relative to evaluation methodologies before Problem 7 is assigned.

PROBLEM 6. COUNSELING AN UNSATISFACTORY EMPLOYEE

Supervisor's reports on one of the interns have indicated a quality
of work below that considered satisfactory. If the employee is to be
terminated at the end of the internship instead of hired on a permanent basis, she must be warned ninety days before the end of the internship. The Library Director must counsel the intern in such a
way as to motivate her to change her behavior and to improve the
quality of her work. The Director must know what sources of help
are available to the employee and inform her of them.

Roles: Director, DOE Library
       Intern, Helen Moore

Roleplay time: 15-20 minutes.

Suggestions for preparation: Review:
   1. Regulations relating to employee counseling and termination.
   2. Motivation of employees.
   3. Counseling techniques.

Sources:

   Burke, Ronald J. and Wilcox, Douglas S. "Characteristics of Ef-
      fective Employee Performance Review and Development Inter-
      views," Personnel Psychology 22 (Autumn 1969), 291-305.

   Kirk, E.B. "Appraisee Participation in Performance Interviews,"
      Personnel Journal 44 (January 1965), 22-25.

   Sterner, Frank M. "Motivate—Don't Manipulate," Personnel
      Journal, 48 (August 1969), 623-627.

   Strauss, Paul S. "The Rating Game," Personnel Administration
      32 (January-February 1969), 44-47.

   Thompson, David W. "Performance Reviews: Management Tool or
      Management Excuse," Management Review 58 (June 1969), 62-
      65.

   Zeitlein, L.R. "Planning for a Successful Performance Review
      Program," Personnel Journal 48 (December 1969), 957-961.

Communication 8

Department of Ecology   memorandum

to: Director, DOE Library
from: Chief, Technical Services
subject: Helen Moore, Library Intern
date: May 22, 19x5

Mrs. Moore spent her first period of internship in Technical Services. She has been well trained in technical procedures and

learned our modifications of standard procedures easily. She performed best in routine situations and assisted in several instances
in improving procedures for speed. She applied herself, on assignment, to the development of new procedures as part of a feasibility
study and performed acceptably. Mrs. Moore was not, however, in
spite of her ability, a really satisfactory employee. She tends to be
too sociable, especially with the young technicians and part-time
workers, for whom she appears to want to be some kind of leader.
Although I attempted to speak to her several times about interrupting
and distracting others by her "sociability," she continued to act in
this way the entire time she was in the department. I could not, on
the basis of this experience with her, recommend that she be added
to the permanent staff.

Communication 9

Department of Ecology   memorandum   June 10, 19x5

to: Director, DOE Library

from: Chief, Documentation Services

subject: Helen Moore, Library Intern

I am replying to your request for an evaluation of Mrs. Moore although I feel that, with only ten days behind her in Documentation
Services, it is a bit too soon. The initial experience with Mrs. Moore
has been a disappointing one for me. She was, apparently, poorly prepared in library school for any kind of machine applications to library
work; neither did she have any courses in abstracting or indexing.
She seems uninterested in our computer projects and has not, so far
as I can tell, learned much from the reading material I gave her when
I realized her deficiency. She does the task placed in front of her in
a minimal way and seems to be just putting in the time until she is
rotated to another division. I am planning to try her in the experimental work on our retrieval projects this week, but I foresee little
difference in her attitude or performance. I cannot, as yet, recommend her for the permanent staff.

Communication 10

Department of Ecology   memorandum

to: Helen Moore, Intern

from: Director, DOE Library

subject: First Evaluation of Work

date: June 10, 19x5

As we told you at the beginning of the Internship Program, we plan
to evaluate all interns very carefully, and to talk over staff evaluations of your work with you at frequent intervals. Will you please

come to my office for your first evaluation on June 12, 19x5, at
2:30 p.m. If this appointment time is inconvenient, please call my
secretary for another time. I'm looking forward to talking with you.

Note to Instructor: Problem 6 emphasizes the need to know what to
    say to an employee in a counseling interview and how to say it. The
    roleplay offers an opportunity for practice for the student playing
    the role of the library director. The student playing the role of the
    intern should study Mrs. Moore's application (Problem 3, Com-
    munication 5, Attachment 3) and fabricate an appropriate person-
    ality. In this roleplay the student playing Mrs. Moore is part of
    the problem and does not act as she normally would in such a situ-
    ation. Only the student playing the part of the director should play
    as he himself would act.

The debriefing should center on both the substance of the interview and the communications techniques employed. This is an
excellent roleplay opportunity for an immature or inexperienced
student to play the role of the library director. The debriefing
can then include replays in which other students play the director
to demonstrate alternative approaches or in which the original director tries again, this time utilizing ideas from the discussion.
Problem 6 can be extended to include the design of intern evaluation forms.

PROBLEM 7. COORDINATION OF DIVISION PLANS

The Director of the DOE Library must work with his Division Chiefs
to unify their individual quality control plans into an overall plan
for the library.

Roles: Director
        Chief, Bibliographic Services
        Chief, Documentation Services
        Chief, Circulation Services
        Chief, Acquisition Services

Roleplay time: 45 minutes - 1 hour

Suggestions for preparation: Review:
    1. Design of a user study.
    2. Design of a product study.
    3. Design of a technology feasibility study.
    4. Work-load indicators.

Sources:

Cochran, M.L., et al. "Application of Managerial Cost Accounting
    to a Science Information Center," Journal of the American
    Society for Information Science 21 (March 1970), 163-164.

Conference on the Present Status and Future Prospects of Ref-
    erence/Information Service. Columbia University, March 30-
    April 1, 1966. Chicago: American Library Association, 1967.

Cuadra, C.A. and Katter, R.V. "Implications of Relevance Re-
    search for Library Operations and Training," Special Li-
    braries 59 (September 1968), 503-507.

Dougherty, Richard M. and Heinritz, Fred J. Scientific Manage-
    ment of Library Operations. New York: Scarecrow Press,
    1966.

King, B.G. "Cost-Effectiveness Analysis: Implications for Ac-
    countants," Journal of Accountancy 129 (March 1970), 43-49.

Landau, H.B. "Methodology of a Technical Information Use
    Study," Special Libraries 60 (July-August 1969), 340-346.

Lindberg, Roy A. "The Unfamiliar Art of Controlling," Man-
    agement Review 58 (August 1969), 49-54.

Morse, Philip M. Library Effectiveness: A Systems Approach.
    Cambridge: MIT Press, 1968.

Wills, G. and Christopher, M. "Cost/Benefit Analysis of Company
    Information Needs," UNESCO Library Bulletin 24 (January-
    February 1970), 9-22.

Communication 11

Department of Ecology   memorandum

to: Division Chiefs
from: Director, DOE Library
subject: Coordination of Plans for Library Performance Review
date: June 18, 19x5

. . . .

I would like to schedule our meeting to coordinate your plans for the
library performance review for July 2, 2-4 p.m. If there is a conflict
for anyone, please let my secretary know immediately.

You, or your division representative, will be asked to give a brief
report on your plans before the general discussion begins. Please
turn in your complete report by June 26 for reproduction and distribution by my office.

Note to Instructor: Make a special point of reproducing and distributing the statements of division plans in time for all students to
study them carefully. The debriefing must focus on both the substance of the plans and the interpersonal action of the roleplay.
The way in which the director and the group plan to mold four separate plans into one integrated plan for the entire library must be
feasible. Similarly, the way in which each individual presents his
division plan, defends it, criticizes the other plans and perceives
what is necessary to coordinate all the plans must be realistic.

PROBLEM 8. RESPONSE TO COMPLAINT

The head of one of DOE's subagencies has complained in writing to
his supervisor, Assistant Secretary for Ecologic Art, about some
material in the library. The Assistant Secretary has asked the Library Director to prepare a reply for his signature, and has informed
the Assistant Secretary for Administration of the bruhaha. In this
roleplay, the Library Director is to talk over the complaint and his
suggested response with the Assistant Secretary for Administration.
The Assistant Secretary should instruct his secretary, when the Library Director arrives for his appointment, that they are not to be
disturbed.

It should be assumed that there is something to the complaint, the details of which are in some instances factually correct, in others open
to individual interpretation. It should also be assumed, however, that
there are some plus values to the publication, and the Library Director should be prepared to state what they are. Over-all, the vehe-
mence of the complaint seems out of proportion.

Roles: Assistant Secretary for   Director, DOE Library
            Administration   Secretary

Roleplay time: 10 minutes

Suggestions for Preparation: Review:

1. DOE Library Policy (Federal Library Model, Document F).
2. Principles of book selection.
3. Techniques of persuasive communication.

Sources:

Anderson, John. "Giving and Receiving Feedback," Personnel
    Administration 31 (March-April 1968), 21-27.

Burke, Ronald J. "Methods of Resolving Interpersonal Conflict,"
    Personnel Administration 32 (July-August 1969), 48-55.

Burnes, Bruce B. "How to Become a More Persuasive Manager,"
    Management Review 58 (September 1969), 34-40.

Kelly, Joe. "Make Conflict Work for You," Harvard Business Re-
    view 48 (July-August 1970), 103-113.

Mendheim, John M. "Dealing with Executive Conflict," Manage-
    ment Review 58 (July 1969), 22-28.

Pemberton, William H. "Talk Patterns of People in Crises,"
    Personnel Administration 32 (March-April 1969), 36-40.

Communication 12

Department of Ecology   Phone Message

to: Director, DOE Library   July 13, 19x5

from: Assistant Secretary for Administration

Concerned about July 12 memo from Assistant Secretary for Ecologic
Art. Please contact him as soon as possible about it.

> I took the liberty of making an appointment
> with him for you at 3:30 this afternoon.
>
> Marge

Communication 13

Department of Ecology   memorandum   July 12, 19x5

to: Director, DOE Library

from: Assistant Secretary for Ecologic Art

subject: Outdoor Sculpture

Attached is a copy of a letter which concerns me. Please prepare a
response for my signature at your earliest convenience.

Attachment

cc: Assistant Secretary for Administration

. . . .

Communication 13: attachment

DEPARTMENT OF ECOLOGY

Garden Club Bureau
July 11, 19x5

Assistant Secretary for Ecologic Art
Department of Ecology
Ecology Building
Washington, D.C.

Dear Sir:

I feel I must inform you of a situation which exists in the Department
Library. The Library insists upon subscribing to--in fact, has just
renewed its subscription to--a publication that is contrary to the aims
and purposes of this Bureau and, indeed, of the Department of Ecology

itself. I refer to <u>Outdoor Sculpture</u>. I have called the Bureau's position to the attention of the Librarian on more than one occasion, but
the publication has not been deleted from the subscription list.

All members of the Bureau staff are in agreement with me that this
publication is of no value. The editorial quality is poor, the printing
worse. Its photographic reproductions are unbelievably bad in this
day of skilled technology. Furthermore, it is the policy of this publication to accept advertising from anyone. As a consequence, it includes ads from manufacturers who violate recognized ecologic principles in their manufacturing processes. In the May 19x5 issue, on
page 27, there is an advertisement from the International Hose Company, a firm which is at the present time in litigation with the Department of Justice at the instigation of our own Department.

These reasons (I could add more if you want them) indicate clearly
to me the inadvisability of spending government money to subscribe
to <u>Outdoor Sculpture</u>. Besides, nobody on my staff would use it.

I trust you will use your influence to rid us of this undesirable publication. Thank you.

Sincerely,

Ray Etatson

Chief, Garden Club Bureau

<u>Note to Instructor</u>: Give out the following role-cards in advance so
that the students assigned to the roles can prepare:

Problem 8: Response to Complaint
Role: Assistant Secretary for Administration

You are in the position of both defender and arbiter. Naturally,
if one of the units under your jurisdiction is attacked unjustly,
you want to defend it. A complaint that goes up through channels reflects on you. But you want to be sure of your facts.
You are responsible to see that the library serves **DOE** well,
and if it is not doing so, you need to know and to make some
changes. So you're listening, willing to be convinced, but need-
ing specific answers to specific questions. If it comes to a confrontation between two subagencies, you will probably have to
serve as an arbiter along with the Assistant Secretary for Ecologic Art, who realizes this and has been kind enough to notify
you of the problem by way of carbon copies of correspondence.

Problem 8: Response to Complaint
Role: Library Director

You have restudied the publication in question and are convinced
that, though it is not the best in the field, it needs to be in the
library. It is widely read inside **DOE** and by industry and general public. It is listed in standard bibliographies; it must be

included in Ecology Literature (library-initiated index); and it is currently being used by DOE and Justice personnel in preparing cases against several manufacturers. You realize the Assistant Secretary for Administration is preparing to help you by talking with you, and you want to cooperate with him. Apparently the Assistant Secretary for Ecologic Art also wants to help you since he's asked you to prepare his reply to the Garden Club Bureau Chief--or, he may be simply using this means of learning your position. Naturally you want to cooperate with him also. Know your position; be helpful; be firm.

In this problem, the roleplay stage must be set so that action unanticipated by the class can take place. The Assistant Secretary and the Library Director need space to be seated at a desk or table. Some distance away, as if in a reception room, the secretary is seated at a desk or table. The class must be informed of the real physical plan even though that plan is shown only symbolically through props.

When the Library Director presents himself for his interview, the secretary conducts him into the Assistant Secretary's office, is told, "See that we're not disturbed," and returns to the outer office. After the interview has proceeded long enough for a discussion of the issues from the Library's point of view, but before the conclusion of the interview, the Chief of the Garden Club Bureau appears in the reception room. This role should have been privately assigned and instructed by means of the role card below. He may discuss his role with the teacher, but not with any member of the class. (In fact, the teacher may wish to bring in a student in theatre arts to give a more realistic performance than could be expected from a member of the class.)

Problem 8: Response to Complaint
Role: Chief, Garden Club Bureau

You are mad and showing it. You want the publication Outdoor Sculpture out of the Library. Use the reasons stated in your letter, plus any others you can think of. Logic doesn't matter after a point. If you don't always make sense in what you're saying, so much the better. Obviously there is more to this than meets the eye. You don't want anyone to know it, but some years back you were the editor of a rival publication that failed. This professional failure was a setback in your career and you blame the rival editor. You resent helping him by even one subscription. Do everything you can, short of physical violence or personal abusiveness, to get your way. You may question the Library Director's competence.

The Bureau Chief, if he is a member of the class, should sit near the secretary's desk so that he can rise and begin to talk to her simultaneously. If the Bureau Chief is not a member of the class, he should be right outside the door ready to enter on cue from the teacher. The idea is to surprise both class and roleplayers and to move very quickly to a confrontation. The action proceeds as follows:

Bureau Chief (pushy and insistent): I want to see Mr. _____
(or Miss _____; using the real name of the student playing
the role of the Assistant Secretary).

Secretary (will probably respond somewhat as follows): I'm
sorry; he's in conference.

Bureau Chief (annoyed): It's very important. I must see him
at once.

Secretary: I'm sorry, but he can't be disturbed. I'll be glad to
make an appointment for you.

Bureau Chief (breaking in angrily): I'm a Bureau Chief in this
Division and I have to see him now. (Pushes past secretary into office): I've got to talk with you immediately. (Seeing Library Director): Oh, you're here. Good. We can settle this
whole matter right now. (Launches into his beef, going on and
on, becoming less and less logical.)

Though this problem is set up to appear to the students like a reasonable complaint, it is actually an experience in dealing with an
unreasonable complaint and a confrontation. Legitimate complaints
from reasonable people are relatively easy to work out; it is the
unreasonable complaint from the prejudiced, defensive, aggressive
or otherwise hung-up individual that causes trouble. If the student
playing the role of the Assistant Secretary is experienced or quick
on his feet, he may realize there is more to this situation than
meets the eye.

Let the action play itself out if it is making progress. If, however,
neither the Assistant Secretary nor the Library Director is able to
get the leadership away from the Bureau Chief, the teacher may
have to stop the action. Either way, the debriefing should bring out
as many alternatives as possible and may well incorporate several
replays. A complete discussion of the attitudes displayed by the
three players as well as their methods of handling the situation is
in order. The phenomenon of overreaction should also be studied.

PROBLEM 9. INITIATION OF A COMPLAINT

A list of twenty-two journals not available from standard microform
sources was requisitioned, with specifications, from the DOE Procurement Office. When the material arrived in the library, it was
found to be unusable for the generation of hard copy. The invoice dis-
closed that the material had not been ordered from the vendor recommended by the Library. Permission to return the material because
it did not meet specifications was requested from the Procurement
Officer and denied. The denial brought the further information that
the Procurement Office not only selected its own vendor, but also
changed the Library's specifications. A further plea from the Chief
of the Technical Services Division has been ignored for two weeks.
At this point, the Chief, TSD, reports to the Director, who must now
take some action.

Roles: Director, DOE Library   Chief, Technical Services Division

Roleplay time: 10 minutes

Suggestions for Preparation: Review:
1. Written communication skills.
2. Techniques of persuasive communication.
3. Procurement of Library Materials: An Orientation Aid Pre-
    pared for the Federal Library Committee, by Leslie K. Falk,
    (Washington, D.C. : Federal Library Committee, 1968).

Sources:

  Ammer, Dean. "What Management Expects of Purchasing," Pur-
    chasing 49 (November 21, 1960), 71-73+.

  Boettinger, H.M. "The Art and Craft of Moving Executive Moun-
    tains, " Business Management 36 (July 1969), 22-25+.

  Boyd, Bradford B. "An Analysis of Communication between De-
    partments," Personnel Administration 28 (November-Decem-
    ber), 33-38.

  Farrell, Paul V. "Changing Patterns in Purchasing Management,"
    Purchasing 56 (January 13, 1964), 70-73.

  Feinberg, Mortimer. "The Gentle Art of Executive Persuasion,"
    Dun's Review and Modern Industry 86 (December 1965), 41-47.

  Geist, K.R. "What Other Departments Expect of Purchasing,"
    Purchasing 49 (November 21, 1960), 75-76+.

  Harger, Howard E. "Three Ways to Send Better," Supervision 26
    (July 1964), 4-6.

  Khera, Inder P. and Benson, James D. "Communication and Indus-
    trial Purchasing Behavior," Journal of Purchasing 6 (May 1970),
    5-21.

  Pell, Arthur R. "Are You Getting Through?" Purchasing 50 (April
    24, 1961), 74-76+.

Strauss, George. "Tactics of Lateral Relationship: The Purchasing Agent," Administrative Science Quarterly 7 (September 1962), 161-186.

Zelko, Harold P. "You Can Win Arguments -- Without Arguing," Supervisory Management 7 (November 1962), 38-39.

Communication 14

Department of Ecology   memorandum   July 30, 19x5

to: Director, DOE Library
from: Chief, Technical Services Division, Library
subject: Purchase of Microfilm Copies of 22 Journals

. . . .

Correspondence related to this problem is attached. Notice that the new procurement officer did not accept our endorsement of Norwich Microimages, which submitted the middle bid. Notice also that two weeks have passed since my second memo to him and there has been no reply. We got into this situation because these are all new journals, not yet available from the usual commercial sources for microfilmed journals. All the journals are being indexed here for Ecology Literature Index and are heavily used by our staff and agency personnel. Circulation tells me it is essential that we be able to retain the original journals in the library and circulate reproductions for both current and back volumes.

May I talk with you about our next move?

. . . .

Communication 14: attachment 1

Department of Ecology   memorandum   July 9, 19x5

to: DOE Procurement Officer
from: Chief, Technical Services Division
subject: Requisition 5-2291, Microfilm Copies of 22 Journals

. . . .

Microfilm copies of 22 journals ordered by you from Western Filming Company have arrived in the library and are unsatisfactory. The specifications for this order called for negative microfilm; the company has supplied positive microfilm. May I recall to your attention the fact that the Library recommended acceptance of the bid from Norwich Microimages, Inc., instead of that from Western Filming Company because Western could not document its claimed experience with the microfilming of library materials.

Please send me permission to return the material.

GLS / Problem 9 283

GLS / Problem 9 283

. . . .

Communication 14: attachment 2

Department of Ecology   memorandum   July 12, 19x5

to: Chief, Technical Services Division, DOE Library

from: Procurement Officer, Procurement Office

subject: Requisition 5-2291, Microfilm Copies of 22 Journals

. . . .

The order was given to Western Filming Company because it offered
the low bid, a 5% saving over the bid of Norwich Microimages. To obtain the savings, the specifications were changed from negative to
positive microfilm since both are usable. Economy is essential in
the operation of the agency. Permission to return the microfilm
copies of 22 journals is not granted.

. . . .

Communication 14: attachment 3

Department of Ecology   memorandum

to: DOE Procurement Officer

from: Chief, Technical Services Division, DOE Library

subject: Requisition 5-2291, Microfilm Copies of 22 Journals

date: July 13, 19x5

Positive and negative microfilm may be equally usable from the standpoint of reading with optical equipment. However, DOE personnel
characteristically request printouts of significant material to use at
their desks along with other materials when they use micro-materials.
All of our reader-printers have been purchased on the evidence of this
increasing demand.

The library's reader-printers handle only negative microfilm. In order to be able to supply our users with print-outs from positive microfilm, we would have to buy new equipment (an expenditure of not less
than $1000). Reader-printers for positive microfilm are nowhere
near the technical proficiency of the reader-printers for negative microfilm, so there is every reason to believe that even with the finest
equipment available we would not be able to give our users service
comparable to that which they receive from the reader-printers we
already have—which require negative microfilm.

Again, the library requests permission to return the positive microfilm to Western Filming Company.

Communication 15

Department of Ecology   Phone Message

to: Chief, TSD, Library
from: Library Director's Secretary
message: The Boss will see you at 3:15 today about the microfilm-
           ing problem.

Note to Instructors: The argument between the Library and the Procurement Office in this problem is on the usability of the product,
   not on the technicality of the specifications, on the authority to
   choose a bidder, or any other side issue. Actually, if determina-
   tion of usability of a product were a problem in this agency, it
   should have been worked out long ago. Therefore, to lend realism
   to the roleplay, assume a newly appointed Procurement Officer
   who arrived in the agency only a short time before Requisition
   5-2291 was submitted. This is the first time the question of who
   decides on the usability of a product has arisen with this Procurement Officer. It is therefore, an important test.

The first roleplay situation is a review of facts and a planning session. The teacher should be prepared to move the class into a second roleplay situation which should be a confrontation with the Procurement Officer. To that end the following role card should be
used:

   Problem 9: Initiation of a Complaint
   Role: Procurement Officer

   You are relatively new to government service, from industry.
   Your mandate, from the Assistant Secretary of Administration
   is "Economy," and you are going about this as you did in industry. Your attitude is not belligerent, but very, very defensive. You would rather cover up than back up. You use the
   tactic of getting your opponents off on side issues if you can.

The confrontation may take place by phone or in person. If a phone
call, it should be limited to 10 minutes at the most. If the roleplaying students opt for a visit to the Procurement Office, 20 minutes
is the limit. If there is no resolution within these times, the
teacher should stop the play.

Again, the debriefing focuses on attitudes and methods of handling
complaint but this time the shoe is on the other foot and the librarian is the complainant. This is a good opportunity for role
reversal.

PROBLEM 10. REFUSAL OF A STAFF MEMBER TO HELP A USER

DOE is preparing information for the use of the U.S. Attorney General in litigation against the Major Metallurgical Company on a charge of despoilage of natural resources. All members of the staff have been assisting in this work, including the interns, as they have been rotating through the divisions.

One day a library user identifies himself to John Blalock, intern on duty at the reference desk, as a company lawyer of the Major Metallurgical Company. The lawyer wants copies of the legislative histories of certain ecological laws, and he wants John to search through publications of DOE and its predecessor agencies for material that will show the government's position over a period of years on the point under contention. John gives the lawyer minimum service because of both DOE's interest in the case and his own personal philosophy about ecology. The lawyer complains to the Director of the Library, who then takes action. His first step is to talk with the Chief of the Bibliographic Services Division, under whom John was working at the time of the incident. The Director must then proceed on the basis of this conversation. Sooner or later, someone must talk to John about it.

Roles: Director, DOE Library   Chief, Bibliographic
        Intern John Blalock   Services Division

Roleplay time: 10-15 minutes

Suggestions for Preparation: Review:

   1. DOE Library policy
   2. Principles of information service
   3. Counseling techniques

Sources:

   Feinberg, Mortimer R. and Tarrant, John J. "Dealing with Subordinates' Personal Problems, "Management Review 59 (June 1970), 52-55.

   Krug, Judith F. and Harvey, James A. "Intellectual Freedom: Statement of ALA Intellectual Freedom Committee to Activities Committee on New Directions for ALA, "American Libraries 1 (June 1970), 533-535.

   Nouri, Clement J. "The Viability of Conformity and Creativity," Personnel Journal 48 (September 1969), 716-721, 731.

   Strauss, Paul S. "The Professional Attitude," Personnel Administration 33 (March-April 1970), 33-36.

   Van Horne, R.D. "Discipline: Purpose and Effect," Personnel Journal 48 (September 1969), 728-731.

Communication 16

MAJOR METALLURGICAL COMPANY
Legal Division

August 3, 19x5

Director, DOE Library
Ecology Building
Washington, D.C.

Dear Sir:

I feel I must report to you an incident that happened to me yesterday
as I was attempting to use the DOE Library to gather information
needed by me in a company legal matter that is pending.

On that occasion one of your staff members, a Mr. Blalock, refused
to assist me. I needed to trace the government's position over a number of years in relation to reforestation of public lands leased to private industry. When I asked Mr. Blalock to search for this information for me, he informed me that I could use the catalogs and stacks
myself.

I know that the policy of executive department libraries requires that
assistance be given to members of the public who request it. I hope
you will clear up this matter and let me know, as soon as possible,
when I can obtain the needed help.

Thank you for your attention to this matter.

Sincerely,

Thomas E. Sinclair, Attorney

———————

Communication 17

Doe Library Phone Message   August 7, 19x5
                                                 10:20 a.m.

to: Chief, Bibliographic Services

from: Director, DOE Library

Something has come up that requires our immediate attention. Can
you come to my office right away? Please bring the Division public
service desk log for August 2.

Communication 18

DOE LIBRARY: BIBLIOGRAPHIC SERVICES DIVISION
Public Service Desk Log
August 2, 19x5

Time	Patron Name and Address	Request	Disposition	User Status	DOE / Federal Liaison / Outside
8:10	Howard Lewis	Photocopy of story in yesterday's Times	Filled	DOE	
8:12	Nancy Gibbons	List of journal articles by author of Ecological Future Shock (E.R.Heintz)	Filled	DOE	
8:15	John Threlkel	Who is Walt Goodnow?	Filled		Liaison-Toledo
8:20	Thomas Sinclair	Two legislative histories	Filled		Outside
8:40	" (Major Metal- lurgical Co.)	Information on federal position re reforestation of public lands leased to private industry, as far back as possible.	Filled		Outside
8:45	Eastern University Lib.	Address of DOE Office in Houston	Filled		Outside
8:50	SE Regional Ecological Research Co. Dr. Richardson	Name of expert on recycling small glass containers (chemistry equipment needed)	Referred		Outside
9:05	William Huffman	Address for Dr. Everett Reedy	NA-called Smithsonian	DOE	

Note to Instructors: The following role card should be given to the student who plays John Blalock:

Problem 10: Refusal to Help a User
Role: Intern John Blalock

You understand the library's policy and feel you helped the user. That is why you indicated on the log that the request had been filled. You see no reason why you have to go beyond the letter of library policy to help a company that is polluting the environment. You have very strong feelings on this subject and,

when challenged, it becomes a matter between your rights and
the company's rights. You have filled the letter of the policy
by directing the user to the material. Why do more?

The matter of individual right to dissent, even against administration policy, is of growing importance in federal libraries. The
matter of disqualifying oneself from working on an information
request is also of concern to reference librarians. This problem
provides an opportunity for discussion. It also highlights the
phenomenon of differing perceptions of a situation by participants
and observers. The latter consideration lends itself to reverse
roleplaying or substitution of players in one role at a time. Especially if the roleplay develops into a three-way conversation
that represents the library's position, the intern's position and
the user's position, substitution of one roleplayer will show how
one person can affect the outcome of a situation.

PROBLEM 11. TERMINATING A PROBATIONARY EMPLOYEE

Before the end of the internship, the Assistant Secretary for Administration has informed the Library Director that, because of the merger of the OAES Library staff with the DOE Library staff, no additional positions for the Library will be authorized at this time. Un-
expectedly, but fortunately for the Library in its dilemma, Mrs.
Goodman's husband is transferred and the Library Director is able
to find her a job in a liaison agency close to where her husband will
be stationed. The Director then tried, and succeeded, in justifying
another position on the basis of additional workload because of OAES
staff exposure to the DOE Library services. This position is half-
time for Bibliographic Services, where public services have felt the
strain, and half-time Documentation Services, where foreign lan-
guages are badly needed. Either John Blalock or Mrs. Moore must
be chosen. The one not chosen must be terminated.

Roles: Director, DOE Library
        Chief, Documentation Services Division
        Chief, Bibliographic Services Division
        One intern

Roleplay time:
In this roleplay, the two steps of (1) conference with supervisors and
(2) interview with employee to be terminated must be carried out in
sequence. First roleplay time: 20 minutes; second roleplay time:
10 minutes.

Suggestions for Preparation: Review:

1. Employee rights.
2. Interview techniques.
3. Termination paperwork requirements.

Sources:

Fortune. The Executive Life. Garden City, N.Y.: Doubleday and
    Company, 1956. Chapter 11, "How to Fire Executives,"
    Chapter 12, "How to Retire Executives."

Lefkowitz, Joel and Katz, Myron L. "Validity of Exit Interviews,"
    Personnel Psychology 22 (Winter 1969), 445-455.

Leonard, John W. "Guidelines for Off-the-Job Discipline and
    Discharge," Personnel Administration 32 (November-December
    1969), 39-43.

Malouf, A.G. and Lee, W.T. "The Positive Approach to Firing,"
    Administrative Management 25 (July 1964), 12.

Trueman, Allen K. "Cut Turnover with Exit Interviews,"
    Administrative Management 25 (May 1964), 12-14.

Communication 19

Department of Ecology   memorandum   September 4, 19x5

to: Chief, Bibliographic Services
             Division
         Chief, Documentation Services
             Division

from: Director, Library

subject: Filling new position.

. . . .

My conferences with the Assistant Secretary for Administration and
our Personnel Officer have worked out well. One additional position
has been authorized for the library, to be filled by one of our interns,
either John Blalock or Helen Moore. Please come to my office on
September 10 at 2 p.m. with your recommendation. Remember that
whichever intern is not chosen for this position must be terminated.
Bring along your evaluations of the interns for our use in making the
decision and in justifying it.

Note to Instructors: Notice that each Chief must supply evaluations
    of John Blalock and Helen Moore. These should be prepared and
    distributed in advance. If the class agreed on a performance
    evaluation form in an earlier problem, that form should be used.
    Otherwise, each Chief may present his evaluation as he chooses.

    There are two distinct aspects of termination which must be in-
    cluded in the roleplay. First is the liaison with the agency Per-
    sonnel Office and the required paperwork. Second is considera-
    tion of the employee in the interview and in helping him adjust.
    The Library Director must be knowledgeable, and he must com-
    municate empathy.

    There is a good possibility here for paperwork follow-up. This
    might be in the form of a letter of justification to the Personnel
    Office, a letter for the file of the intern to be terminated, a let-
    ter of inquiry about jobs for the intern (directed to other federal
    agencies or to the Director's friends), and a letter of recom-
    mendation for the intern who has been terminated. Each of these
    would present a problem of communication.

PROBLEM 12. ALLOCATION OF NEW EQUIPMENT

The inventory and appraisal of equipment in the OAES Library prior
to the merger showed that one typewriter was not worth moving.
Funds are included in the DOE Library budget (and not yet spent) for
one electric typewriter. Inasmuch as the Director is being pushed,
he must now decide who is to get the new typewriter.

Roles:

This is a class exercise in which each member of the class simultaneously plays the role of Director, studies the documentation and
makes a decision. Each Director must decide how he is going to let
the people affected know of the decision, and he must prepare the communications.

Roleplay time: 15 minutes

Suggestions for Preparation:

This problem calls for the subtle application of techniques of planning
and interpersonal relationships already studied rather than additional
preparation. If review is needed, appropriate readings should be self-
selected from those suggested in the Professional Bookshelf (Federal
Library Model, Document J) or in the Sources of earlier problems.

. . . .

Communication 20   memorandum   October 15, 19x5

To: Director, DOE Library

From: Specialist in Aerial Survey Cartography,* Library

Subject: Typewriter

It was my understanding that the five-year-old typewriter I had used
in the former OAES Library was to be discarded because of its condition, and that I would receive a new typewriter when I became part
of the DOE Library staff. It has not worked out that way, however.
My old typewriter was moved and assigned to me here. It is un-
suitable for use in typing entries for direct reproduction in bibliographies—part of my present responsibility—and I am forced to
scrounge some other typewriter when I am ready to type. This is
doing nothing to improve the inhospitable situation in which I find myself here in DOE.

May I request your immediate attention to this problem?

———————————

*Former Head, OAES Library

<u>Communication 21</u>

Department of Ecology   memorandum   June 15, 19x5

to: Director, DOE Library
from: Chief, Circulation Services Division
subject: Inventory of Typewriters

· · · · · · · · · · · ·

Attached is my inventory and appraisal of typewriters in the combined DOE and OAES Libraries as of this date, per your request of
June 1.

Attachment

· · · · · · · · · · · ·

Communication 21: attachment

INVENTORY AND APPRAISAL OF TYPEWRITERS

Inventory Number	Make, Type and Year	Presently Assigned to:	Condition
I. Director's Office			
06594	Remington Standard 19x1	Library Director	Poor
10583	IBM Electric 19x4	Secretary	Good
II. Bibliographic Services Division			
06583	IBM Electric 19x1	Chief, BSD	Fair
08921	SCM Electric 19x2	Subject Specialist	Good
08922	Royal Standard 19x2	Subject Specialist	Fair
06586	Remington Standard 19x1	ILL Technician and Workroom	Fair
09436	Royal Standard 19x3	Clerk/Typist	Fair
	N.B. Clerk/Typist has been promised next electric.		
III. Documentation Services Division			
09444	IBM Electric 19x3	Chief, DSD	Excellent
08941	SCM Electric 19x2	Abstractor/Indexer	Good
06587	Royal Standard 19x1	Technician	Good
IV. Circulation Services Division			
06589	SCM Electric 19x1	Chief, DSD	Good
V. Acquisition Services Division			
09446	SCM Electric 19x3	Chief, ASD	Excellent
06590	Remington Standard 19x1	Technician	Fair
10582	SCM Electric 19x4	Clerk/Typist	Excellent
VI. OAES Library			
S-3197	Underwood Standard 19x1	Library Director	N.G. Must be discarded
S-6891	Remington Standard 19x3	Subject Specialist	Good
S-5423	Underwood Standard 19x2	Technician	Good

Note to Instructors: As indicated at the beginning of the problem, each student acts as the Director and works independently. The debriefing must give each one an opportunity to state his solution and to identify the kinds of communications he has prepared. The ingenuity of the solution and consideration for all affected personnel are the crucial points. The actual communications can be studied and discussed also.

Index